Ancillary Relief

ANCILLARY RELIEF

Practice and Precedents

Andrew Newbury, Shona Alexander
and Ann Corrigan

The Law Society

Contents

Table of cases   x
Table of statutes   xiii
Table of statutory instruments   xv

1   First meeting with the client   1
Shona Alexander

1.1   First meeting   1
1.2   Setting the scene   1
1.3   Basic information   2
1.4   Jurisdiction   3
1.5   Data collection   4
1.6   Financial claims   6
1.7   Immediate action   7
1.8   Interim financial provision   8
1.9   Occupation of the home   9
1.10   The way forward   10
1.11   Concluding the interview   11

2   Disclosure   13
Andrew Newbury

2.1   Basic principles   13
2.2   Pre-action protocol   14
2.3   Requests for further disclosure   17
2.4   Settling cases without full disclosure   17

3   Procedure   19
Andrew Newbury

3.1   Why make an application?   19
3.2   Pre-action protocol   19

3.3	Family Proceedings Rules 1991	20
3.4	Form A	21
3.5	Drafting of Form E	25
3.6	First Appointment documents	29
3.7	Failure to comply with court timetable	32
3.8	First Appointment	33
3.9	Financial dispute resolution hearing	36
3.10	Applications for directions/further disclosure	38
3.11	Third party dislosure	39
3.12	Preparation for final ancillary relief hearing	41
3.13	Final ancillary relief hearing	42

4	**Powers of the court**	**44**

Ann Corrigan

4.1	Orders available under the Matrimonial Causes Act 1973	44
4.2	General duty and the law post-*White*	44
4.3	Spousal maintenance	46
4.4	Secured periodical payments	49
4.5	Lump sum and lump sums	49
4.6	Property adjustment	53
4.7	Pensions	55
4.8	Orders in favour of children	62
4.9	Child maintenance orders	64
4.10	The duty to consider a clean break	67

5	**Experts and valuations**	**69**

Andrew Newbury

5.1	Introduction	69
5.2	Instruction of experts	69
5.3	Part 35 Civil Procedure Rules 1998	71
5.4	Practice Direction 35	73
5.5	President's Best Practice Guide	74
5.6	Practical considerations when instructing experts	76
5.7	Instruction of accountants	77
5.8	Instruction of surveyors	79
5.9	Instruction of pension experts	80

6   Agreements between the spouses   **83**
Ann Corrigan

6.1   Pre-nuptial agreements   83
6.2   Post-nuptial agreements   87
6.3   '*Xydhias* agreements'   91
6.4   Consent orders   92

7   Unusual considerations   **94**
Shona Alexander

7.1   Introduction   94
7.2   Capital gains tax   94
7.3   Overseas assets   96
7.4   Tracing information   97
7.5   Company pension schemes   98

8   The route to settlement   **99**
Andrew Newbury

8.1   Approaches to negotiations   99
8.2   Negotiations between the parties   102
8.3   Roundtable meetings   103
8.4   Negotiating tactics   104
8.5   Tips on drafting consent orders   106

9   Interim applications and orders   **109**
Andrew Newbury

9.1   Introduction   109
9.2   No power to order interim lump sums   109
9.3   Applications for maintenance pending suit   109
9.4   Provision for legal fees   111
9.5   Procedure for making an application   112
9.6   Guidance on sworn statements   113
9.7   Injunctions to secure the preservation of assets   115

10   Costs   **119**
Andrew Newbury

10.1   Costs information to be given to the client   119
10.2   Funding of litigation   121
10.3   Costs orders within family proceedings   125

10.4   Interaction with the Civil Procedure Rules 1998   127
10.5   Form H   128
10.6   Drafting statements of costs   128
10.7   Proportionality of costs   130

11 Future applications   132
Shona Alexander

11.1   Variation   132
11.2   Periodical payments and maintenance pending suit   133
11.3   What does the court consider?   135
11.4   Situation upon death   135
11.5   Pensions   136
11.6   Termination of payment   136
11.7   Procedure   136
11.8   Variation of lump sum orders   136
11.9   Appeals   137
11.10 Applications to set aside   139

Appendices

1   First meeting checklist   143
2   Ancillary relief checklist   150
3   First letter to client following first meeting   157
4   First letter to other spouse following first meeting   160
5   Disclosure schedule (voluntary disclosure)   161
6   Form A   163
7   Schedule of expenditure   165
8   Statement of issues   167
9   Letter instructing accountant to value a family business   169
10   Letter instructing pensions expert   172
11   Letter instructing surveyor   175
12   First appointment order   177
13   Notice of application for further directions   179
14   Notice of application for maintenance pending suit/interim
     periodical payments   181
15   Notice of application for penal notice   182
16   Notice of application for an adjournment   183
17   Offer letter   184
18   FDR bundle index   186
19   Ancillary relief – pre-application protocol (25 May 2000)   188

20	President's Direction, Court bundles (26 July 2000)	192
21	Best Practice Guide for Instructing a Single Joint Expert	198
22	Civil Procedure Rules, Part 35, Experts and assessors	201
23	Extracts of Matrimonial Causes Act 1973 (as amended at 1 October 2009)	205
24	Extracts of Family Proceedings Rules 1991 (as amended at 1 October 2009)	223

Index   241

Table of cases

A v. A [2004] EWHC 2818 (Fam); [2006] 2 FLR 115 . . . . .89, 141
A v. A (Maintenance Pending Suit: Provision for Legal Fees) *sub nom:*
   A v. A (Maintenance Pending Suit: Provision for Legal Costs)
   [2001] 1 WLR 605; [2001] 1 FLR 377 . . . . .111, 123
B v. B (No.2) (Production Appointment: Procedure) [1995] 1 FLR 913 40
B v. P *sub nom:* VB v. JP [2008] EWHC 112 (Fam) 135
Barder v. Caluori *sub nom:* Barder v. Barder [1988] AC 20; [1987]
   2 FLR 480 . . . . .139, 141
Behzadi v. Behzadi [2008] EWCA Civ 1070 54
Burns v. Burns [2004] EWCA Civ 1258; [2004] 3 FCR 263 140
C v. C (Maintenance Pending Suit: Legal Costs) [2006] 2 FLR 1207 . . . . . . .111, 124
C v. C (Variation of Post Nuptial Settlement: Company Shares)
   [2003] EWHC 1222 (Fam); [2003] 2 FLR 493 55
C v. F (Disabled Child: Maintenance Orders) *sub nom:* C v. F
   (Child Maintenance) [1998] 2 FLR 1 63
Cornick v. Cornick (No.1) [1994] 2 FLR 530 . . . . .141, 142
Cornick v. Cornick (No.3) [2001] 2 FLR 1240 134
Crossley v. Crossley [2007] EWCA Civ 1491; [2008] 1 FLR 1467 84
Currey v. Currey [2006] EWCA Civ 1338 . . . . .111, 124
D v. D [2007] EWHC 278 (Fam); [2007] 2 FLR 653 78
D v. D (Financial Provision: Lump Sum Order) [2001] 1 FLR 633 52
David Truex (A Firm) v. Kitchin *sub nom:* Truex v. Kitchin [2007]
   EWCA Civ 618 120
Den Heyer v. Newby [2005] EWCA Civ 1311; [2006] 1 FLR 1114 140
Dorney-Kingdom v. Dorney-Kingdom [2000] 2 FLR 855 65
Dutfield v. Gilbert H Stephens and Sons [1988] Fam Law 473 18
Duxbury v. Duxbury [1987] 1 FLR 7 52
Edgar v. Edgar [1980] 1 WLR 1410; [1980] 3 All ER 887 . . . . .87, 90, 91
Edmonds v. Edmonds [1990] 2 FLR 202 141
F v. F (Clean Break: Balance of Fairness) [2003] 1 FLR 847 67
Flavell v. Flavell [1997] 1 FLR 353 67
Fleming v. Fleming [2003] EWCA Civ 1841; [2004] 1 FLR 667 . . . . .107, 136
G v. G (Financial Provision: Equal Division) [2002] EWHC 1339 (Fam) 96
G v. R (Pre-Nuptial Contract) *sub nom:* NG v. KR (Pre-Nuptial
   Contract); Radmacher v. Granatino [2009] EWCA Civ 649 . . . . .84, 85

G (Financial Provision: Liberty to Restore Application for Lump Sum),
   Re [2004] EWHC 88 (Fam); [2004] 1 FLR 997 52
Gojkovic v. Gojkovic (No.2) [1992] Fam 40; [1991] 3 WLR 621 . . . . .99, 100
Hamlin v. Hamlin [1986] Fam 11; [1986] 1 FLR 61 116
Hildebrand v. Hildebrand [1992] 1 FLR 244 31
J-P v. J-AF [1955] P215 13
J (SR) v. J (DW) sub nom: SRJ v. DWJ [1999] 2 FLR 176 67
Jenkins v. Livesey (formerly Jenkins) [1985] AC 424; [1985]
   1 All ER 106 . . . . .13, 139, 140
K v. K (Ancillary Relief: Prenuptial Agreement) [2003] 1 FLR 120 84
K v. K (Periodical Payment: Cohabitation) [2005] EWHC 2886 (Fam) 48
Khanna v. Lovell White Durrant [1995] 1 WLR 121; [1994] 4 All ER 267 41
L v. L (Lump Sum: Interest) [1994] 2 FLR 324 50
L v. L [2007] EWHC 140 (QB) 98
Lambert v. Lambert sub nom: L v. L (Financial Provision: Contributions)
   [2002] EWCA Civ 1685 46
Lamont v. Lamont unreported 13 October 2006 . . . . .53, 107, 137
Lauder v. Lauder [2007] EWHC 1227 (Fam); [2007] 2 FLR 802 135
Livesey v. Jenkins see Jenkins v. Livesey (formerly Jenkins)
M v. M (Prenuptial Agreement) [2002] 1 FLR 654 83
MacDonald v. Taree Holdings Ltd [2001] CPLR 439 129
MacLeod v. MacLeod [2008] UKPC 64; [2009] 3 WLR 437; [2009]
   1 FLR 641 . . . . .84, 90
Mareva Compania Naviera SA v. International Bulk Carriers SA
   (The Mareva) [1980] 1 All ER 213 117
Martin v. Martin [1978] 3 All ER 764; (1978) 122 SJ 366 55
Mastercigars Direct Ltd v. Withers LLP [2009] EWHC 651 120
Mesher v. Mesher [1980] 1 All ER 126 (Note) 54
Miller v. Miller sub nom: M v. M (Short Marriage: Clean Break)
   Joined Cases: McFarlane v. McFarlane [2006] UKHL 24 . . . . .7, 46, 135
Moses-Taiga v. Taiga sub nom: Taiga v. Taiga [2005] EWCA Civ
   1013; [2006] 1 FLR 1074 . . . . .111, 123, 124
Myerson v. Myerson [2009] EWCA Civ 282 141
N v. N (Financial Provision: Sale of Company) [2001] 2 FLR 69 89
Newton v. Newton [1990] 1 FLR 33 51
North v. North [2007] EWCA Civ 760 135
Pearce v. Pearce [2003] EWCA Civ 1054; [2003] 2 FLR 1144 134
Piglowska v. Piglowski [1999] 1 WLR 1360; [1999] 2 FLR 763 . . . . .45, 138
Poon v. Poon [1994] 2 FLR 857 118
Practice Direction (Fam Div: Ancillary Relief: Costs) [2006] 1 WLR 634 125
Practice Direction (Fam Div: Ancillary Relief Procedure) [2000]
   1 WLR 1480; [2000] 1 FLR 997 . . . . .14, 74
Practice Direction (Fam Div: Family Proceedings: Court Bundles)
   [2006] 1 WLR 2843 . . . . .37, 42
R v. R (Lump Sum Repayments) [2003] EWHC 3197 (Fam); [2004]
   1 FLR 928 137
Radmacher v. Granatino see G v. R (Pre-Nuptial Contract) sub nom:
   NG v. KR (Pre-Nuptial Contract)

Reynolds v. Stone Rowe Brewer (A Firm) [2008] EWHC 497 (QB) 120, 121
Rose v. Rose (Divorce: Consent Orders) (No.1) [2002] EWCA Civ 208;
    [2002] 1 FLR 978 91
Rose v. Rose (Divorce: Consent Orders) (No.2) [2003] EWHC 505 (Fam);
    [2003] 2 FLR 19 140
SRJ v. DWJ see J (SR) v. J (DW)
SW v. RC see W v. C
Sears Tooth v. Payne Hicks Beach [1997] 2 FLR 116 ....111, 122
Shaw (Jayne) v. Shaw (Philip) [2002] EWCA Civ 1298 ....139, 140
Shipman v. Shipman [1991] 1 FLR 250 118
T v. T (Consent Order: Procedure to Set Aside) [1996] 2 FLR 640 140
TL v. ML (Ancillary Relief: Claim against Assets of
    Extended Family) [2005] EWHC 2860 (Fam) 110, 111, 113, 123, 124
Tebbutt v. Haynes [1981] 2 All ER 238 41
Tee v. Tee Joined Cases: Tee v. Hillman [1999] 2 FLR 613; [1999]
    3 FCR 409 109
Thomas v. Thomas [1995] 2 FLR 668 51
VB v. JP see B v. P
Vicary v. Vicary [1992] 2 FLR 271 140
W v. C sub nom: SW v. RC [2008] EWHC 73 (Fam) 51
Walkden v. Walkden [2009] EWCA Civ 627 ....13, 142
Westbury v. Sampson [2001] EWCA Civ 407; [2002] 1 FLR 166 ....53, 107, 137
White v. White see White (Pamela) v. White (Martin)
White (Pamela) v. White (Martin) [2001] 1 AC 596; [2000]
    2 FLR 981 ....28, 45, 46, 55
White v. Withers [2008] EWHC 2821 (QB) 98
Wicks v. Wicks [1999] Fam. 65; [1998] 1 FLR 470 ....109, 118
Xydhias v. Xydhias 1999] 2 All ER 386; [1999] 1 FLR 683 91

Table of statutes

Child Maintenance and
Other Payments Act 2008 . . . . .64, 65
Child Support Act 1991 . . . . . .63, 64, 66
   s.4 66
   s.8 64
      (3) 66
      (5) 66, 93
      (6) 65
      (7) 65
        (a) 65
      (8) 66
      (9) 66
Computer Misuse Act 1990 . . . . . .6, 98
County Courts Act 1984
   s.38 117
   s.77 138
Data Protection Act 1998 6
Family Law Act 1996 . . . . .109, 205
   Part IV 9
   Sched.2 para.3 50
Human Rights Act 1998 6
Inheritance (Provision for
Family and Dependants)
   Act 1975 .7, 67
   s.1(1)(b) .67
   s.15(1) 68
Married Women's Property
Act 1882
   s.17 109
Matrimonial Causes
   Act 1973 . . . . .44, 55, 109,
                   132, 205
   Part II 205
   s.1(2)(d) 88
   s.21 205
   s.21A(1) 56, 206

      (a) 56, 206
      (b) 56, 206
      (2) 206
   s.21B 206
   s.21C 206
   s.22 . . . . .109, 110, 207
   s.23 . . . . .44, 49, 158, 207
      (1) 49, 207
        (a)–(c) 44
        (a) 46, 67, 108, 207
        (b) 49, 67, 207
        (c) 51, 55, 207
        (d) 46, 55, 65, 207
        (e) 49, 207
        (f) 207
      (2) 207
      (3) 208
        (a) 50, 208
      (4)–(6) 208
      (6) 49, 50
   s.24 . . . . .41, 44, 208
      (1)(a) 53, 208
        (b) 54, 209
        (c)–(d) 209
   s.24A 44, 54,
                   107, 209
   s.24B 44, 55, 210
   s.24C 210
   s.24D 210
   s.24E 211
   s.24F 212
   s.24G 212
   s.25 . . . . .3, 28, 46, 48, 52,
             57, 64, 83, 84, 87,
             91, 92, 135, 212
      (1) 44, 212

(2) 3, 31, 44, 45, 51,
                  67, 209, 212
(3) 6, 209, 213
(4) 213
s.25A 45, 55, 67, 213
s.25B 44, 214
  (1)–(3)
  (4) 60, 136, 214
  (5)–(6) 214
  (7)–(7C) 215
s.25C 44, 136, 215
  (1) 215
  (2) 215
    (b) 61, 215
  (3) 215
  (4) 216
s.25D .216
s.25E 217
s.27 88
s.28 . . . . .48, 219
s.28(1A) 6, 47, 107, 133,
                168, 185, 220
  (1B) .220
  (2) 220
  (3) 24, 220
s.29(1) 63, 220
  (2) 63, 220
  (3) 63, 220
  (4) 63, 221
  (5)–(8) 221
s.31 . . . . .21, 53, 107, 132,
              133, 135, 136,
                 137, 222
  (1) 132, 133, 222

(2) 132, 133, 136, 222
  (a)–(c) 222
  (d) 53, 132, 137, 222
  (dd) 136, 222
  (e)–(g) 222
  (2A) 133, 222
  (2B) .222
  (3)–(4) 222
  (5)–(6) 223
  (7) 133, 223
  (7A) 134, 223
  (7B) 134, 223
  (7C)–(H) 224
  (8) 136, 223
  (9) 224
  (10)–(15) 225
s.34(2) 87
s.35(1) 87
s.37 . . . . .19, 115, 116, 117
  (2)(a) 115
    (b) 115
  (4) 115
  (5) 116
s.52(1) 63
Regulation of Investigatory
  Powers Act 2000 6
Supreme Court Act 1981
  s.37 .117, 118
Taxation of Chargeable Gains
  Act 1992
  s.58(1) 94
  s.223(1) .95
Welfare Reform and Pensions
  Act 1999 55

Table of statutory instruments

Civil Procedure Rules 1998 (SI 1998/3132) 5, 20, 69, 127, 137, 171, 173
    rule 2.1 138
    Part 7 192
    Part 8 192
    Part 25 117
    Part 25D 117
    Part 35 . . . . .5, 17, 20, 58, 70, 71, 73,
                                           74, 79, 81, 199, 200, 201
    rule 35.1 . . . . .71, 201
    rule 35.2 . . . . .71, 201
    rule 35.3 . . . . .71, 201
    rule 35.4 . . . . .71, 201
    rule 35.4(1) 71, 201
    rule 35.4(2) 71, 201
    rule 35.4(3) 71, 201
    rule 35.4(4) 71, 201
    rule 35.5(1) 72, 201
    rule 35.5(2) 71, 201
    rule 35.6 . . . . .72, 201
    rule 35.6(1) 201
    rule 35.6(2) 72, 202
    rule 35.6(3) 72, 202
    rule 35.6(4) 72, 202
    rule 35.7 . . . . .72, 202
    rule 35.7(1) 202
    rule 35.7(2) 202
    rule 35.7(3) 202
    rule 35.7(3)(a) 199, 202
    rule 35.8 . . . . .72, 202
    rule 35.8(1)–(2) 202
    rule 35.8(3) 72, 202
    rule 35.8(4) 202
    rule 35.8(4)(b) 71
    rule 35.8(5) 202
    rule 35.9 . . . . .72, 203
    rule 35.10 203

rule 35.11 . . . . .73, 203
rule 35.12 . . . . .73, 203
rule 35.13 . . . . .73, 204
rule 35.14 . . . . .73, 76, 200, 204
rule 35.15 204
Part 35D 73, 75
Part 39 191
Part 44 20
rule 44.3 127
    (1)–(5) 127
    (1) 190
    (6)–9) 127
    (6) 127
    (8) 127
    (9) 127
rule 44.4(2) 128
    (3) 128
rule 44.8 127
Part 45 20
rule 47 . . . . .127, 128
rule 48.7 196
Part 52 137
County Court Remedies Regulations 1991 (SI 1991/1222) 118
County Court Rules 1981 (SI 1981/1687) 20
    Ord. 20 rule 12 41
    Ord. 37 rule 1 . . . . .138, 142
        rule 6(2) 138
County Courts (Interest on Judgment Debts) Order 1991 (SI 1991/1184) 50
Divorce etc. (Pensions) Regulations 2000 (SI 2000/1123) 23
Family Proceedings (Amendment No.2) Rules 1999 (SI 1999/3491) 188
Family Proceedings (Amendment) (No. 5) Rules 2005 (SI 2005/2922) 60
    rule 118(f)(i) 60
Family Proceedings (Amendment) Rules 2006 (SI 2006/352) 125, 126
Family Proceedings Rules 1991 (SI 1991/1247) 5, 20, 29, 31, 58, 99,
                                                                    127, 137, 227
    rule 1.2 188
    (1) 136
    rule 1.4 227
    rule 1.5 . . . . .20, 227
    rules 2.51A–2.70 20
    rule 251B 189, 228
    rule 2.51D 20, 130, 228
    (1) 130, 228
    (2)–(6) 228
    rule 2.52 229
    rule 2.53 229
    (1) 229
    (d) 58, 229

(2)–(3) 229
rule 2.54 229
rule 2.57 230
rule 2.59 . . . . .53, 230
  (2) 230
    (a) 21, 230
    (b) 21, 230
  (3) 41, 230
  (4) 23, 230
  (5) 230
  (6) 231
rule 2.60 231
rule 2.61 . . . . .92, 231
  (1) 231
    (a)–(f) 92
  (2) 231
  (3) 232
  (7) 39
rule 2.61A 22, 232
  (1)–(2) 232
  (3) 58, 232
  (4) 23, 232
    (a) 22, 232
rule 2.61B 232
  (1) 232
  (2) 22, 29, 232
  (3) 28, 29, 232
  (4) 29, 232
  (5) 233
  (6) 29, 233
  (7) 22, 29, 233
    (a) 31, 233
    (c) 30, 233
  (9) 233
rule 2.61C 71, 233
rule 2.61D 33, 38, 233
  (1) 33, 233
  (2) 233
    (b) 76, 233
    (e) 36, 233
  (3) 38, 234
  (4) 39, 234
    (a) 77, 234
  (5) 234
rule 2.61E 36, 99, 126, 234
  (1) 38, 234
  (2)–(3) 234
  (4)–(9) 235

rule 2.61F 128, 235
   (2) 128, 235
rule 2.62 235
   (2)–(3) 235
   (4) 40, 235
   (4A) 235
   (7)–(8) 235
   (9) 236
rule 2.64 236
rule 2.65 236
rule 2.66 . . . . .42, 236
rule 2.67 236
rule 2.68 237
rule 2.69 100
rule 2.69E 42, 99, 237
rule 2.69F 112, 113, 116, 237
   (1) 237
   (2) 112, 237
   (3) 237
   (4)–(8) 238
rule 2.70 . . . . .24, 27, 29, 238
   (1) 238
   (2) 23, 59, 238
   (3)–(5) 238
   (6) 58, 238
   (7) 23, 58, 239
   (8) 59, 60, 239
   (9) 60, 239
   (10) 60, 239
   (11)–(12) 239
   (13) 61, 240
   (16)–(18) 240
rule 2.70A 241
rule 2.71 . . . . .72, 100, 125, 126, 127, 128, 242
   (1) 127, 242
   (2)–(3) 242
   (4) 242
      (a) 125, 242
      (b) 125, 126, 242
   (5) 125, 242
      (b) 101, 126, 242
   (6) 242
rule 8.1 138
   (2) 138
   (3)(a) 138
Pension Sharing (Valuation) Regulations 2000 (SI 2000/1052)
  reg. 2(5) 60
  reg. 2(6) 60

reg. 2(7) 60
reg. 4 . . . . .57, 60
reg. 5 57
reg. 6 57
reg. 7 57
Pensions on Divorce etc. (Charging) Regulations 2000 (SI 2000/1049)
  reg. 2(2) 59
Pensions on Divorce etc (Provision of Information)
  Regulations 2000 (SI 2000/1048) 58
  reg. 2(2) 23
Rules of the Supreme Court 1965 (SI 1965/1776) 20
  Ord. 15 rule 6(2)(b) 41
  Ord. 32 rule 7 40
  Ord. 38 rule 14 40
  Ord. 58 rule 1 139
    rule 3 139

CHAPTER 1

First meeting with the client

Shona Alexander

1.1 FIRST MEETING

The first meeting is one of the most important that you will have with the client, and there are many topics which will need to be covered with the client at this meeting. The first meeting should enable you to understand the individual goals that the client seeks to achieve and place realistic expectations on such goals. It is essential that client management begins at this meeting. This, together with the provision of accurate, relevant and appropriate legal advice, should avoid many problems and potential complaints at a later stage. It should also help to keep the case focused and avoid unnecessary legal costs for the client.

This first meeting can be an overwhelming and upsetting experience for many clients, who may have had little previous contact with the legal profession but now find themselves having to discuss difficult and emotional issues. It is important to be sensitive to this, whilst also gathering the necessary information in order to be able to advise your client.

1.2 SETTING THE SCENE

The client should be allowed a period at the commencement of the meeting in which to set out what he or she understands the current position to be and what is sought from this meeting. This, however, needs to be realistic in light of the time available and the information provided. Is the client contemplating separation, so that all that is needed today is information on what options are open and what are the possible outcomes of any financial claim? Is the client already separated and, if so, was that the client's choice or was it imposed upon him or her? If so, how long ago was this separation and where are the parties now living? Does the client anticipate imminent divorce/dissolution proceedings? Have any proceedings already been commenced and, if so, has there been correspondence from another solicitor or from the court? It is important to frame the meeting in the right context, to avoid falling into the trap of providing information and advice which is not relevant. This first

1

meeting can be an overwhelming experience for the client and unnecessary information can detract from the advice that the client needs to receive and understand.

1.3 BASIC INFORMATION

The opportunity should be taken at the outset of the first meeting to take as much relevant information from the client as possible. This task may often also help to settle clients who are feeling emotional or nervous. The information requested should include, but is not limited to, the following:

1. full names of both parties, together with dates of birth and addresses;
2. adults' respective National Insurance numbers (this will be useful when dealing with pension issues and any communication with the Child Maintenance and Enforcement Commission (CMEC)), if known;
3. occupations, property details, details of any assets and other financial details;
4. full names of all children of the family and dates of birth;
5. children's school details;
6. details of any ill health or physical or mental disability of any party or child;
7. date of marriage/partnership and length of any prior cohabitation;
8. date of separation.

Additional details should be taken of the values, as far as the client is aware, of the home, all other assets including those referred to in Form E, all income (from whatever source) of the parties, and their respective liabilities, such as loans, credit card debts, finance agreements or 'soft loans' from friends or family. Without this basic information it will be difficult to provide any realistic or accurate advice. (Comprehensive guidance regarding the drafting of Form E and the documents to be exhibited can be found at **3.5** onwards.)

It is essential to note that you should not be tempted to give detailed advice until you have a full picture of the financial position of both parties. Clients do not always bring detailed information on these matters to the first interview, and therefore any advice should be prefaced with the caveat that the advice is given on the limited information available and may change once the full details become clear. A client with complex circumstances should be encouraged to provide a schedule of such information in advance of the first meeting, as this is likely to result in a far more productive meeting and will save time and expense.

1.3.1 Section 25 considerations

The court has a very wide discretion as to what order it can make when dealing with any application for ancillary relief, but in deciding which of those orders is appropriate it is directed by the Matrimonial Causes Act (MCA) 1973, s.25(2) to have regard to certain factors (see **4.2**). Not all of these are strictly financial, for example, the standard of living enjoyed by the parties, any conduct which might be considered relevant, or contributions which either party has made or may make to the marriage or partnership. Some details may be more relevant than others, but remember that a client may not know what or how much to tell you. When taking basic information at the first meeting it is essential to cover the s.25 factors in as much detail as possible. It is often helpful to have a copy of the s.25 factors available at the first meeting to show to clients so that they can see themselves what factors the court will take into account.

Future contact details are essential. It may be necessary to consider communicating with the client at a different address from that of the marital home, or on a different telephone number. In this day and age it may also be appropriate to communicate via email, but the client may wish to use a work email address or set up a new webmail account with a secure password.

A checklist for use at the first meeting can be found at **Appendix 1**. It is not designed to be definitive or exhaustive, as each meeting will be different because each relationship and the parties' circumstances are different in every case.

1.4 JURISDICTION

Two important questions should always be borne in mind during a first meeting. Is the court of England and Wales the correct jurisdiction for this case? Are there any alternative jurisdictions that would be available for this case? In the majority of cases the only jurisdiction that will be relevant is that of England and Wales. Practitioners should be reminded that Scotland and Northern Ireland are separate legal jurisdictions. It is not intended in this book to cover multi-jurisdictional cases as reference should be made to specialist reference books. If the issue of a foreign jurisdiction arises, it is prudent to take urgent advice from a lawyer in that jurisdiction, particularly to ascertain whether it would be more advantageous for your client to issue in England and Wales or the foreign jurisdiction. Details of experienced family lawyers in foreign jurisdictions can be found on the website of the International Academy of Matrimonial Lawyers (**www.iaml.org**).

Although it is self-evident in most cases, it is also essential to ensure that the family court in England and Wales has jurisdiction to deal with the proposed divorce, judicial separation or nullity proceedings. It is necessary for the client to be able to establish one of the following jurisdictional grounds:

- the husband and the wife are both habitually resident in England and Wales;

- the husband and the wife were last habitually resident in England and Wales and one party still resides here;
- the proposed respondent is habitually resident in England and Wales;
- the proposed petitioner is habitually resident in England and Wales and has resided here for at least one year immediately prior to the presentation of the petition;
- the proposed petitioner is domiciled and habitually resident in England and Wales and has resided here for at least six months prior to the presentation of the petition;
- both the husband and the wife are both domiciled in England and Wales;
- no other court of a contracting state has jurisdiction under Council Regulation (EC) No. 1347 of 2000 and either the husband or the wife is domiciled in England and Wales.

As at August 2009 the contracting states are Belgium, Bulgaria, Cyprus, Czech Republic, Germany, Greece, Spain, Estonia, France, Hungary, Ireland, Italy, Latvia, Lithuania, Luxemburg, Malta, Netherlands, Austria, Poland, Romania, Portugal, Slovakia, Slovenia, Finland, Sweden and the UK.

1.5 DATA COLLECTION

Due to the length of time it can take to obtain certain information or documentation it is important at the outset of the case (preferably at the first meeting), where relevant, to provide a copy of Form E and ask your client to start collating the information required. In particular the client should be asked to deal with the matters set out below (although some clients may prefer you to take these steps on their behalf, so it is advisable to ensure that you have letters of authority available for clients to sign).

1.5.1 Pension information

The client (or you on the client's behalf) should write to all pension providers of any nature as early as possible to seek the up-to-date cash equivalent transfer value (CETV as it is known) for each pension. This can usefully be done by sending Form P and a copy of paragraph 2.13 of Form E so it is clear exactly what information is needed. A copy of the letter should be retained by the client so that if a significant delay occurs in receiving the information, this can be annexed to Form E to prove that a request has been made.

Additionally, clients should be asked to complete Form BR20 which is a request for the Department for Work and Pensions to provide a valuation of their SERPS pension (otherwise known as SP2 or second state pension). This is their state earnings related pension which is additional to the basic state pension entitlement and can relate to the amount of national insurance paid if the client has not contracted out of SERPS. It is important that all pension valuations including SERPS are obtained for a number of reasons.

Firstly, each client has a duty of full financial disclosure and a SERPS pension is an asset like any other. Furthermore, clients may wish to pension share or offset within a financial settlement and figures would be inaccurate if the SERPS valuation is not included.

A client of 50 years or over should also be asked to complete Form BR19, which is a request that the Department of Work and Pensions provide a full state pension forecast, i.e. what amount the client may expect to receive when retiring at state retirement age. It is important to make clear that the request is being made with the view to a divorce or dissolution, as one spouse can rely upon the other's higher national insurance contributions made for the duration of the marriage to enhance his or her own pension entitlement.

1.5.2 Up-to-date information

Information which is out of date is of little relevance for anyone, and will simply be met with a questionnaire from the other party requesting up-to-date information. A client who is primed at the outset to obtain the current values of any bank accounts, savings, investment policies and such like can save time and costs in the disclosure and negotiation process.

Clients with complex assets should be encouraged to liaise with their accountants at an early stage as up-to-date business or trust accounts management information and tax returns will be necessary.

It is not advisable for up-to-date valuations of major assets such as the home, other property or businesses to be obtained by one party at huge cost at the outset of the case. The Civil Procedure Rules (CPR) 1998 Part 35 (set out at **Appendix 22**) has largely been adopted by the court in ancillary relief proceedings, despite these proceedings being governed by the Family Proceedings Rules (FPR) 1991. In an effort to achieve cost saving and to avoid duplication, the approach of the court is likely to be that (in default of an agreement between the parties) a valuation of major assets should be carried out by a single joint expert on the basis of joint instruction and joint expense of the parties, which would generally be ordered at the First Appointment hearing. Parties could be criticised for obtaining their own expert reports disregarding the CPR requirements, although if a report has already been prepared for other reasons it can be helpful to attach this to Form E to assist the parties in reaching agreement rather than spending money on a fresh report.

1.5.3 Preservation, collation and copying of documents

At the first meeting clients should be encouraged to obtain and retain their bank statements, as statements for at least the last 12 months will be required for Form E. If these are not available it can sometimes take time to acquire duplicates.

Clients often enquire whether they can take away or copy information and documentation belonging to their spouses. This has become much more of an issue in our modern technological age and particularly in family law, where disclosure plays an essential role in any case and the court is looking for a 'fair' result. It is, however, important to remember that although the family courts have taken a more relaxed approach to this issue (although there are limits), your client – or even you – could be in breach of data protection laws which can lead to claims in tort and criminal proceedings. It is therefore important to familiarise yourself with the provisions of the Computer Misuse Act 1990, Data Protection Act 1998, Regulation of Investigatory Powers Act 2000, copyright and privacy laws and, of course, the Humans Right Act 1998. The position then also needs to be made clear to your client.

1.6 FINANCIAL CLAIMS

It is important for a client to understand the exact nature of the financial claims available within ancillary relief and how the court will consider these. These should be discussed at some stage during the meeting (as appropriate) as this will help the client to focus on how the case will be conducted and the reasons for this.

Rather than set out all the possible orders that can be made by the court, it may be wise to explain the court's approach to settlement by grouping these into property issues, capital claims, income claims and future claims upon death. Clients are generally concerned about the matrimonial home, its occupation and who will retain the property in the future. The matrimonial home is often the main asset and it is therefore essential to get as much information as possible, such as estimated sale price and most recent mortgage figure (if applicable).

There is a wealth of case law setting out the court's approach to capital claims but the client at first meeting is unlikely to have the capacity or interest to take in such detailed information. Those clients who do will no doubt ask probing questions. It is perhaps sufficient to state at this early stage that the court seeks to achieve a 'fair' settlement of capital issues, which is not necessarily the same as equality. It should be made clear that the court, pursuant to MCA 1973, s.25(3), must bear in mind the financial needs of any child(ren) of the family (in particular the need to be housed). An early review of possible settlement terms can then be discussed with the client, although anything more detailed should wait until full disclosure has been provided.

Similarly, a brief consideration of income claims should be made where relevant, including the difference between interim orders, joint lives and term orders and those term orders which are non-extendable, i.e. subject to the s.28(1A) bar. In order to enable clients to start to think in terms of relevant income issues, it is always advisable to provide a budget schedule template at the first meeting and ask them to complete it. Even if income claims are not going to be made by the client, whether on an interim basis or otherwise, Form E requires clients to set out their income needs in any event. Of course, following *Miller* v. *Miller; McFarlane* v. *McFarlane* [2006] UKHL 24 claims for spousal maintenance are not now limited to a party's income needs in those cases where the income of the parties is above and beyond what both parties reasonably need.

It should be made clear to clients when discussing the various heads of claim that if a spouse remains financially dependent upon the client post settlement, then reasonable financial provision has to be made by the client in his or her will, otherwise the client's estate could be subject to a claim pursuant to the Inheritance (Provision for Family and Dependants) Act 1975.

Additionally, there may be a claim for child maintenance which could have a bearing upon any income orders. Where there are natural children of the relationship the claim for child maintenance will currently be outside the jurisdiction of the court and will be the responsibility of the Child Support Agency in the event of a dispute. The functions of the Child Support Agency were transferred to a new body called the Child Maintenance and Enforcement Commission (CMEC) on 1 November 2008. Although the CSA/CMEC have jurisdiction to deal with the payment and collection of child support in the majority of cases, many couples are able to agree an appropriate level of child support by applying the CSA formula, which is yet to be replaced by the new CMEC formula. Clients should be advised about the practical benefits of provision for child support being included in a consent order as part of an overall settlement which also includes provision for division of the assets of the marriage, payment of spousal maintenance, etc.

It is perhaps at this stage of the meeting that some discussion should take place about the client's goals. For example, the client may wish to retain the family home at all costs, or to achieve a clean break at the earliest possible moment. A client's approach will usually be clear by now but aspirations may not be so clear. In any event, these must be kept under review at all times during the case. It is most important not to give the client unrealistic expectations, as this will lead to an unhappy client whatever the outcome. If it is more than likely that the family home will have to be sold, state so clearly at this stage. A good first meeting is as much about managing the client's expectations as the delivery of relevant information and advice. Clients do not seek your advice merely to hear what they want to hear.

1.7 IMMEDIATE ACTION

Preservation of assets and limitation of liabilities is a good maxim for clients who are about to embark upon court proceedings to dissolve a marriage or partnership. In order to achieve this, it is worth considering the following, particularly if there is a lack of trust between the parties:

- any issues over joint bank accounts and credit cards;
- interim financial provision including applications for benefit;
- occupation of the home;
- necessity of injunction proceedings; and
- severance of a joint tenancy.

1.7.1 Joint accounts

Some clients can work together with their spouse and continue to operate a joint account as they did throughout their relationship. However, consideration should be given to this at the first meeting, and if the client feels that there is simply not sufficient trust between them to allow this to continue it may be necessary to place a stop on the account. However, this can have serious ramifications particularly if standing orders, direct debits, etc. are being paid out of that account. Banks and other financial institutions are sometimes too proactive in this respect and make their own decisions to stop accounts at the slightest hint of difficulty between the parties. Others may refuse point blank to action a request for the account to be stopped. In those cases, written notification that the client is no longer willing to be jointly and severally liable for any overdraft on the account usually brings about action on the part of the bank.

These days the types of accounts available have become far more complicated. Online accounts requiring passwords are commonplace and if the other party is aware of the password on an account, problems could occur. Clients should consider changing any passwords as soon as possible.

Similarly, there are mortgages with immediately available draw down facilities or offset accounts which can be manipulated by one party to the detriment of the other. Again, written notification to the bank or building society should be advised, to prevent further draw down or movement on those accounts.

The use of second cards on a client's credit card account is not uncommon and consideration should be given at the first meeting to discontinuing such a facility.

The client should always be advised that any instructions to the bank or other financial institution should be given not only verbally but also followed up in writing with a request for written acknowledgement of receipt. It is good practice to notify the spouse in writing of the stopping or amendment of any banking or credit facilities so as not to cause unnecessary embarrassment and to avoid the other side taking costly formal steps, e.g. applying for an injunction.

1.8 INTERIM FINANCIAL PROVISION

This chapter is not intended to provide detailed information on procedural aspects of interim court applications or benefits available. However, it is important at the first meeting to determine how the financial needs of clients are to be met in the first instance if they do not have sufficient income of their own to meet their needs.

Notifying clients of the state benefits which may be available and referring them to the local DSS office for the full details of an application for benefit is the role of a good family lawyer. Below are just some of the benefits which may be relevant and which could significantly help some clients:

- working tax credit;
- child tax credit; and
- council tax benefit.

Not only will these be of assistance to the client, but upon consideration of any formal application for interim maintenance, the other party and the court will almost certainly ask whether an application for state benefits has been made, and if not, why not. These benefits should be discussed at an early stage and any application made as soon as possible as they may take some time to process.

1.8.1 Income support

If no benefits are available or if they still do not meet the financial needs of the client, then consideration must be given to an interim application for maintenance. The first stage of any such application is to provide the other party or his or her solicitor with a detailed budget schedule and details of what income can be generated by the client him or herself. This will usually be in affidavit form as it is unlikely that Form Es will have been exchanged by this stage. If they have, then they should be used. It may not be possible to take these details within the first meeting, but the procedure should be made clear to the client and set in motion. It is important to inform the client that any claim for maintenance, whether interim or otherwise, will have to be balanced against the other party's ability to pay.

1.9 OCCUPATION OF THE HOME

It is, of course, hoped that in the majority of cases occupation of the home is not a matter of dispute. However, where dispute arises in the face of violence or significant risk of violence the relevant law is found within Part IV of the Family Law Act 1996.

Even where there is no immediate dispute, there is an important issue when the home is held in the name of only one spouse. If there is any element of doubt as to the ownership of the home then an office copy of the Land Registry entry should be obtained as soon as possible. If your client is not the proprietor, then you should discuss with the client the need to register a charge on the property. The client should secure his or her own position as soon as possible but be aware that the other party will be notified of this.

The effect of the registration of such charge will be to prevent any dealing with the property whether by sale, transfer or re-mortgage pending resolutions to financial settlement. The charge will cease upon decree absolute, so will need to be reviewed at that time. In the absence of any occupation order to the contrary, a spouse has the right to occupy the matrimonial home until decree absolute. However, you should make your client aware that the right of occupation as a spouse ceases upon decree absolute. If decree absolute is anticipated prior to financial settlement having been resolved, then you should consider making an application for extension of the right of occupation after decree absolute. Such an application must be issued by the court prior to decree absolute, so a diary entry for review is essential.

1.9.1 The need for injunction proceedings/emergency steps

In addition to the injunctive relief of an occupation order, you should, where necessary, consider with the client at the first meeting whether any other injunctive relief or emergency steps may prove necessary, particularly in respect of any children.

Good practice generally requires a letter to be written to the other party prior to making an application for interim relief; however, in certain cases an application without notice may be appropriate. In some courts such applications are kept to a bare minimum with the threat of costs orders against solicitors. Clients will need to be advised about court procedure, the cost involved and the implications of an adverse costs order against them.

1.9.2 Severance of the joint tenancy and wills

Severance of a joint tenancy may be necessary to protect the client's interest in the home, although a check should first be carried out at the Land Registry to ensure that property is, in fact, held as joint tenants. Clients should also be advised to consider making a new will as under any current one the other party will be treated as having died following decree absolute. Further, given that the relationship has broken down, clients may not wish their old will to be implemented in the event of their death.

1.10   THE WAY FORWARD

It is important to inform the client at the first meeting as to the way forward and the next steps to be taken. It may be that agreement is reached that no action will be taken at this stage. A file note will be made and an account rendered. It may be that the preparation of a draft letter for the client's approval is required. In some cases a detailed 'to do list' may be necessary, as clients who are in a distressed state will rarely remember all that has been discussed. It is always advisable to send a follow-up letter outlining what has been discussed, the advice given and the action to be taken by either yourself or the client. The client is also likely to want time to consider the options before making a decision (unless there is an urgent issue). Possible outcomes should also be outlined briefly to the client, where relevant, to manage the client's expectations.

1.10.1 Codes and protocol

Any way forward agreed with the client should ideally comply with both the Resolution Code of Practice and the Law Society's pre-action protocol (see **2.2**). If the client's instructions do not comply with those practices it is wise to advise the client of the existence of the Code and protocol, as this may lead the client subsequently to be criticised by the court, and in the worst cases the action may be visited by a costs order.

1.11 CONCLUDING THE INTERVIEW

It is also important in any first meeting to deal with what could be termed 'administrative' matters. Again, this will avoid any misunderstanding and problems at a later stage.

1.11.1 Cost and timescale

It is essential to discuss with the client the manner in which costs will be incurred. For most this will include provision of information of the hourly rate of the fee earners likely to be working on the case, when accounts will be rendered and when payment will be due. It may also include how the costs are going to be funded – by the other party, from a bank facility or some other manner.

The client will most likely want an estimate of how much the case is going to cost and the timescale. It is unlikely to be possible to be precise at the outset as it is not known what amount of work the case may entail and whether the case will be dealt with by agreement or litigation. It is acceptable to say this but perhaps set a limit at which the case will be reviewed and also to give an estimate as far as possible in broad terms depending on whether the matters are resolved by agreement or by litigation.

Subsequent to any meeting, and before taking a client on formally, the Law Society requires solicitors to send a letter in accordance with Rule 2 of the Solicitors' Code of Conduct 2007.

1.11.2 Legal Services Commission

Those firms with a Legal Aid franchise will be able to offer different types of assistance to certain clients depending upon the merit of their case and their individual financial circumstances. If your firm does not have a franchise as such it is not possible to offer this form of assistance. In this situation, it must be made clear to clients that they should make enquiries of another firm if they believe they are entitled to such assistance with fees.

1.11.3 Money laundering requirements

Prior to the first meeting, clients should be asked to bring with them sufficient documentation to comply with the firm's money laundering requirements.

1.11.4 Other agencies/assistance

It is appropriate to consider with any client at the first meeting whether different forms of assistance over and above legal advice may be appropriate in the circumstances. For example, counselling may be helpful to some clients. Not all clients who ask for legal advice want to end their marriage or partnership, and in some cases counselling may enable the relationship to be saved. Similarly, some clients may be experiencing significant difficulty in dealing with the breakdown of their relationship and would benefit from professional help. This may be sought from one of the charitable agencies or private counsellors, and may involve individual counselling or counselling with their spousal partner. Consider holding contact details for local counsellors and relevant charities in the office so that these can be provided to clients where appropriate.

Mediation may provide a way forward for some couples to resolve the issues between them. This may involve 'all issues' mediation, covering the financial aspects of the separation as well as dealing with issues concerning children. Alternatively, clients may feel it is more appropriate to deal with financial issues via solicitors but to use mediation for the issues relating to the children. Mediators may be legally qualified or non-legally qualified; however, it is likely that each party will require his or her own legal advice in the background.

Collaborative law is fast developing across the country, enabling solicitors to facilitate an environment in which the parties and their solicitors work through to resolution of their problems together in four-way face-to-face meetings. This may not be appropriate to every client, but information about this approach and the other alternative services should be provided at the first meeting.

CHAPTER 2

Disclosure

Andrew Newbury

2.1 BASIC PRINCIPLES

Financial disclosure is the bedrock of final proceedings within divorce or separation. Without full financial disclosure being provided, it is impossible for solicitors to advise upon terms of settlement. Realistically speaking, proposals for settlement can neither be submitted nor considered until full disclosure has been given.

Both a husband and a wife are under an obligation to give full and frank disclosure. That obligation is enshrined in case law (*Jenkins* v. *Livesey (formerly Jenkins)* [1985] AC 424). Clients should be advised clearly and emphatically of the need to give full and frank disclosure. They should also be advised of the consequences of failing to give full disclosure. In particular, any final ancillary relief order, whether made by consent or after a contested final hearing is capable of challenge and being re-opened if full and frank disclosure has not been provided.

The obligation is to provide 'full, frank and clear' disclosure – see *J-P* v. *J-AF* [1955] P 215. Also note the more recent comments of Wall LJ in *Walkden* v. *Walkden* [2009] EWCA Civ 627.

Circumstances may arise where clients do not wish to pursue full and frank disclosure and are willing to settle their financial claims without full disclosure being sought. This issue is considered further at **2.4**.

Clients should also be clearly advised that the obligation to give disclosure is ongoing throughout the proceedings. For example, should their circumstances change, they must advise their spouse of that change of circumstances. Some clients occasionally fall under the misapprehension that once they have provided their disclosure, they do not need to provide further information, and the position must be made clear to them. It is sensible to advise clients that when a draft consent order is lodged with the court, it must be accompanied by a statement of information setting out their relevant financial circumstances at that time. A statement of information will therefore capture any changes of circumstances since initial disclosure was made.

Disclosure is usually provided within a divorce in one of two ways. These are:

(a) by way of voluntary disclosure. The various forms of voluntary disclosure are considered in this chapter; and

(b) in the context of formal ancillary relief proceedings. This is considered further in **Chapter 3**.

2.2 PRE-ACTION PROTOCOL

Guidelines for the provision of financial disclosure outside of the framework of ancillary relief proceedings are set out in the pre-application protocol for ancillary relief (annexed to *Practice Direction (Ancillary Relief Procedure)* [2000] 1 FLR 997) which is contained in the Family Law protocol published by the Law Society. It should, however, be noted that the protocol does not set out rigid rules, but is simply a protocol to assist with the early settlement of cases. Paragraph 1.2 of the protocol states that its aim is to ensure that pre-action disclosure and negotiation takes place in appropriate cases, that such disclosure and negotiation is dealt with cost effectively and in line with the overriding objective set out in the FPR, and to ensure that the parties are in a position to settle the case fairly and early without litigation.

2.2.1 Is it necessary to always comply?

Rule 2.2 of the protocol specifically states that when considering the option of pre-application disclosure and negotiation, solicitors should bear in mind the advantage of having a court timetable and court-managed process. It goes on to state that 'the option of pre-application disclosure and negotiation has risks of excessive and uncontrolled expenditure and delay'.

The following may be circumstances where it is preferable to have a court-managed timetable as opposed to voluntary disclosure:

1. It is a complex or big money case where extensive disclosure and/or the instruction of experts will be required. It is often preferable if such issues are dealt with in the context of a clearly defined court timetable.

2. There is a belief that the other party may be reluctant to provide prompt disclosure or may be unwilling to give full and frank disclosure. Your client may therefore prefer the security of court orders directing the provision of disclosure.

3. There may be a fundamental issue of principle between the parties which will not easily be resolved in negotiation (for example, whether there should be a clean break or provision for ongoing spousal maintenance). In such cases, judicial intervention and an early financial dispute resolution hearing (FDR) can be essential in reaching a negotiated settlement. By contrast, without the court structure, ongoing negotiations may prove to be fruitless. Clients may understandably be frustrated and unhappy

if they have spent six months in voluntary disclosure and negotiations only to then issue an application for ancillary relief. It is inevitable that settlement will be delayed and potentially costs duplicated.

It should also be noted at paragraph 2.4 of the protocol that it is stated that making an application to the court 'should not be regarded as a hostile step or as a last resort'. It can be a way of controlling disclosure and endeavouring to avoid a costly final hearing. The protocol does, however, say at paragraph 2.6 that an application should not be issued when a settlement is a reasonable prospect.

2.2.2 Format of voluntary disclosure

The pre-action protocol at paragraph 3.5 states that 'the parties should exchange schedules of assets, income, liabilities and other material facts, using Form E as a guide to the format of the disclosure'. It also states that documents should only be disclosed to the extent that they are required by Form E. Excessive or disproportionate costs should not be incurred.

Many solicitors therefore prefer to use Form E for voluntary disclosure. For some straightforward cases, Form E can appear cumbersome, although one of the benefits of using Form E is that if subsequent ancillary relief proceedings are issued, then Form E can be updated with relatively little additional cost. Where Form E is used for voluntary disclosure, sometimes an agreement is reached between solicitors that the completion of the form should be limited to the sections dealing with disclosure. It may be possible to agree that it is unnecessary to give a breakdown of income needs, nor will it be necessary to complete the sections towards the end dealing with contributions, etc.

It can also be agreed between solicitors that Forms E do not require swearing by the parties. For example, it could be agreed that Forms E are unsigned or simply signed, but not sworn by the parties.

Some other solicitors prefer for voluntary disclosure to be kept on a simpler basis. A schedule of assets, liabilities and income can be disclosed with the Form E disclosure exhibited to it. An example of a disclosure schedule can be found at **Appendix 5**.

Whatever the format of voluntary disclosure, the following are sensible points to note:

1. The format of the disclosure should be agreed in advance between the parties, including the extent to which documents in support need to be produced.
2. To avoid delay, a date for exchanging disclosure should also be agreed. One of the inherent problems of voluntary disclosure is delay, as there is no external pressure from a court timetable.

It may also be sensible to agree prior to the exchange of Forms E or schedules that reasonable questions regarding disclosure raised thereafter will be answered. Some practitioners may unreasonably insist that once disclosure has been provided in Form E, then the pre-action protocol has been complied with and therefore no further disclosure is required. Clearly, if reasonable questions are being raised, then reasonable steps should be taken to answer them. Whether in the context of voluntary disclosure or contested ancillary relief proceedings, the overriding principle is that both parties must give full and frank disclosure.

2.2.3 First letter and subsequent correspondence

The pre-action protocol deals with correspondence, although in any event particular care should be taken over both the content and extent of correspondence. Few clients will thank solicitors for extensive *inter partes* correspondence and such letters are rarely, if ever, produced to the court at a final hearing.

Paragraphs 2.5, 3.6 and 3.7 of the protocol deal with correspondence. The tone and content of the first letter sent by a solicitor to the other spouse is important. A letter to an unrepresented party should always recommend that they seek independent legal advice and a second copy of the letter should be enclosed so that it can be passed to any solicitor instructed. A reasonable time limit for a response is suggested to be 14 days. A precedent letter is included at **Appendix 4**.

The protocol does not deal with solicitor/client correspondence. Correspondence should be kept clear and free of legal jargon. The client must always be kept advised of all steps and the client's instructions should be taken before any significant step is taken. Any important letters should first be sent to the client in draft form for approval.

2.2.4 Instruction of experts

Even where disclosure is being dealt with on a voluntary basis, experts may still need to be instructed, particularly where the parties cannot agree or do not know the value of a significant asset.

Even outside of the ambit of ancillary relief proceedings, the costs of any valuation or expert evidence must be proportionate to the sums in dispute. Where possible, expert reports should be obtained from a single valuer instructed by both parties. Particular reference should be made to the contents of *Family Division: Best Practice Guide for Instructing a Single Joint Expert* dated November 2002 which can be found in Appendix 14 to the Family Law protocol. The Guide applies where experts are being instructed either in the context of voluntary disclosure or within ancillary relief proceedings, and is considered in more detail in **Chapter 5** in the context of instruction of experts.

The pre-action protocol itself provides the following guidance on the instruction of experts:

1. Where one party wishes to instruct an expert, he or she should give to the other party a list of names of experts in the relevant speciality whom he or

she considers to be suitable. Within 14 days the other party may indicate an objection to one or more of the named experts and, if so, that party should supply the names of one or more experts whom he or she considers to be suitable. A common practice is for one party to put forward names of three suggested experts and for the other party to pick one of those names.

2. Where the identity of the expert is agreed, the parties should agree the terms of a joint letter of instruction. Sample draft letters of instruction are included at **Appendices 9, 10** and **11**.

3. Where no agreement can be reached about the identity of an expert, in view of the costs, each party should think carefully about instructing his or her own expert.

4. Where either a joint expert's report has been commissioned or each party has instructed their own expert, the expert should be prepared to answer reasonable questions raised by either party.

5. Even where reports are commissioned pre-application and CPR Part 35 does not apply, the expert should be told that in due course he or she may be obliged to report to the court and may therefore may be bound by Part 35 in the future.

6. Where the parties propose to instruct a joint expert, there is a duty on the parties to disclose whether they have already consulted their expert about the assets in issue.

7. If the parties agree to instruct separate experts, the parties should be encouraged to agree in advance that the reports will be disclosed.

2.3   REQUESTS FOR FURTHER DISCLOSURE

The pre-action protocol is silent on the issue of requests for further disclosure. After Forms E or schedules of assets have been disclosed, it is often the case that further questions are raised. Outside of the ambit of court proceedings, there is no obligation upon either party to answer such questions. It may therefore be a good idea in advance to establish in correspondence that both parties will be willing to answer any reasonable questions that may arise from initial disclosure. If either party indicates an unwillingness to answer such questions, then voluntary disclosure may be unsuitable and it may be preferable to issue Form A instead.

2.4   SETTLING CASES WITHOUT FULL DISCLOSURE

A relatively common scenario which may arise is where a party wishes to enter into a settlement with his or her spouse without having obtained full and frank disclosure from the other party. In some cases the situation may seem quite straightforward: for example a young childless couple who have relatively limited means, whose financial circumstances are transparent and who are both fully aware of the other's means. By contrast, a more troubling area is where you have been instructed by a wife whom you believe may be entering into a settlement under duress.

In any event, clear advice in writing must be given to the client stating that he or she should not be entering into a settlement without having obtained full and frank disclosure from his or her spouse. It must also be clearly stated in writing that you cannot advise the client upon terms of settlement without having the benefit of such disclosure and that the client is entering into the proposed settlement contrary to your specific advice.

Certainly in circumstances where you are acting for a wife who appears to have been placed under duress, you should try and arrange a prompt meeting with her to discuss the issues face to face. Advice given in person is often more effective than advice simply given in writing. Following on from such a meeting, you should always record your advice in writing to the client. When sending the disclaimer letter to the client, the client should be advised to seek independent legal advice on the letter before signing it. Although it is unlikely that the client will in fact obtain independent legal advice, the client should still be recommended to do so in any event.

On this difficult issue, you should be aware of case law where solicitors have failed to advise clients to obtain full and frank disclosure before entering into a settlement (*Dutfield* v. *Gilbert H Stephens & Sons* [1988] Fam Law 473). Another issue to consider is whether it is appropriate to remove yourself from the court record before any draft consent order is lodged with the court. Some solicitors feel that it is inappropriate for them to countersign a draft consent order which contains terms which they have specifically advised against. If you do wish to remove yourself from the court record, note should be had of the following:

1. The circumstances in which you cease acting for a client are limited and are regulated by the Solicitors' Code of Conduct 2007.
2. Where a client is acting in person when a draft consent order is lodged with the court, some courts will require an appointment to be made before a district judge for the client to be given advice upon the order before it is approved by the court.

CHAPTER 3

Procedure

Andrew Newbury

3.1 WHY MAKE AN APPLICATION?

In many divorces, a financial settlement may be secured without the necessity for a court timetabled ancillary relief application. In straightforward situations, an agreement can often be reached using the voluntary disclosure process or by negotiation between the solicitors and/or the parties. The following are common reasons for making an application for ancillary relief:

1. The other party refuses to provide full and frank disclosure on a voluntary basis.
2. Negotiations have broken down, or there does not appear to be a reasonable prospect of settlement.
3. The financial circumstances of the parties are complex. In complex divorces where extensive disclosure and expert evidence is required, the parties may in fact benefit from an ancillary relief timetable to ensure that prompt progress is made. Complex cases can sometimes be difficult to manage in the context of voluntary disclosure.
4. It is necessary to make an application for maintenance pending suit or for an injunction under MCA 1973, s.37. Such applications can only be made in the context of an ancillary relief application.

3.2 PRE-ACTION PROTOCOL

Although parties and solicitors are obliged to consider the pre-action protocol and to provide disclosure on a voluntary basis where appropriate, paragraph 2.2 of the pre-action protocol specifically states that the parties may benefit from a court-structured ancillary relief timetable. For any of the reasons set out at **3.1**, it may therefore be viewed as wholly appropriate to make an application for ancillary relief.

3.3   FAMILY PROCEEDINGS RULES 1991

3.3.1 Overview

If in doubt about any aspect of ancillary relief procedure, or for that matter, family procedure generally, the first point of reference must be the Family Proceedings Rules (FPR) 1991. They are the cornerstone of family procedure and will usually provide the answer to any given question. They have been updated and amended on several occasions since they were first introduced in 1991, so care should be taken to ensure that reference is always made to the up-to-date rules in force at any time. Rules 2.51A–2.70 deal with ancillary relief proceedings.

The leading practical procedural guide is *Family Court Practice* which is updated each year. It is commonly known as the 'Red Book'.

3.3.2 Interaction between the FPR, CPR, Green Book and White Book

Where the FPR are silent on any procedural issue, reference should then be made to the County Court Rules (CCR) 1981 (where the proceedings are in the county court – see *The Civil Court Practice*, commonly known as the 'Green Book') and the Rules of the Supreme Court (RSC) 1965 (where the proceedings are in the High Court – see *Civil Procedure*, commonly known as the 'White Book'). Although neither of these apply to civil proceedings, they do still apply to family proceedings. The Civil Procedure Rules (CPR) 1998 have very limited application to family proceedings. They apply only where specifically referred to by the FPR. Broadly speaking, only CPR Part 35 (experts) and most of CPR Parts 44 and 45 (costs) apply to ancillary relief proceedings.

3.3.3 The overriding objective

Care should be taken to read the overriding objective of the ancillary relief rules set out in FPR rule 2.51D. Particular emphasis is placed upon saving expense, ensuring that the case is dealt with proportionately, expeditiously and fairly. Reference is also made to active case management and what that entails. Specific guidelines and comments in the overriding objective are useful tools to use within ancillary relief proceedings, for example, at a First Appointment when contesting the relevance of questions in a questionnaire or the appropriateness of the instruction of an expert.

Practical tip

A careful reading of FPR rule 1.5 which deals with the computation of time is recommended. For example, periods of seven days or less referred to in the FPR should exclude days which are not a business day (i.e. weekends and bank holidays). Seven-day time periods under the FPR are therefore slightly longer than you may think.

3.4 FORM A

An application for ancillary relief is commenced by either the petitioner or the respondent filing Form A in triplicate (together with the requisite fee payable) with the court where divorce proceedings are pending.

3.4.1 Drafting of Form A

As it is such a straightforward document, often little thought is given to the proper completion of Form A. **Appendix 6** is an example of Form A completed with the appropriate information where there are children of the family and a full range of ancillary relief is sought. The following are practical points to note in completing Form A:

1. Ensure that the appropriate statement is made at the commencement of the form and the correct option is deleted, i.e., is your client intending 'to apply to the court for' ancillary relief (the option to choose if your client is the respondent in the main suit and has not issued an answer), or is your client intending to 'proceed with the application in the [Petition] [Answer] for'? In the case of a variation application under MCA 1973, s.31, does your client intend 'to apply to vary'?

2. When ticking the appropriate boxes setting out the relief required, the box referring to 'an order for maintenance pending suit' should only be ticked where such an application is being made. Some courts will automatically list an application for maintenance pending suit where that box has been ticked.

3. In the blank box under the application for a property adjustment order, addresses of all properties should be given, to include Land Registry title numbers where known. 'Property adjustment orders' include an application for a property transfer, order for sale and variation of an ante-nuptial or post-nuptial settlement. Where a variation of a settlement is sought, the full name of the settlement (where known) should be included. Note that under FPR rule 2.59(2)(a), where land is registered, the Land Registry title number must specifically be included in Form A. Under rule 2.59(2)(b), where the property is subject to a mortgage, full particulars should likewise be given where they are known.

4. Where an application for pension attachment or pension sharing is sought, details of the pensions should be listed under the appropriate box, for example, 'Scottish Widows policy no. XY123456'. It will often be the case that when Form A is issued, information has not been received in respect of the spouse's pensions, and so details cannot be included in Form A. Once that information has been received, Form A can be amended and re-lodged with the court with the appropriate pension details inserted.

21

5. Where there are children of the family, care should be taken to ensure that the appropriate boxes towards the foot of the form are likewise ticked. The most common box to tick is in respect of an application for a school fees order, i.e. 'to meet expenses incurred by a child in being educated or training for work'.

3.4.2 Amending Form A

It is often the case when an application for ancillary relief is made, that it is at an early stage of the divorce when disclosure has not been provided. Accordingly, when acting for the applicant, property details may not be known, or more commonly pension details will not have been disclosed. When appropriate information is received at a later date in the proceedings, Form A can be amended, marked up in red and then filed with the court for re-issue. No fee is payable on filing an amended Form A.

When lodging an amended Form A with the court, the position should be explained in the covering letter to the court.

3.4.3 Filing and service of Form A

Form A is lodged with the court in which the divorce proceedings are pending. The form must be lodged in triplicate together with a cheque for the fee payable, which at the time of writing (August 2009) is £210.00. Upon the filing of Form A, the court must serve a copy on the respondent within four days of the date of filing (FPR rule 2.61A), although in reality, taking into account the backlog with some courts, this time limit is not usually complied with.

When processing Form A, the court must also produce Form C setting out the first part of the ancillary relief timetable as follows:

1. The date of the First Appointment which must be not less than 12 weeks and not more than 16 weeks after the date of filing Form A (FPR rule 2.61A(4)(a)).
2. The date for the filing and exchange of Forms E, which in accordance with rule 2.61B(2) must not be less than 35 days before the date of the First Appointment.
3. The date for the filing and service of statement of issues, chronology, questionnaires and Form G, which in accordance with rule 2.61(B)(7) must be at least 14 days before the date of the First Appointment.

Practical tip

As soon as Form C has been issued by the court, you should advise your client immediately and take the following steps:

1. Write to your client and inform them of the dates which have been fixed by the court. In particular, point out the time and date of the First Appointment and explain that they must attend that hearing.

---

2. Send a blank Form E to your client to be completed, together with a schedule setting out all of the documents that the client will need to produce. It is a good idea to send to the client the short booklet produced by the court which contains guidelines for completing Form E.
3. Some clients have real difficulty in starting to complete Form E – when presented with the form, they simply panic. If that is the case, it may help if you provide the client with the form filled in as far as possible with the information on your file. Alternatively, it may be helpful to arrange for the client to visit your office so that you can go through the form together.
4. Where your client has pension provision, the client should be asked to sign Form P forthwith so that pension information can be requested immediately. Note should be had of the procedural requirements under FPR rule 2.70(2). More detailed consideration of procedural issues in respect of pensions is set out at **3.4.4**.

3.4.4 Service of Form A: mortgagees and pension providers

Although rule 2.61A(4) specifies that the obligation is on the court to serve the respondent with Form A, it is good practice when acting for the applicant to serve the respondent's solicitors with Form A and Form C to ensure that they have been properly notified of the dates.

Of particular importance is the need to serve Form A upon pension trustees and mortgagees. As far as mortgagees are concerned, in accordance with FPR rule 2.59(4), they must be served with Form A where an application is made in Form A for either a property adjustment order or an avoidance of disposition order.

As far as pension trustees are concerned, the procedure is more complex and is set out in FPR rule 2.70(7). Upon making an application for ancillary relief, the applicant must send to the pension trustees the following:

(a) a copy of Form A;
(b) an address to which notice is to be served in accordance with the Divorce etc. (Pension) Regulations 2000, SI 2000/1123 (this can be either the client's own address or the solicitor's address);
(c) an address to which any payment is to be sent by the pension trustees;
(d) where the address in paragraph (c) is that of a bank, sufficient details to enable payment to be made into the account of the applicant.

Practitioners should also be aware that obligations are placed upon spouses with pension rights when they receive notification that a First Appointment has been fixed. In accordance with FPR rule 2.70(2), within seven days of receiving Form C, they must contact the person responsible for each of their pensions and request that they provide the information set out in the Pensions on Divorce etc. (Provision of Information) Regulations 2000, SI 2000/1048, reg.2(2). Such information is now requested in Form P. A copy of Form P should be sent to the client, with Section A fully completed. The client must sign and return the form so that it can then immediately be served on the pension provider.

3.4.5 Cross-applications using Form A

A cross-application in Form A may be appropriate in certain circumstances, outlined below.

Pension sharing

On occasions, Form A may be issued by the spouse with pension rights (usually the husband). Within that ancillary relief application the court has the power to make orders in favour of the wife, although when acting for the wife in such circumstances, it may be prudent to make a cross-application in Form A specifying details of the husband's pensions so that Form A can be served upon the pension trustees in accordance with rule 2.70. The same procedure applies when making a cross-application in Form A, although in a covering letter the court should be notified that it should simply be consolidated with the pre-existing ancillary relief application.

Acting for the respondent – avoiding the re-marriage trap

This is one of the most common areas of negligence for family lawyers. By virtue of MCA 1973, s.28(3), an application for ancillary relief cannot be brought after re-marriage. A claim for ancillary relief made before re-marriage can, however, be brought to a conclusion after re-marriage. Where a petitioner has sought all forms of ancillary relief in the prayer of the petition, such claims will have been brought before re-marriage and therefore they will not be adversely affected by s.28(3) (save for not being able to pursue claims for spousal maintenance which are automatically dismissed by virtue of the re-marriage). Where acting for a respondent who intends to re-marry, the respondent must bring an application in Form A before the date of the re-marriage to ensure that the claim is before the court.

Where claims are being brought by the respondent which are not sought by the applicant

Strictly speaking, the issue of a petition for divorce will trigger all claims that either party has against the other arising upon the breakdown of a marriage. Some courts, however, take a different view. For example, if an applicant has issued Form A and is only seeking, say, lump sum provision and periodical payments, the court will insist that the respondent files his or her own Form A if the respondent is seeking, say, property adjustment and pension sharing orders. This approach is, however, uncommon.

3.5   DRAFTING OF FORM E

3.5.1 Basic principles

The completion of Form E is largely self-explanatory. The following are a few basic principles:

1. To minimise costs, it is usually a good idea to send a blank Form E to the client to complete, together with the explanatory booklet which is provided by the court. The client's attention should be drawn to the detailed footnotes in Form E and in particular the schedule on the last page which sets out the documents which should be exhibited. Clients should be asked to complete the form in manuscript as far as they are able and return it with documents which can then be copied and exhibited to Form E.
2. Be aware that some clients struggle with completing such forms. They may be unfamiliar with them and may find the task daunting.
3. Where a client may be unable to complete Form E from scratch without assistance, one option would be to have a meeting with the client to go through the form together, with a view to advising the client on the disclosure he or she needs to obtain. An alternative approach would be to complete Form E as far as possible on the client's behalf and then specifically address with the client the outstanding information required.
4. Clients often have particular difficulty in completing Section 3.1.1 requiring them to detail their income needs. It can be useful to send to the client a pro-forma schedule of income needs to assist the client in providing a full breakdown. A precedent schedule of expenditure can be found at **Appendix 7**.
5. As the date for completing Form E is often two to three months after issuing Form A, there is a natural temptation to delay its completion. A properly completed Form E often takes longer than anticipated and the client should be urged to start work upon it as soon as possible.
6. The importance of Form E cannot be underestimated. It is often the first document to which a district judge will refer and therefore it must be correct. It is also the client's first – and often best – opportunity to properly present and plead his or her case. Do not therefore overlook the importance of properly completing Sections 4 and 5 at the end of Form E.
7. It is not only the client's responsibility to ensure that Form E is accurate: onus is also placed upon the solicitor. Practitioners often spend a great deal of time and care in checking the other side's disclosure, but fail to check thoroughly their own client's documents.

3.5.2 Practical tips for completing Form E

The following is not intended as a comprehensive overview for completing Form E, but simply deals with sections of the form where uncertainty sometimes arises.

1. **Paragraph 1.11** – details of health. The footnote specifically requests that details of the state of health should be given 'if you think this should be taken into account'. Clients should therefore be advised to think carefully about making reference to any stress, anxiety or depression arising from the breakdown of the marriage. Usually health concerns will only be relevant if they have an impact upon earning capacity or income requirements if medical treatment or expenses need to be taken into account.

2. **Paragraph 1.13** – this paragraph invites not only details of CSA assessments to be given, but also where there is no such assessment, a calculation of the estimated liability. Where details of the absent parent's income are available, the anticipated assessment can be easily calculated using the present formula.

3. **Paragraph 2.1** – when including an estimate of the value of the matrimonial home or any other property at paragraph 2.2, it is sensible for clients to speak to local estate agents to seek a free and informal estimate of the value of any given property. Clients should be advised to request that estate agents give their opinion as to the open market value of the property as opposed to the figure at which it should be placed on the market. Enquiries of no more than two or three estate agents should suffice. Where their view is given in writing they must be exhibited to Form E. Clients should also be advised not to speak to too many estate agents in case a formal valuation may be required in due course as the spouse may object to formally instructing a firm that has already been informally instructed by your client.

   As far as costs of sale are confirmed, specific figures should be included where available, although as a rule of thumb in many parts of the country, practitioners use a figure of 3 per cent (inclusive of VAT, legal fees and disbursements) of the selling price.

4. **Paragraph 2.8** – clients often give a great deal of attention to the value of personal items and contents, whereas such issues are rarely of particular interest to the court. It is inappropriate and unnecessary to give a global value of the contents of the former matrimonial home or any other property – only items with a value in excess of £500 need be included. Realistic open market second hand values should be given. Insurance values should not be relied upon as they are usually far in excess of the second hand value of an item. As far as cars are concerned, *Parker's Car Price Guide* or similar publications usually give a broadly realistic estimate of value. For antiques, it is not usually necessary to obtain a formal valuation at the outset. If antiques or works of art are of substantial value, a formal valuation carried out by a single joint expert following on from the First Appointment may be appropriate.

5. **Paragraph 2.10** – capital gains tax (CGT) liabilities can often be significant, particularly where second homes are owned. CGT liabilities are taken into account as a relevant liability, regardless of whether an

immediate charge is to arise or not. Where a realistic value of an asset is known, an enquiry should be made of an accountant to calculate the CGT liability. Where the situation is more complex, for example, where there may be a jointly held property portfolio, it may be more logical to seek direction at the First Appointment for an accountant instructed as single joint expert to carry out the CGT calculations once the properties have been formally valued.

6. **Paragraph 2.11** – it would be sensible to ask the client's accountant to complete this page prior to filing Form E. Unless that accountant has experience in calculating business values, it may be advisable not to place a value upon the business interests at that juncture. Where larger or more complex business interests are involved, it will be more prudent to remain silent on that issue and for the business to be valued by a jointly instructed forensic accountant following on from a direction at the First Appointment.

7. **Paragraph 2.13** – upon issuing Form A, the first step that must be put in motion is a request for pension information. As a calculation of cash equivalent transfer value can often take several weeks to be produced, the request must be made forthwith after issuing Form A (see **3.4.4**). In accordance with the procedural requirements of FPR rule 2.70, Form P must be sent to the client to sign in respect of each pension policy. Once signed by the client, the form must be sent to each pension provider immediately. The client should also be sent Form BR20 to complete so that an estimate of SERPS can be obtained. This is often overlooked.

8. **Paragraph 2.18** – when including details of state benefits, the availability of working tax credit and child tax credit should not be overlooked. Particularly where a couple have separated and are living in separate homes, one or both households may be eligible to claim tax credits, or to increase their entitlement to tax credits. The level of tax credits receivable by a household can have a profound effect upon applications for maintenance pending suit and also quantifying maintenance entitlements in the long term.

9. **Paragraph 3.1** – as suggested at point 4 of **3.5.1**, clients should be provided with a pro-forma schedule of income needs to assist them in calculating their income requirements. In fact, it may be a good idea to provide two schedules: one to enable them to calculate their present/interim needs and another to enable them to calculate their longer-term future requirements. A great deal of care and attention should be spent in completing this section for the following reasons:

   (a) Clients often believe that to maximise their claims on divorce, they should likewise maximise their income needs, thus putting forward a schedule that is wholly unrealistic. District judges are usually exceedingly critical of such expenditure schedules and view them as 'wish lists'.

27

(b) Those principles apply whether acting for a husband or a wife. For example, a husband submitting a monthly income requirement of, say, £5,000 would be put in a difficult position if he were to contend that his wife had an income requirement of, say, only £2,000 per month.

(c) Although care must be taken in assisting the client to provide a schedule which is accurate, ultimately, it should be a breakdown of what the client believes his or her needs to be. District judges have been known to ask parties at final hearings whether the schedule in their Form E has been prepared by them or by their solicitors.

(d) A distinction needs to be drawn between current/interim needs and future needs. A monthly figure for car depreciation/car replacement fund or replacement of furniture, house redecoration, etc. may be perfectly appropriate as longer-term needs, but is rarely appropriate on an interim basis.

10. **Paragraph 4.3** – it would seem logical that any contributions which are to be included are limited to those which are reasonably likely to be taken into account by the court. Note should be had of the comments of case law in *White* v. *White* [2000] 2 FLR 981 onwards. For example, under present case law, relevant contributions could be assets acquired prior to the marriage or post-separation. Inherited assets may also reflect a relevant contribution. By contrast, an argument that one party was the major breadwinner and therefore made a relevant contribution to the marriage is unlikely to find favour with the court.

11. **Paragraph 4.4** – clients must be firmly advised only to raise conduct arguments where relevant. A clear explanation must be given to clients of the limited circumstances where conduct arguments will be taken into account under MCA 1973, s.25.

12. **Paragraph 5.1** – often, it is impossible to give specific details of the ultimate orders being sought from the court. That is usually because until Forms E have been exchanged, full disclosure has not been obtained. Having said that, however, it is helpful for a case to be clearly pleaded at this early stage if this is possible. Even if quantum of spousal maintenance cannot be stated, a broad indication will assist the court at this stage.

3.5.3 Documents to be exhibited to Form E

Rule 2.61B(3) is specific about the documents which must be exhibited to Form E. They are as follows:

1. Any document required by Form E, i.e. those documents specified in the footnotes and the index at the rear.

2. Any other documents necessary to explain or clarify any of the information contained in Form E. This provision is not further explained or expanded

upon by the FPR, but could extend to such items as a letter/report from an accountant giving an estimate of the value of a family business, details in respect of family trusts, etc.

3. Any documents produced by a pension provider in accordance with FPR rule 2.70.

Note should also be had of rule 2.61B(4) which clearly states that no other documents must be attached to Form E other than those referred to at rule 2.61B(3).

Where somebody has been unavoidably prevented from sending any document with Form E, that person must serve a copy of the document on the other party at the earliest opportunity, and also file a copy of the document with the court together with a statement explaining the failure to send it with Form E.

3.5.4 Additional disclosure and requests for disclosure prior to the First Appointment

Rule 2.61B(6) is clear. No disclosure may be requested or given between filing Form A and the First Appointment, save for those documents served with Form E and the subsequent service of the questionnaire, statement of issues, etc. prior to the First Appointment.

3.6 FIRST APPOINTMENT DOCUMENTS

In accordance with FPR rule 2.61B(7), each party must file with the court and serve on the other a statement of issues, chronology, questionnaire and Form G. It is worth noting that although rule 2.61B(2) refers to Forms E being exchanged, rule 2.61B(7) refers to the First Appointment documents being served. There is therefore no requirement that they be mutually exchanged. Arguably, they should be served even if the other party is not ready, although general practice is that such documents are served by way of exchange.

3.6.1 Questionnaire

This is arguably the most important of the First Appointment documents. In most divorce cases, this will be the one opportunity to ask questions about the other party's relevant financial circumstances. Although it is necessary to seek full disclosure and cover all relevant issues, the questions must be relevant to the issues in the case. District judges are particularly wary of questionnaires which are little more than fishing expeditions. When drafting questionnaires, the following practical points should be noted:

1. Rule 2.61B(7)(c) specifically states that the questionnaire must be set out 'by reference to the concise statement of issues'. Accordingly, one document must tie in with the other.

2. In terms of layout, it is often a good idea for the questionnaire to be broken down into relevant sections, for example, a section seeking disclosure in respect of bank accounts and savings, etc., another in respect of income and earning capacity, and another section in respect of pensions, etc. Some practitioners prefer to draft questionnaires so that the questions specifically relate to the numbered sections of Form E.

3. It is inappropriate to ask questions where your clients can obtain the information themselves. For example, questions should not usually be asked in respect of a joint bank account if your client can obtain the appropriate information directly from the bank.

4. When looking through bank statements, the following points should be noted when raising questions:

    (a) Are bank transfers being made to any other account which has not been disclosed?

    (b) Is there a full and continuous run of statements for each account or are any statements missing?

    (c) When asking questions about any significant debits or credits, consider issues of proportionality. For example, in specific cases is it really appropriate to ask about transactions of less than, say, £1,000?

    (d) If new accounts have been opened during the last 12 months, check whether there are any old accounts which have been closed. If so, statements for that account within the last 12 months up to the date of closure should be produced.

    (e) Do the bank accounts disclosed show normal day-to-day expenditure, such as household bills, mortgage payments, food shopping, etc.? If not, from what account are such payments made?

5. When referring to bank accounts, policies, etc. in a questionnaire, it is always a good idea to quote or make reference to the full policy number. That approach should also be carried through into correspondence. By always quoting full account numbers, it is easier to cross-reference documents in due course, for example, when preparing for an FDR.

6. Always keep in mind the overriding objective and proportionality of costs. It is important to consider not only whether a question is relevant to the issues in the case, but whether the time and cost in answering the question are proportionate to the sums in dispute.

7. Where a person is being asked to produce a document, is that document in that person's possession or control? Could he or she reasonably be expected to obtain it?

8. Many district judges are reluctant to order the disclosure of credit card statements unless there is good reason, for example, where there has

been a significant increase in credit card debt post-separation. They may only order the disclosure of up-to-date statements to confirm present balances.

9. Many district judges are also reluctant to order that either party answers questions raised about their expenditure requirements in Form E. Such issues are usually dealt with in cross-examination at the final hearing.

10. Also bear in mind that entrapment is inappropriate. Where documents which belong to the other party have been obtained, they must immediately be returned in accordance with *Hildebrand* v. *Hildebrand* [1992] 1 FLR 244. After disclosing the existence of those documents, questions may then be asked. It is, however, inappropriate to retain those documents and ask questions of the other side without disclosing their existence.

3.6.2 Statements of issues

Note that rule 2.61B(7)(a) refers to filing and serving a 'concise' statement of issues. The purpose of the document is not to fully plead the case, but to give the district judge a brief overview of the issues between the parties.

The format which should be adopted is not specified by the FPR, although a common practice is to break the document into sections dealing with each issue in turn and setting out the respective positions of the husband and the wife. An alternative way in which to approach this statement of issues is by reference to the MCA 1973, s.25(2) checklist. Attached at **Appendix 8** is an example of a draft statement of issues.

3.6.3 Chronology

It is understood that different district judges take different approaches to the chronology. The most popular approach seems to be a concise chronology simply setting out the key dates. Some district judges prefer the chronology to be more detailed, providing some background information but that does, however, appear to be the minority view.

It should be borne in mind that there may be little point in setting out dates which may be relatively easily ascertainable from the court file, such as date of issue of Form A and dates of Forms E, etc. What is more useful to the court are those dates which may be of particular relevance, but are not otherwise obvious from Form E. For example, the date that a property was acquired or a business was started may be relevant, as may be the date that one of the parties was made redundant. The date of the parties' pre-marriage cohabitation would clearly be relevant, as would the date when any inherited assets fell in. Where there has been a long period of separation, the date of the acquisition or disposal of properties during the separation period will also be of importance.

3.6.4 Form G

This is a simple procedural document in which the parties advise each other and the court whether they are able to use the First Appointment as an FDR. In most cases it will not be possible to proceed directly to an FDR as disclosure and valuations will be required. Where a party does wish to proceed straight to an FDR, the position should be made clear not only in Form G, but also in the covering letter to the court and to the other side. Practical considerations should, however, be borne in mind. The time allotted by the court for a First Appointment is usually far shorter than the time allocated for an FDR. Even if both parties agree that the First Appointment should be used as an FDR, the court may not be able to accommodate that request. Enquiries should be made of court listing.

3.7 FAILURE TO COMPLY WITH COURT TIMETABLE

A common concern amongst many practitioners is the delay in filing and serving documents. The timetable between exchanging Forms E, questionnaires, etc. and the First Appointment is tight. It is also becoming common practice for deadlines to be missed by several days.

The only immediate remedy available to either of the parties is an application for a penal notice to enforce the timetable set out in Form C.

The following are practical points to note when applying for a penal notice:

1. Many courts will insist that an application is dealt with on notice and therefore will require notice of application to be filed together with the appropriate fee. Listing considerations then arise as courts may not be able to accommodate the application prior to, say, the First Appointment. A certificate of urgency filed with the notice of application may, however, ensure an early hearing date.
2. Where possible, it is worth making enquiries of the local court listing office and district judges to ascertain whether they would be wiling to deal with applications for penal notices on a 'without notice' basis. Some district judges are known to be willing to deal with such applications by way of a letter and therefore applications for penal notices can be dealt with urgently.
3. Where an order for a penal notice has been granted, it must be served personally upon the person against whom the order has been made. The time for them to comply with the order runs from the date of service, not from the date the order was made.
4. Where either no Form E has been served prior to a First Appointment or it has been served so late in the day that the First Appointment is

ineffective, the most practical remedies at the First Appointment are as follows:

(a) An order for costs should be sought at the First Appointment. As a summary assessment of costs may be appropriate, it is therefore necessary to file and serve a costs schedule at least 24 hours before the hearing.

(b) An order for a penal notice to be attached to any subsequent directions should be requested.

(c) A request for a further First Appointment may be necessary to consider any subsequent questionnaire, etc.

3.8   FIRST APPOINTMENT

The purpose of the First Appointment is clearly set out in FPR rule 2.61D(1): the First Appointment must be conducted with the objective of defining the issues and saving costs. When considering what a district judge must do in accordance with rule 2.61D, the purpose of the First Appointment becomes clear:

1. The district judge must determine the extent to which the questionnaires must be answered and which documents requested in those questionnaires must be produced. He may also give directions for the production of such further documents as may be necessary.

2. The district judge must also give directions about the valuation of assets, the obtaining and exchanging of expert evidence and evidence to be adduced by each party, to include any further chronologies or schedules to be filed by each party.

3. The district judge must list the matter for an FDR appointment, unless he or she feels that is not appropriate. Where an FDR is not appropriate, the district judge may make one of the following orders:

   (a) List the matter for a further directions appointment/adjourned First Appointment.

   (b) List the matter for the making of an interim order, such as a hearing for maintenance pending suit.

   (c) Fix the matter for a final hearing.

   (d) Adjourn the application for mediation or private negotiation, or in exceptional circumstances adjourn the case generally. This latter approach is, however, somewhat rare.

3.8.1 Practical steps for preparation

Some First Appointments need more preparation than others. The following are practical steps which are worth considering:

33

1. Just before the hearing itself, set aside time to prepare for that hearing. Ensure that you are familiar with the facts of the case and that you have all relevant information at your fingertips. If you are acting for the applicant, you may need to set out some relevant background for the district judge. Ensure that you are familiar with basic information such as the length of the marriage, the names and ages of any children, etc.
2. Where expert evidence is to be required (for example, a surveyor to value the matrimonial home or an accountant to value the family business), if the expert is to be instructed as a single joint expert it is worthwhile trying agree upon the identity of the expert prior to the hearing.
3. Prior to the First Appointment and in accordance with the *Best Practice Guide (Instructing a Single Joint Expert)* [2003] 1 FLR 573 (dated December 2002) (see **Appendix 21**), the experts you would wish to instruct should be asked to provide details of their suitability as set out in the Best Practice Guide. A letter from the expert should include confirmation that there is no conflict of interest, that the matter is within the range of expertise of the expert, the expert's availability to provide the report within a specified timescale, the fee rate, etc. Although not specified in the Best Practice Guide, it is often a worthwhile idea to submit the names of three possible experts and to provide the details set out above in respect of each expert. It is a good idea to request the expert's CV and send it to the other side. Some solicitors keep a database of CVs of their preferred experts.
4. Based upon the information submitted prior to the First Appointment, the district judge should then be invited at the First Appointment to identify the expert to be instructed.
5. Where there could be a delay in agreeing the contents of the letter of instruction, or the contents of that letter of instruction could be contentious, it may be prudent to prepare prior to the First Appointment a draft letter of instruction and to serve it upon the other party. See precedents at **Appendices 10, 11** and **12**. At the First Appointment the district judge should then be invited to direct that the specified single joint expert be instructed by a specific date in accordance with the terms of the letter of instruction.
6. If specific counsel has been involved in the case, and if it is intended that counsel will be used at the FDR, it can be sensible to take a note of counsel's availability for the First Appointment and to ask the court to fix the FDR hearing there and then subject to counsel's availability.
7. Thought should also be given to the timetabling of matters after the First Appointment and how the provision of information will tie in with the instruction of experts. For example, the husband may need to provide his replies to questionnaire before a forensic accountant can be formally instructed. Likewise, if a family business owns premises, those premises may need to be valued by a surveyor before the accountant's calculations can be finalised.

8. The client should also be prepared for the First Appointment. It is important to talk clients through what will happen at court that day. For many clients, it will be their first attendance in a court room and it may be the first time they have seen their spouse for many months. Clients should be assured that it is usually a short procedural hearing and that they are unlikely to have to say anything.

9. It is a good idea to take a draft order to the First Appointment setting out the directions you are seeking. It may well endear you and your client to the district judge and can be used as a template by the district judge. When setting out deadlines in the draft order, it is preferable to include specific dates as opposed to timescales. For example, instead of stating that replies to questionnaire should be filed and served 'within 28 days of the date of the order', it is better to state that, for example, they should be filed and served 'by 4pm on 21st January'.

3.8.2 Practical steps for attending

Where possible, it is often advisable to agree with your opposite number to attend at court at least half an hour or so before the First Appointment. Discussions before entering into the court room can often narrow the issues between the parties and in some cases directions can be agreed whilst in the court building.

By way of example, it may be possible to agree which questions in the questionnaire should be deleted or amended. Likewise, the identity of valuers can often be agreed, as can final wording of letters of instruction.

The length and format of a First Appointment can vary considerably depending upon the complexity of the matter and the approach adopted by the individual district judge. If directions have been agreed in advance, many district judges will be happy to make an order in the terms agreed. Other district judges may, however, adopt a different approach: even where questionnaires have been agreed, they may have their own view as to which questions should or should not be answered. They may also have different views as to the appropriateness of expert evidence or otherwise. It is important to advise clients that whatever may be agreed in advance, it is ultimately the district judge who is making the order and who has final say.

3.8.3 Costs issues

It is necessary to provide to the court and to the other party a completed Form H costs estimate at the First Appointment. The documents do not need to be served and filed in advance. Where the proceedings were commenced before 3 April 2006, Form H in the old format should be used. Where the proceedings were issued on or after 3 April 2006, the revised Form H should be used.

Costs orders are uncommon at First Appointments, but may be made where either party has not complied with the rules, in accordance with FPR rule 2.61D(2)(e).

3.9 FINANCIAL DISPUTE RESOLUTION HEARING

Very little guidance is given in the FPR about the format and conduct of FDR appointments. The only guidance is set out in FPR rule 2.61E.

The only procedural step that must be complied with prior to the FDR in accordance with rule 2.61E is that not less than seven days before the FDR, the applicant must file with the court details of all offers and proposals and responses to them. That includes all without prejudice correspondence as well as open offers.

In some courts directions are also made for the filing of an agreed schedule of assets or updated statements of issues and chronologies prior to the FDR. Note must be had of any specific provisions contained in the order made at the First Appointment.

Although the FPR provide for proposals for settlement to be submitted prior to the FDR, that does not mean that there is an obligation upon the parties to make offers before the FDR itself. It is, however; undoubtedly the case that an FDR has a greater chance of success if proposals for settlement have been submitted by the parties prior to the hearing. Where the parties attend at court for an FDR and no parameters have been set by offers for settlement, negotiations are starting cold and even though issues may be narrowed, the prospects of a settlement being reached are reduced.

3.9.1 Steps to be taken in advance

In addition to the desirability of having exchanged and submitted proposals for settlement, the following are steps which should also be considered and which may assist in negotiations at an FDR:

1. All disclosure including experts' reports and replies to questionnaire must be considered carefully as far in advance of the FDR as possible. Where any questions or issues arise in respect of that disclosure, they should be raised and dealt with as soon as possible. It is a common problem that disclosure is not considered until immediately prior to the FDR, questions are then raised days before the FDR and it is impossible for any outstanding information to be provided in advance of the hearing. Lack of full disclosure often hinders negotiations.

2. Even where not specifically directed by the court, it is good practice to prepare a schedule of assets, liabilities and income based upon the disclosure produced to date. The other party should be invited to agree that

schedule of assets. It is often the case that negotiations are more fruitful and productive where the asset base has been agreed and therefore the factual issues have been narrowed.

3.   If an issue regarding a spouse's reasonable housing requirements is anticipated, then appropriate estate agents' particulars should be obtained and served prior to the FDR.

4.   Where up-to-date information has been obtained or the input of third parties obtained, such information should be produced as far in advance of the FDR as possible to enable the other party to respond or consider that information. Producing crucial information at the FDR itself will often hinder negotiations.

5.   Where possible, clients must be advised candidly and as far in advance of the FDR as possible about potential parameters of settlement. Clients with a realistic view of settlement and the orders available to them should be more amenable to negotiation and more open to agreeing a realistic settlement. If the input of counsel is to be required at the FDR, it is sensible to have a conference with counsel at least a few weeks in advance of that FDR.

6.   Clients should be advised to be as open minded as possible about what may happen at the FDR itself. The format is fluid: some FDRs involve an attendance at court all day with little or no input of the district judge, whereas other FDRs are largely based around seeking the views of the district judge. Where possible, neither the representatives nor the parties should have any other commitments during the day which would prevent ongoing negotiations.

7.   Usually, FDR hearings are only fixed to last for an hour and therefore there is no obligation to prepare a bundle in accordance with the President's Direction of 27 July 2006. Where FDR hearings are listed for more than an hour, a bundle must be produced in accordance with that direction. In more complex cases, it can in any event be a good idea to prepare a core bundle which may assist the district judge and the parties. The district judge will not have a substantial amount of time to consider the bundle and it should be kept as short as possible. A good idea would be to limit a bundle to the following documents:

(a)   without prejudice and open offers;
(b)   agreed schedule of assets;
(c)   statements of issues;
(d)   Forms E, without enclosures;
(e)   replies to questionnaire, without enclosures;
(f)   any relevant experts' reports or other documents which will be useful in negotiations.

3.9.2 Conduct of FDRs

As stated above, the format varies dramatically from case to case and court to court. The following are of note:

1. Rule 2.61E(1) simply states that the FDR appointment must be treated as a meeting held for the purposes of discussion and negotiation.
2. Care must be taken to ensure that the client's agreement is secured before any proposals for settlement are submitted at the FDR. It is also important that the client understands the nature of discussions and feels comfortable with what is happening. Undue pressure must not be placed upon the client with a view to securing the settlement.
3. It may be the case that even where a final settlement cannot be achieved, the issues in a case have been substantially narrowed by discussions at an FDR. The narrowing of those issues and moving on from intractable positions can often be the spur to settlement being reached in the forthcoming weeks.
4. On occasions where discussions are progressing constructively, the district judge may be invited not to express a view. On occasions, the district judge's view may be quite different from the format of the settlement being envisaged by the parties. At other times, however, the district judge's view is the catalyst which leads to settlement. Accordingly, the district judge may be invited to give a view on certain aspects of the case but asked not to comment on others.
5. Where agreement has not been reached at the FDR, careful consideration needs to be given to the directions which are to be required from the court. Most commonly, the matter will need setting down for a final hearing, or if there is a prospect of settlement being reached in the foreseeable future, the court could be asked to list the matter for a further FDR or a short directions hearing which could be used to obtain the court's approval of a draft consent order.

3.10 APPLICATIONS FOR DIRECTIONS/FURTHER DISCLOSURE

In most straightforward cases, all appropriate disclosure and directions will be dealt with at the First Appointment. The questionnaire served prior to the First Appointment should be the only substantive request for further disclosure in most ancillary relief cases. In some cases, however, further requests for disclosure will arise. Circumstances may change considerably during the ancillary relief proceedings, or further issues may come to light which need investigating. Sometimes replies to questionnaire may give rise to further issues which need to be addressed in a supplemental questionnaire.

The rules dealing with further directions and requests for disclosure are set out in FPR rule 2.61D. By virtue of rule 2.61D(3), after the First

Appointment, a party is not entitled to the production of any further documents (other than those ordered at the First Appointment) other than with permission of the court. In accordance with rule 2.61D(4), at any stage either party may apply to the court for further directions and the court may give further directions as appropriate.

Accordingly, strictly speaking a request for further disclosure, whether in a supplemental questionnaire or done by way of a letter should only be made with the appropriate order of a court. In practice, however, practitioners will tend to serve a supplemental questionnaire, although if the other party refuses to reply to that questionnaire, an application needs to be made to the court by way of a notice of application (see **Appendix 13**). The matter will then be decided by way of an appropriate directions hearing.

Where disputes arise in respect of expert evidence, further applications may also be made to the court under rule 2.61D(4), although that issue is dealt with in **Chapter 5.**

3.11 THIRD PARTY DISLOSURE

Such applications are surprisingly uncommon within ancillary relief proceedings. Disclosure issues are usually dealt with between the husband and the wife. Where circumstances warrant it, however, the court does have the power to order disclosure from third parties by way of a subpoena (in the High Court), a witness summons (in the County Court) or an inspection appointment.

3.11.1 Inspection appointment

Inspection appointments (previously known as production appointments) are dealt with by FPR rule 2.61(7). This provision states that either party may apply to the court that any person must attend an appointment (an inspection appointment) before the court and produce any documents to be specified or described in the order, the inspection of which appears to the court to be necessary for disposing fairly of the application for ancillary relief or for saving costs.

Examples of appropriate third parties against whom an inspection appointment may be brought are as follows:

1. A cohabitee or new spouse where it is contested that their financial circumstances are a relevant resource to be taken into account within the ancillary relief proceedings.
2. An employer if information has not been produced regarding a party's remuneration package, benefits, share options, etc.
3. An accountant if the accountant holds information relevant to a party's financial affairs which has not otherwise been disclosed.

4. A bank manager where information has not been disclosed in respect of a party's bank records.
5. A parent if there are relevant financial dealings between a party and his or her parent.

Procedure for applying for an inspection appointment

The procedure for an inspection appointment is set out in *B* v. *B (Production Appointment: Procedure)* [1995] 1 FLR 913 and is as follows:

1. The initial application is made on notice to the other party to the proceedings with a sworn statement in support. The sworn statement should set out details of the nature of the proceedings, the need for the production of the documents, the exact documents sought and whether the applicant intends to call the witness at the hearing.
2. The application is then considered by the district judge. It is suggested that it should usually be heard either at the First Appointment or at the end of the FDR. If the order is made, the third party will then be ordered to attend a subsequent hearing, bringing the documents which he or she has been ordered to produce.
3. It is at this second hearing that the third party can be represented and may object to the production of the documents. The court is compelled to balance the interest of the parties to the suit as against the importance of privacy to the third party. It should be borne in mind that the third party is not a party to the substantive proceedings.

The inspection appointment was introduced to bring forward the time at which disclosure from third parties could be ordered. Previously, such disclosure had only been produced at final hearings following on from the issue of a subpoena or witness summons.

3.11.2 Applications for subpoena/witness summons

Aside from the power of the court to order attendance by way of a subpoena or witness summons, at a final ancillary relief hearing a district judge can order the attendance of any third party by virtue of FPR rule 2.62(4).

Subpoenas

In High Court proceedings, an application to compel a party to attend at a hearing is made by way of a subpoena under RSC Ord. 38 rule 14. If the proceedings are in chambers, Ord. 32, rule 7 applies: leave is required before the subpoena may be issued.

A subpoena issued to compel a witness to attend to give evidence is a *subpoena ad testificandum*. A subpoena issued to compel a party to produce documents at a hearing is a *subpoena duces tecum*.

It should be noted that if you issue a subpoena and that party is called to give evidence, then that party is your witness and therefore usually cannot be cross-examined.

Witness summons

In the county court the corresponding process is to issue a witness summons under CCR Ord. 20 rule 12, although leave is not required in the county court unless the witness is being called to give evidence at a directions hearing in chambers.

It has been held in the Chancery Division (*Khanna* v. *Lovell White Durrant (a firm)* [1994] 4 All ER 267) that the *subpoena duces tecum* may validly require the production of documents at a date in advance of the trial. In theory, there is no reason why such principles should not apply to witness summonses in the county court.

3.11.3 Joining of third parties

This is an application which is relatively rare within ancillary relief proceedings. Third parties may be joined in, for example, where they jointly own property with either the husband or the wife (for example, parents), or they are the trustees of a settlement of which a party is seeking a variation in accordance with MCA 1973, s.24.

There is no provision in FPR for the joining of third parties. The only provision is in RSC Ord. 15 rule 6(2)(b).

An application to join in a third party is not clearly defined by the rules, but the appropriate approach would be to issue a notice of application together with a sworn statement in support. That application should be served upon the other party to the proceedings as well as the third party who is to be joined. The third party will then attend at the return date of that application.

Where a third party has been made a party to the proceedings, an order made within ancillary relief proceedings will be binding upon them in accordance with *Tebbut* v. *Haynes* [1981] 2 All ER 238.

Note should also be made of the wording of FPR rule 2.59(3) – where a third party does have an interest a district judge should be asked to direct that Forms A and E are served upon that third party.

3.12 PREPARATION FOR FINAL ANCILLARY RELIEF HEARING

The comments set out at **3.9.1** with regards to the preparation for an FDR apply equally, if not more so, to preparation for a final ancillary relief hearing. Great care must be taken to ensure that all disclosure has been provided and, where necessary, updated.

3.12.1 Open offers

Some information with regards to arrangements for final hearing is set out in FPR rule 2.66, although particular regard should be had for rule 2.69E and the need to submit open proposals for settlement prior to the final hearing. Not less than 14 days before the final hearing, the applicant must file with the court and serve on the respondent an open statement setting out concisely the order sought together with the sums involved. The respondent must respond not more than seven days thereafter.

3.12.2 Instructing counsel

Most solicitors will instruct counsel to represent the client at a final contested hearing. The following are practical points which should be borne in mind:

1. If counsel has not previously been involved in the matter, a conference with counsel should be arranged at least a month or two before the final hearing to review the overall approach to the case.
2. The brief to counsel should be delivered well in advance of the final hearing to enable counsel to prepare properly. Taking into account the President's Direction dated 27 July 2006 in respect of trial bundles, counsel may be involved in preparing preliminary documents for that bundle.
3. Some chambers operate a system of deemed delivery of briefs which may mean that the client could be liable for the brief fee even if the final hearing does not go ahead. Where counsel is instructed subject to deemed delivery, the client must be fully advised of the dates and financial implications.

3.12.3 Preparation of bundles

Reference must be had to the President's Direction dated 27 July 2006 entitled 'Family Proceedings – Court Bundles (Universal Practice To Be Applied In All Courts Other Than The Family Proceedings Court)'. The President's Direction is detailed and sets out the documents which must be included in bundles for hearings lasting more than an hour. Specific deadlines are set out for the preparation and delivery of bundles. Note should also be had of the costs implications of failing to comply with the President's Direction.

3.13 FINAL ANCILLARY RELIEF HEARING

Many ancillary relief hearings can be disposed of in a day, although a realistic time estimate for the listing of the hearing should have been given when fixed, usually at the FDR. Where there are complex issues or expert evidence involved, final hearings can last two or more days.

As a matter of course, clients should be advised of the risk of hearings over-running or going part-heard. Whilst that should be avoided at all costs, it is a risk, particularly where issues arise during the course of a hearing. A more likely scenario is that the judge may wish to reserve judgment and hand down the judgment at a later date. That may happen where there is insufficient time for the judge to give the judgment, or where the judge wishes to consider the case before judgment can be given. The judgment may then simply be sent to solicitors in due course either by email or by post; alternatively some judges prefer to fix a further short hearing whereby they hand down their judgment orally.

It is usual practice these days for final hearing listings to include some time for the district judge to read the bundle. Complex matters may involve at least half a day of reading time.

Solicitors and counsel cannot influence a client's evidence, nor should clients be tutored in giving evidence, but basic principles should nonetheless be explained to the client. The client should be encouraged to answer questions clearly and truthfully, but also keeping to the point. It is important to ensure that clients understand that the purpose of giving evidence is to assist the court in adducing factual information – it is not the client's responsibility to put forward his or her case whilst giving evidence.

3.13.1 Attendance of witnesses/experts

In cases where experts and/or witnesses are to attend to give evidence, it is often a good idea to try and agree a template/timetable for when those witnesses must be in attendance at court. Witnesses and experts must be notified as far in advance as possible of the dates of the hearing and nearer the time of the hearing should be given a clearer estimate of when they will be expected to attend at court.

3.13.2 Costs issues

With the introduction of the new costs rules with effect from April 2006 onwards, there is the potential for complex issues to arise where costs orders are being sought. Where there is the potential for pursuing costs orders, time must be allowed in the listing of the final hearing. It is also a good idea for a separate concise bundle to be prepared setting out documents and skeleton arguments that may be relevant on the issue of costs.

CHAPTER 4

Powers of the court

Ann Corrigan

4.1 ORDERS AVAILABLE UNDER THE MATRIMONIAL CAUSES ACT 1973

The court has the power to make a variety of orders in favour of either party to the marriage. This chapter deals with the long-term ancillary relief orders that are available.

The orders available are set out in MCA 1973, ss.23, 24, 24A, 24B, 25B and 25C. A petitioner and/or a respondent in a suit for divorce, judicial separation or annulment may apply to the court for an order with regard to the financial aspects of their separation. Pension sharing orders are not available in judicial separation proceedings.

The court does not make orders of its own motion but waits for an application by either of the parties and the court cannot exercise its powers under MCA 1973 until a decree has been granted although terms of an agreement can, of course, be submitted to the judge in advance of the decree. The judge may give approval to the proposed order provided it is either post-dated or directed to remain on the court file until the decree nisi has been granted.

4.2 GENERAL DUTY AND THE LAW POST-*WHITE*

The court's general duty in all applications for ancillary relief is set out in MCA 1973, s.25(1) which states that:

> It shall be the duty of the court in deciding whether to exercise its powers under section 23, 24, 24A or 24B above and, if so, in what manner, to have regard to all the circumstances of the case, first consideration being given to the welfare while a minor of any child of the family who has not attained the age of eighteen.

Having taken on board the welfare of any children, the court must then have regard to those matters set out in MCA 1973, s.25(2) which states:

> As regards the exercise of the powers of the court under section 23(1)(a), (b) or (c), 24, 24A or 24B above in relation to a party to a marriage, the court shall in particular have regard to the following matters –

(a) the income, earning capacity, property and other financial resources which each of the parties to the marriage has or is likely to have in the foreseeable future, including in the case of earning capacity, any increase in that capacity which it would in the opinion of the court be reasonable to expect a party to the marriage to take steps to acquire;

(b) the financial needs, obligations and responsibilities which each of the parties to the marriage has or is likely to have in the foreseeable future;

(c) the standard of living enjoyed by the family before the breakdown of the marriage;

(d) the age of each party and the duration of the marriage;

(e) any physical or mental disability of either of the parties to the marriage;

(f) the contributions which each of the parties to the marriage has made or is likely in the foreseeable future to make to the welfare of the family, including any contribution by looking after the home or caring for the family;

(g) the conduct of the parties, if that conduct is such that it would in the opinion of the court be inequitable to disregard it;

(h) in the case of proceedings for divorce or nullity of marriage, the value to each of the parties to the marriage of any benefit which, by reason of the dissolution of the marriage, that party will lose the chance of acquiring.

As far as the s.25(2) criteria are concerned, the House of Lords held in *Piglowska* v. *Piglowski* [1999] 2 FLR 763 that, with the exception of the first consideration being given to the children of the family, there was no hierarchical order to the s.25(2) factors and that each is of equal value and must be considered in turn.

In addition the court has a duty under s.25A to consider whether a clean break can be achieved, thus giving each party financial independence either immediately or at some later date. This should be borne in mind when considering any application for ancillary relief. Clean break orders are dealt with in more detail later in this chapter.

The landmark case of *White* v. *White* [2000] 2 FLR 981 remains the leading authority in ancillary relief and its application will be well known to practitioners. Lord Nicholls of Birkenhead gave judgment from which the following emerges:

1. **The yardstick of equality**. The judge should first consider and apply those matters set out in the s.25(2) checklist and then check any decision against the 'yardstick of equality'. If there is to be an uneven distribution of the matrimonial assets, good reason must be shown. A long marriage case where assets outweigh need may attract an equal division but in limited asset cases, given the statutory requirement to consider the welfare of the children first, the housing needs of the children and the parent with care are likely to result in a departure from equality.

2. **Reasonable requirements**. Pre-*White* cases that dealt with significant assets were concerned with meeting the needs of the applicant regardless of the value of the assets available for division. In *White* this was held to be unfair and discriminatory.

3. **Contributions**. The House of Lords made it clear that there should not be any discrimination between the roles of the breadwinner and the homemaker. In most cases, contribution arguments will be unnecessary although there will be cases where they are relevant, for example, if one party has brought significant wealth into the marriage.
4. **Fairness**. This was the overriding hallmark of the decision in *White* and has been repeated subsequently. In *Lambert* v. *Lambert* [2002] EWCA Civ 1685 Thorpe J said that the duty under s.25 to assess each of the statutory factors does not require a detailed appraisal of the performance of each party and the aim of the court is to achieve fairness between the parties.
5. **Inherited wealth**. In most cases the fact that some assets were inherited by one party will carry little weight, particularly as the court's first consideration is the children's needs. Where the assets outweigh needs, inherited assets may be treated differently from assets acquired by the parties jointly and where possible should be retained by that party.

Miller and McFarlane

The main post-*White* authority is *Miller* v. *Miller; McFarlane* v. *McFarlane* [2006] UKHL 24 from where the following principles are drawn:

1. The three principles that should guide the court when making a financial award are need, compensation and sharing. There cannot be a hard and fast rule about whether the court should start with equal sharing and then depart if need or compensation supply a reason for doing so, or whether the court should start with need and compensation and then share the balance.
2. A periodical payments order can be made not only to meet the spouse's needs, but also to compensate them. The principle of compensation is aimed at redressing any significant prospective economic disparity which may arise from the way in which the parties conducted their marriage.
3. Arguments in respect of conduct or special/stellar contributions should only be pursued in cases where the contribution was so marked that to disregard it would be inequitable.
4. The principles of *White* (equal sharing) apply as much to short marriages as to long marriages.

4.3 SPOUSAL MAINTENANCE

4.3.1 Periodical payments

An order for periodical payments under MCA 1973, s.23(1)(a) and (d) is an order for the payment of a regular sum of money by one party to the other or to or for a child of the family. The latter is considered later in this chapter. Payments will generally be expressed at weekly or monthly intervals.

4.3.2 Types of periodical payment orders

There are essentially seven different types of order which the court has the power to make:

(a) a substantive order of a certain amount per week/month/year;
(b) a nominal order of, say, 5p per annum which preserves a spouse's right to apply to vary at a later date;
(c) a term order, i.e. payments for a specified length of time to enable a spouse to adjust without undue hardship to a termination of financial dependence. The term of such an order might be expressed as coming to an end on the happening of an event such as a party's cohabitation with another person or until a child reaches the age of 18 or ceases full-time education. If it is necessary to apply to extend an order of this nature, it must be done before the order comes to an end;
(d) a term order as above but with a direction under MCA 1973, s.28(1A) that the recipient cannot later apply for any extension to the term;
(e) an order adjourning the application;
(f) a deferred periodical payments order, intended to come into effect on a specified date, e.g. on the retirement of the other party;
(g) an order dismissing the claim with a direction that the applicant shall not be entitled to make any further application in relation to the marriage.

4.3.3 Timing of the application

The court has no jurisdiction to make a periodical payments order until a decree nisi in divorce or a decree of judicial separation has been granted. In divorce proceedings the order does not take effect until decree absolute. It may be that the court has already made an interim order providing protection until decree absolute (a maintenance pending suit order, dealt with in **Chapter 9**).

Although an order cannot take effect until decree absolute, it can be backdated to the date of the application, which will usually have been made in the petition – providing, of course, that the prayer in the petition contains such an application. No reliance, however, should be placed on obtaining a backdated order and if needs demand it, an application should be made for maintenance pending suit.

An order for periodical payments cannot extend beyond the joint lives of the parties or the remarriage of the applicant, nor beyond the expiry of any fixed term where there is a direction under s.28(1A).

4.3.4 Level of payments

The applicant's financial needs, obligations and responsibilities will be the starting point for the court. An applicant's own income must be factored into the level of payments ordered. Income derived from state benefits should not be overlooked. A comprehensive overview of tax credits can be found on the Directgov website (**www.direct.gov.uk**).

The respondent's ability to pay must be assessed in terms of the respondent's own financial needs, obligations and responsibilities, particularly as payments will be made from net income. There is no tax relief available to the payer and no tax payable by the recipient.

A net effect schedule should be prepared from the Form E information given by both parties. This involves adding together the net incomes of both parties and deducting or adding the amount of the proposed order. This will give an indication of the total which each party will be left with; this in turn can then be compared against each party's financial needs.

4.3.5 Income needs

A schedule of anticipated income needs should be prepared and, if necessary, updated as the case progresses. At final hearing the schedule of the applicant's budget will be under close scrutiny and, whilst it is not the only factor which the court will take into account, it is an essential tool for the judge, who will be considering the split of capital at the same time.

Income and earning capacity is part of the court's statutory consideration under s.25. For this reason the court will be considering not only the applicant's present circumstances but whether the applicant could be taking steps to improve his or her position. How much weight will be attached to this will be dependent upon the circumstances. A wife caring for young children will not necessarily be expected to work full time and in these circumstances the court may consider a term order with a view to a clean break at a later date.

Similarly, an applicant who is looking for work would be well advised to keep and produce job applications, letters of rejection and even a CV.

4.3.6 Cohabitation

As noted above, an entitlement to spousal periodical payments ceases upon remarriage but if the applicant is cohabiting, this does not prevent the applicant from applying for periodical payments; the cohabitation is one of the circumstances of the case that the court will consider. In *K* v. *K* [2005] EWHC 2886 (Fam) Coleridge J held that MCA 1973, s.28 did not prohibit the courts from ordering the termination of continuing periodical payments to a spouse who was cohabiting. He stated that if cohabitation was to be the 'social norm' then financial independence had to go with it. In this case the paying husband had applied to vary an earlier order to a nominal sum or in any event to a drastically reduced sum. Although the court agreed that the wife's cohabitation of three years merited a variation, it would have had too drastic an effect upon the wife if the payments were stopped altogether and instead the payments were reduced gradually to allow the wife to adjust without undue hardship.

4.4   SECURED PERIODICAL PAYMENTS

If there is concern that there may be difficulty in enforcing an order for periodical payments, MCA 1973, s.23(1)(b) and (e) provides for the payments to be secured.

The manner in which a secured order operates varies depending upon the circumstances of the case and the assets available. It may be that the asset which provides the security is income producing, such as a shareholding or it may be a non-income producing asset such as a property. If the paying party defaults, any arrears will form a charge over the property which the recipient can seek to realise by forcing a sale of the property. Whilst the order for secured periodical payments is in force, the asset cannot be disposed of. Once the order comes to an end, the assets revert to the payer without further encumbrance.

Secured periodical payments are relatively rare save in cases of considerable wealth or where there is evidence of persistent non-payment of maintenance in the past.

4.5   LUMP SUM AND LUMP SUMS

Section 23 of MCA 1973 provides that:

(1)   On granting a decree of divorce, a decree of nullity of marriage or a decree of judicial separation or at any time thereafter . . . the court may make any one or more of the following orders, that is to say . . . .

   (c)   an order that either party to the marriage shall pay to the other such lump sum or sums as may be so specified . . .

   (f)   an order that a party to the marriage shall pay to such person as may be so specified for the benefit of such a child, or to such child, such lump sum as may be so specified . . .

(6)   Where the court –

   (a)   makes an order under this section for the payment of a lump sum, and
   (b)   directs –

      (i)   that payment of that sum or any part of it shall be deferred; or
      (ii)   that that sum or any part of it shall be paid by instalments,

the court may order that the amount deferred or the instalments shall carry interest at such rate as may be specified by the order from such date, not earlier than the date of the order, as may be so specified, until the date when payment of it is completed.

The court can order the payment of a lump sum or lump sums from one party to the other. The court can only make a lump sum order on one occasion, although on that occasion it is possible for the court to order a series of lump sums to be paid. It is important to be aware of the difference between an order for a series of lump sums and an order for a lump sum payable by instalments. They may appear to be the same but an order for a series of lump sums cannot be varied at a later date. In contrast and in certain circumstances, an order for payment of a lump sum by instalments can be varied.

Lump sums may be ordered for a variety of reasons, for example, payment in lieu of maintenance, a payment to buy out an interest in the family home, house contents, savings, endowment policies, investment and/or in lieu of pension provision.

The application for a lump sum order should be made in the petition (or answer) but if, for any reason, it has been omitted, it may still be made with the court's permission providing the applicant has not remarried before the application is made.

4.5.1 Interest on lump sums

If a lump sum is not to be paid in full immediately, the court may order that the amount deferred or the instalments shall carry interest at a rate and period specified by the court not commencing earlier than the date of the order (s.23(6)). When obtaining an order for a lump sum payable by a certain date, consideration should always be given to including a clause requiring interest to be paid in the event of default. In *L* v. *L* [1994] 2 FLR 324 Ewbank J held that where inefficient drafting of a consent order failed to specify a time when the lump sum should be paid, a wife could not have retrospective interest to cover two years' loss of the use of the money.

By the County Courts (Interest on Judgment Debts) Order 1991, SI 1991/1184, in the absence of any provision to the contrary in the order, any lump sum over £5,000 that remains unpaid carries interest at the judgment rate from the date upon which the payment was due until it is paid. The judgment rate is currently 8 per cent per annum but the court may take a pragmatic view and specify a different rate. If, for example, the delayed lump sum is to enable a wife to purchase a property, there is argument to suggest that the interest should enable her to keep pace with the price of property. If she simply intends to invest the money, then the court may take the view that the interest should be no higher than the bank or building society rate with some adjustment to cover the wife's liability for tax on the income. The important issue is to give consideration to the question of interest at the time of the drafting of the order.

4.5.2 Interim lump sums

At one time it was envisaged that, by virtue of the Family Law Act 1996, Sched. 2 para. 3, the court would have the power to order interim lump sums. That part of the Act was never brought into force and as such the case remains that the court has no power to order interim lump sums save under s.23(3)(a) for meeting expenses for maintaining the applicant or a child before applying for an order under s.23(1)(c). This is a limited type of order, which cannot be made until after decree nisi and which does not become effective until after decree absolute.

4.5.3 Factors to be taken into account

As in every case where the court is making financial provision, it must take into account those factors set out in MCA 1973, s.25(2) before making an order. The size of the lump sum must be determined in the context of resources available. These will include not only resources which are available at the time of the making of the order but also assets which may be available to the parties in the foreseeable future and assets which the parties could take steps to acquire. This may therefore involve the respondent borrowing funds either commercially or from other third parties or by selling property or possessions to enable a lump sum to be paid.

A respondent to an application for a lump sum will be well advised to make proper enquiries as to what funds are available.

In practical terms it is essential to have as much information available for the court as possible. Evidence of a respondent's borrowing capacity such as mortgage quotes, credit applications and any rejections of applications for finance should be obtained when attempting to raise a defence of inability to pay a lump sum; otherwise the court is entitled to draw an adverse inference as in *Newton* v. *Newton* [1990] 1 FLR 33 and in the variation of maintenance case of *SW* v. *RC* [2008] EWHC 73 (Fam) where a father was unable to prove that he had reached his credit raising limit.

Moreover, it is not for the applicant to make enquiries as to the respondent's ability to pay a lump sum as stated in *Thomas* v. *Thomas* [1995] 1 FLR 668:

> where the court was confronted by a husband with immediate liquidity problems but possessing substantial means, the onus was on him to satisfy the court that all means of access to funds to support suitable outright provision for his wife had been thoroughly explored and found to be impossible.

4.5.4 Limited resource cases

There are no specific guidelines but in limited resource cases where assets do not exceed needs consideration should be given to the effect of the receipt of a lump sum. A wife in receipt of state benefits may be disadvantaged if she receives a lump sum. Her entitlement to benefit will cease if she has capital of £6,000 or more. Capital of between £6,000 and £16,000 will mean a reduction in benefit of £1 in every £250 and capital of £16,000 or more will extinguish entitlement to income support, housing and council tax benefits altogether.

In cases such as this where funds are scarce, the court will look to meet the most pressing needs of the parties, but first consideration will usually be to provide a home for the parent with care and any children.

4.5.5 *Duxbury* funds

It may be that a husband wishes to capitalise his wife's maintenance claims by paying a lump sum or sums in place of ongoing periodical payments.

In a big money case where there is sufficient capital to satisfy one party's lifetime income needs, it is necessary to establish what those needs are and to calculate how much is needed in terms of a lump sum to provide an inflation-proof amount to satisfy those needs. The calculation is based on a computer program taking account of the recipient's age, and which makes assumptions as to tax bands and inflation rates. In the case itself (*Duxbury* v. *Duxbury* [1987] 1 FLR 7) the wife received a large lump sum which was intended, amongst other things, to provide funds for new accommodation and to be invested to provide her with an income. Since *Duxbury*, courts have been concerned that the calculation of such lump sums should not become the preserve of experts but must remain a matter of judicial discretion. As such, the *Duxbury* tables remain a useful tool but should be approached with flexibility, particularly as the calculation is based partly on life expectancy which may mean that an older spouse may receive less than a younger spouse. Since the courts are now directed to apply the 'yardstick of equality' after *White*, this is less likely to be problematic.

The *Duxbury* tables appear in the Family Law Bar Association's 'At A Glance' which is updated annually and is an indispensable aid to every practitioner (see **www.flba.co.uk/at_a_glance**).

4.5.6 Adjourning lump sum applications

As can be seen above, the court has the power to make a lump sum order at the time of the granting of a decree or 'at any time thereafter'. Generally, the court will not wish to delay making orders but there may be circumstances where it is desirable to adjourn an application. The test applied on an application to adjourn is two-fold, as per Connell J in *D* v. *D* [2001] 1 FLR 633. First, can justice be done only if there is an adjournment? Secondly, is there a real possibility of capital becoming available from a specific source in the near future? In *D* v. *D*, there was evidence that it was likely the husband's entitlement under a lucrative share option scheme would become known within two years of the wife's application. The case was adjourned to enable the final hearing to take place within two months of the information being available.

In *G* v. *G* [2004] 1 FLR 997 the court adjourned a wife's lump sum application pending the receipt by the husband of an inheritance. The hearing took place eight years after the end of the marriage during which time the wife had remarried (and divorced). The wife recovered a lump sum of £460,000. In that case the judge found that the wife's remarriage was immaterial and merely one of the s.25 factors to be taken into account.

4.5.7 Variation

The court has extremely limited powers to vary capital orders under MCA 1973, s.31. One of the few forms of capital orders which can be varied by the court is an order for the payment of a lump sum by instalments (MCA 1973, s.31(2)(d)). By contrast, it should be noted that the court does not have the power to vary an order for the payment of a series of lump sums. Care should therefore be taken in the drafting of the original order, although note should be had of the unreported decision of Coleridge J in *Lamont* v. *Lamont* (13 October 2006) in which he questioned whether any distinction should be drawn and whether the court's power to vary an order should be excluded by virtue of the mere drafting of the original order.

Under MCA 1973, s.31 the court not only has the power to vary orders, but also to discharge or suspend any provision thereof temporarily. Note should therefore be had that in limited circumstances the court can discharge or suspend outstanding instalments of lump sum payments (*Westbury* v. *Sampson* [2001] EWCA Civ 407).

Variation of ancillary relief orders is dealt with in greater detail in **Chapter 11**.

4.6 PROPERTY ADJUSTMENT

4.6.1 Transfers of property

Most ancillary relief applications will be concerned with the question of the family home. Under MCA 1973, s.24(1)(a) the court has the power to order the transfer of any property between spouses or to (or for the benefit of) any child of the family. (This latter power is rarely used.)

It is not only the matrimonial home that might be the subject of a transfer between spouses. Any property to which a party is entitled either in possession or reversion can be the subject of an order. This might therefore include a tenancy, a holiday home, an endowment policy, shares, bank accounts, vehicles, household contents or other personal possessions.

If a transfer of the matrimonial home is being sought and the application for ancillary relief has been made in Form A, the Form A must be served upon any mortgagee in cases where the property is subject to a mortgage in compliance with FPR rule 2.59. Whilst the court has the power to order either spouse to transfer his or her interest in the property, the court cannot exercise any power over the mortgagee and the mortgagee may not consent to the transfer.

If an application for financial relief is compromised without Form A having been filed, a draft consent order should be prepared and served on the mortgagees at least 14 days before the order is submitted for approval to the court. If no objection is raised by the lender within the 14-day period, it can be assumed that the mortgagee will consent to the transfer and the order can be lodged with the court.

In practical terms, it must be remembered that all lenders apply different criteria when faced with the application to release one party from the mortgage. Some lenders will accept maintenance payments in assessing income, and some will only accept maintenance payments made under a court order. State benefits are accepted by some lenders for purposes of calculating income but others will require six or 12 months' worth of payments to have been made without default by the party seeking the transfer. It is worth checking in advance what the particular lending criteria are and, ideally, the mortgagee's consent should be obtained before any agreement is reached between spouses or in advance of an FDR or final hearing.

4.6.2 Sale of the family home

The court has the power under MCA 1973, s.24A to order a sale of any property but practitioners will mainly be concerned with the sale of the matrimonial home. This power exists providing at least one party has a beneficial interest in the property.

An order for sale may be on the basis that the property is sold 'forthwith' (i.e. immediately or as soon as practicable) or may be deferred until a specified later date.

An order for sale should make provisions for the conduct of the sale (i.e. which firm of solicitors will undertake the conveyancing), which estate agents will be instructed, who will be responsible for the costs of sale and, most importantly, how the sale proceeds are to be divided. In some cases it may be that the entire net sale proceeds are paid to one party, in others a percentage of the proceeds are paid to one party with the balance being paid to the other, or the order may be drafted so as to provide one party with a fixed sum with the balance being paid to the other. For the purposes of calculating costs of sale, following the decision in *Behzadi* v. *Behzadi* [2008] EWCA Civ 1070, unless there is evidence to the contrary, these should be taken to be 3 per cent of the gross sale price.

4.6.3 Settlement of property

Under MCA 1973, s.24(1)(b) the court can order one spouse to settle property to which he or she is entitled for the benefit of the other spouse or for the benefit of any children of the family. Although orders which create the settlement of property are uncommon, where circumstances warrant it, the court may make a *Mesher* order (*Mesher* v. *Mesher* [1980] 1 All ER 126). The court can order the transfer or the variation of title under which the matrimonial home (or other property) is held. The sale of that property may then be postponed until a specific later date such as the remarriage, death or cohabitation of the transferee, or until the youngest child of the family reaches a specified age. Upon the happening of the appropriate event, the trust for sale comes into effect and the proceeds of sale divided in accordance with the order.

In practical terms, particularly in times of economic uncertainty, the *Mesher* order is a useful way of retaining the family home for the children where a sale would provide insufficient capital for an alternative property to be purchased.

A *Martin*-type order (*Martin* v. *Martin* [1978] 3 All ER 764) is one whereby the court postpones sale until the occupying spouse's death, remarriage, cohabitation for a specified period or voluntary removal. *Martin*-type orders are less common following *White* v. *White* but may still be appropriate where, for example, one spouse has obtained alternative accommodation already and has no immediate need to realise his or her capital.

4.6.4 Variation of settlements

Under MCA 1973, s.24(1)(c) and (d) the court has the power to vary for the benefit of the parties or of the children of the family any ante-nuptial or post-nuptial settlement made on the parties to the marriage (including any settlement made by will or codicil). The court also has the power to extinguish altogether or reduce the interest of either spouse in such a settlement. Variation of settlements are uncommon but the reported cases make interesting reading. In *C* v. *C* [2004] 2 FLR 493 the court redistributed interests under a trust held in Grand Cayman even though the settlement expressly reserved jurisdiction to the foreign court.

4.7   PENSIONS

4.7.1 Nature of the available orders

After the matrimonial home, the most valuable asset which a party to a marriage is likely to have is a pension.

Pension attachment orders were introduced on 1 August 1996 and pension sharing orders on 1 December 2000 (under provisions contained in the Welfare Reform and Pensions Act 1999, amending MCA 1973).

There are three possible ways of dealing with pensions in divorce:

1. Off-setting – by adjusting other assets of the marriage to take account of pension rights.
2. Attachment (s. 25A) – by making an order which allows for all or part of any pension or lump sum arising at retirement to be 'earmarked' for the other spouse.
3. Pension sharing (s.24B) – splitting the pension so that the benefits are subdivided at the time of the divorce; the parties will then have two separate pensions to which they can continue to contribute in the future.

4.7.2 Pension sharing orders

A pension sharing order is defined by MCA 1973, s.21A(1) as an order which:

(a) provides that one party's:

    (i) shareable rights under a specified pension arrangement, or

    (ii) shareable state scheme rights,

    be subject to pension sharing for the benefit of the other party, and

(b) specifies the percentage value to be transferred.

This means that a party with pension benefits loses a specified percentage of the pension fund and the other party acquires a pension fund of his or her own.

A pension sharing order can be made where proceedings for divorce, nullity or dissolution are commenced on or after 1 December 2000. As the order can only take effect upon decree absolute, it is not an order available in proceedings for judicial separation.

No order for pension sharing can be made in relation to a pension which, in respect of the marriage in question, has already been subjected to a pension share or is currently liable to an attachment order. The legislation does not exclude claims against a shared pension arising out of a later marriage between the spouse and a third party.

It is not possible to have a pension sharing order and a pension attachment order in respect of the same pension.

4.7.3 Pensions that can be shared

Pensions that can be shared include:

- personal pensions (including SIPPs and stakeholder pensions);
- self-administered schemes;
- SERPS and any second state pensions;
- final salary schemes;
- money purchase schemes;
- income drawdown;
- retirement annuity contracts; and
- AVCs and free-standing AVCs.

4.7.4 Pensions that cannot be shared

Pensions that cannot be shared include:

- basic state pension;
- a lump sum payable on death;
- widow/widower's pension in payment.

4.7.5 Valuation

Pension rights are valued on the basis of the sum (known as the cash equivalent transfer value, or CETV) to which a member would become entitled if his or her employment were terminated or the member opted to leave the scheme. This is the prescribed method of valuation.

The Pension Sharing (Valuation) Regulations 2000, SI 2000/1052, regs. 4 and 5 specify how occupational pension scheme rights are calculated, and regs. 6 and 7 specify the basis of calculation and verification in pension arrangements other than occupational schemes.

The pension provider will value the benefits as at the date of receipt of a request for a valuation but a revised figure will then be calculated at the time of implementation of the order.

The CETV is calculated on the basis that the scheme member is retiring on the date of valuation and as such takes no account of any future event such as increased salary.

4.7.6 Dividing the benefits

The CETV may not necessarily give a true representation of the pension benefits, for example, when dealing with civil service, police or armed forces schemes or defined benefit schemes where the CETV is not necessarily the total value of the fund. In addition, the circumstances of the case itself may warrant further investigation, for example, the ages of the parties, whether the pension is in payment already, if early retirement is an issue or where the pension member's life expectancy is shortened by illness.

In many circumstances the desired outcome is to equalise the pension rights of the parties but this may be achieved in two ways. Either the CETV figure can simply be divided equally or an unequal split which achieves equality of income on retirement may be needed. Actuarial tables show that women have longer life expectancies and as such will require a greater than equal percentage of the CETV.

4.7.7 Instructing an actuary

In these (and any other relevant circumstances) it is advisable (depending upon the size of the pension fund and the costs involved) to seek expert advice from an actuary as to the correct percentage to be transferred. Although there is no case law to support this approach, the court, when carrying out its discretionary exercise under MCA 1973, s.25 must give regard to the income and financial resources available to the parties and, as such, the impact of a pension sharing order on both parties upon retirement must be considered and suitable expert advice obtained. The instruction of a single joint expert can be dealt with at the First Appointment with the court giving a direction as to the timing for the filing of a report in advance of the FDR.

The actuary (or other pension expert such as an independent financial adviser) should be given as much information as possible. It is particularly useful at the outset to obtain letters of authority from both parties as the expert may require further information to enable him to prepare a report. Dealing with this in advance will save time. The requirements of the Practice Direction to CPR Part 35 apply and in addition the expert will require:

- copies of Forms E;
- completed Forms P if obtained from the pension provider;
- court orders relating to the expert's instruction;
- a clear note of the timetable for the report;
- any relevant correspondence;
- a clear statement of how the expert's charges are to be met.

Although Forms E may seem superfluous when the relevant pension sections may suffice, they will provide the expert with the whole picture, and this may enable the expert to offer useful advice taking account of all available assets.

The questions to be put to the expert will, in some respects, be case-specific but will usually include requests to deal with:

- the accuracy and fairness of the CETV;
- whether there is a choice of internal/external transfer;
- the desired outcome and how to achieve it;
- the date upon which benefits can be taken;
- whether a lump sum can be taken;
- anything unusual, relevant or important that may impact in the particular circumstances.

4.7.8 Application to the court – procedural issues

The procedure is governed by FPR and the Pensions on Divorce etc. (Provision of Information) Regulations 2000, SI 2000/1048 ('the regulations')
The summary below highlights the relevant FPR rules:

1. FPR rule 2.53(1)(d) – Application is made in the petition or answer.
2. FPR rule 2.61A(3) – By way of Form A.
3. FPR rule 2.70(6) – A copy of Form A must be served on the pension fund managers or trustee.
4. FPR rule 2.70(7) – If an attachment order is being sought, the following information must be sent in addition to Form A:

    - an address to which any notice that the person responsible (i.e. managers/trustees) is required to serve upon the applicant can be sent;
    - an address to which any payment which the person responsible is required to make to the applicant is to be sent; and

- if the address is that of a bank, building society or the Department of National Savings, sufficient details to enable payments to be made into the account of the applicant.

This information is not always available when acting for an applicant for pension provision but will become apparent from the other party's Form E. As soon as the information is available, Form A and other information required if necessary should be sent without delay to enable the trustees to comply with their obligations to provide information.

4.7.9 Acting for the party with pension rights

Under FPR rule 2.70(2), when the court fixes a First Appointment the party with the pension rights must, within seven days, request from the pension provider the information referred to in the regulations. The required information is:

- a valuation of the pension rights and benefits accrued under the pension arrangement (the CETV);
- a statement summarising the method of calculation;
- a statement of the benefits which have been included in the valuation;
- whether the trustees offer membership to a person entitled to a pension credit, and if so, the types of benefits available to pension credit members under that arrangement;
- whether the trustees intend to discharge the liability for a pension credit other than by offering membership to a person entitled to a pension credit; and
- the schedule of charges that will be levied in accordance with reg.2(2) of the Pensions on Divorce etc. (Charging) Regulations 2000, SI 2000/1049.

If a CETV has been obtained within 12 months, there is no requirement to obtain this information. If a CETV that is less than 12 months old is available, it should be disclosed with Form E. If it is necessary to obtain the information after Form E has been filed without it, it must be sent within seven days to the other party together with the name and address of the trustees or managers of each of the pension arrangements.

4.7.10 What the pension provider may do

1. FPR rule 2.70(8) – A person responsible for a pension arrangement who receives a Form A may within 21 days require the party with the pension rights to provide a copy of section 2.13 of his Form E. The party with the pension rights must provide a copy of section 2.13 at least 35 days before the First Appointment or within 21 days of the request, whichever is the later.

2. FPR rule 2.70(9) – Within 21 days, the pension provider having received a copy of section 2.13 of Form E, may file a statement with the court and serve it on both parties. This gives the pension provider the opportunity of objecting to the application for an order. If the pension provider chooses to raise any objection, it is entitled to be represented at the First Appointment. In accordance with FPR rule 2.70(10), if the court receives a statement, within four days of the date of filing that statement, it must give the pension provider notice of the date of the First Appointment.
3. FPR rule 2.70(8) – Within 21 days of receiving Form A the pension provider is entitled, if an attachment order is being sought in addition to or instead of a sharing order, to request a copy of the completed section 2.13 of the Form E of the pension member.

Within 21 days of being notified that a pension sharing order may be made, the pension provider must provide to the pension member the information set out at reg.2(7) and reg.4.

Within three months of a request for a valuation being received by the pension provider, the information must be provided. That period may be shortened by the court to six weeks or less if needed in connection with proceedings (reg.2(5))

If information (other than a valuation) is requested, it must be provided within one month from the date of the request (reg.2(6)).

4.7.11 Form P

The Family Proceedings (Amendment) (No.5) Rules 2005, SI 2005/2922, came into force on 5 December 2005. Rule 118(f)(i) introduced the Pension Enquiry Form (Form P).

Form P should be used in every case where a pension sharing order might be made. It can be used on a voluntary basis if the scheme member gives authority by signing the front page or as outlined above, completion can be ordered by the court.

The completed Form P should be included in any bundle prepared for the FDR and any subsequent final hearing.

4.7.12 Pension attachment

Under MCA 1973, s.25B(4) the court may order that once the pension becomes payable, the person responsible for the pension arrangement pay part of the pension income and/or lump sum available under that arrangement to the other party to the marriage in question.

This arrangement is known as a pension attachment order. It is a method of securing periodical payments and/or a lump sum against a pension – it is not a separate form of ancillary relief but simply a deferred periodical payment or lump sum order. Pension attachment orders are not available if the petition for divorce was filed before 1 December 1996.

Unlike the position with other periodical payments orders, payments of pension income are taxable in the hands of the recipient.

Many occupational schemes in particular will pay benefits if an employee dies prematurely before retirement (death-in-service benefits) and these may also be the subject of a pension attachment order thus providing security for a surviving former spouse. Under s.25C(2)(b) the court can require the person with pension rights to nominate the other party as the person to whom death-in-service benefits should be paid.

The provisions contain no guidance as to the circumstances in which an attachment order would be appropriate nor as to the amount of the pension income, lump sum or death-in-service benefits to be attached – this is entirely a matter for the court. The only restriction is that the amount to be attached must be expressed as a percentage of the payment due to the person with pension rights.

Pension attachment orders can be impractical, particularly as they undermine the principle of a clean break as there is a continuing commitment to make provision once the pension becomes payable.

By its very nature, attachment is speculative; it may be impossible to predict what the parties' needs might be at the time the pension becomes payable or the value of the asset to be divided and in addition the court is powerless to ensure continuing appropriate levels of contribution.

In practice, pension attachment orders are not a popular remedy and will generally only be considered where the fund is of little value at the time of the proceedings but expected to increase significantly by the date of retirement.

4.7.13 Drafting the order

FPR rule 2.70(13) states that an order for ancillary relief, whether by consent or not, which includes a pension sharing order must:

(a) in the body of the order state that there is to be provision by way of pension sharing or pension attachment in accordance with the annex or annexes to the order; and

(b) be accompanied by an annex in Form P1 (pension sharing annex) or Form P2 (pension attachment annex) as the case may require; and if provision is made in relation to more than one pension arrangement, there must be one annex for each pension arrangement.

The order will not take effect earlier than seven days after the end of the period of filing notice of appeal (21 days) or decree absolute, if later.

The body of the order contains the detail of the pension arrangement (name of provider) and the annex must contain sufficient information to identify the arrangement and the member to which the order relates.

The P1 annex requires information as to any former names by which either party has been known and national insurance numbers. Part C of the form requires the all-important information of the percentage to be transferred and Part D deals with how the pension sharing charges are to be met.

Sufficient information should be available at this stage to complete Part F as to whether an internal or external transfer is sought and if there is to be an external transfer, Part G as to details of the scheme that is to receive the credit. Part G is optional and, in practice, the person in whose favour the order has been made will usually deal with these issues with the benefit of independent financial advice.

The P2 annex requires similar detail as to names and national insurance numbers but also requires details of the bank account into which the payments are to be made and where the order has been arrived at by consent, confirmation that no objection has been made by the pension provider or if an objection has been raised, that it has been considered by the court.

4.7.14 Implementation

Once the pension provider has received the order and the annex(es) from the court (or from either party), the order must be implemented within four months. The four-month period begins on the later of the date on which the pension sharing order takes effect and the date on which the pension provider receives the order and the annex, the decree absolute and all required information (that contained in Form P1).

The pension provider must provide, within 21 days of receipt of the order, a notice of the charges and a list of personal information held. In the event that an order cannot be implemented, the parties must be notified within 21 days.

Once the order has been implemented, the pension provider must issue a notice of discharge to both parties.

4.8 ORDERS IN FAVOUR OF CHILDREN

Child maintenance is largely governed by the Child Maintenance and Enforcement Commission (CMEC) (formerly the Child Support Agency) and capital orders for the benefit of children will only be made if circumstances warrant it. Such orders are rarely sought but the following provisions apply.

4.8.1 Jurisdiction

The court has jurisdiction to make those orders set out in the preceding pages of this chapter for the benefit of a child of the family.

4.8.2 Definition of 'child of the family'

By MCA 1973, s.52(1), 'child of the family' is defined, in relation to the parties to a marriage, as:

(a) a child of both those parties; and
(b) any other child, not being a child who is placed with those parties as foster parents by a local authority or voluntary organisation, who has been treated by both of those parties as a child of their family.

4.8.3 Duration of orders and age limits

Section 29(1) of MCA 1973 provides that no order will be made for a child who has attained the age of 18.

Section 29(2) provides that the term specified in a periodical payments or secured periodical payments order in favour of a child (in cases where the court retains jurisdiction despite the Child Support Act 1991) may begin with the date of the application or at any later date. It is possible therefore for orders to be backdated but they may not:

(a) extend, in the first instance, beyond the child's next birthday after the child attains school-leaving age unless the court considers that in the circumstances of the case, the welfare of the child requires that it should extend to a later date. The present statutory school-leaving age being 16, this means that when first granted, most periodical payments orders will be effective until the child reaches the age of 17 years or until further order; and
(b) shall not in any event extend beyond the child's 18th birthday unless s.29(3) applies.

Section 29(3) provides that orders can be made for children who are over 18 if:

(a) either the child is or will be receiving instruction at an educational establishment or undergoing training for a trade, profession or vocation whether or not the child is also (or will also be) in gainful employment; or
(b) there are special circumstances justifying the making of an order.

A good example of (a) might be where a child is in full-time education at university but working during holiday periods or (b) where a child has a physical or other handicap. In the latter case the court must take account of the expenses attributed to the child's disability in the broadest sense (*C* v. *F* [1998] 2 FLR 1).

Section 29(4) provides that the death of the paying spouse will bring periodical payments in favour of a child to an end unless it is secured and the remarriage of either spouse will not affect orders made in favour of a child.

There is no age limit for the making of orders requiring a settlement of property to be made for the benefit of a child or a variation of a settlement for a child's benefit and no upper age limit for periodical payments provided that the conditions set out in s.29(3) are met.

4.9   CHILD MAINTENANCE ORDERS

Between 2009 and 2014 the Child Maintenance and Other Payments Act 2008 will be phased in. The new legislation has provided the CMEC with objectives that are quite different from those of the Child Support Act (CSA) 1991 and include promoting parents taking financial responsibility for their own children and encouraging parents to make their own private agreements. Much of the new Act deals with the new powers for enforcement and new methods of calculating maintenance.

Although beyond the scope of this book, reference should be made to the Child Maintenance Options Service website (**www.cmoptions.org**) for further information.

CSA 1991 presently provides for the assessment of child maintenance. The Act was effectively designed to exclude the court's jurisdiction and many maintenance issues are resolved by the CMEC (incorporating the Child Support Agency).

The court, however, retains certain powers to deal with child maintenance in limited circumstances.

4.9.1 Jurisdiction of the courts

Under CSA 1991, s.8 the court has the power to make the following orders:

(a)   consent orders, and variation of consent orders predating CSA 1991 and written agreements (i.e. before April 1993);
(b)   'top-up' orders where the maximum liability to pay child support maintenance arises;
(c)   provision for education expenses;
(d)   provision for disability expenses;
(e)   orders once the child reaches the age of 19 or has left secondary education;
(f)   orders for the support of a child in advanced education;
(g)   orders where one of the parties or the child is not habitually resident in the UK;
(h)   orders for the support of step-children or other children of the family, by others than their natural parents;
(i)   orders against the parent with care;
(j)   orders in respect of children looked after by a local authority except for children placed at home by the local authority; and
(k)   orders in respect of children who have no absent parent.

In the limited cases where the court retains jurisdiction, it will have the widest discretion to determine the level of payments. The MCA 1973, s.25 factors will be considered, first consideration being given to the child's welfare.

In practical terms, the court is likely to be persuaded that although a child may not qualify for a maintenance calculation by the CMEC, the child nevertheless needs provision at a level similar to a qualifying child's maintenance. It is therefore worthwhile calculating what a parent would be ordered to pay for a child if a CMEC assessment were possible.

4.9.2 Application for a top-up order

Application is made by Form A alongside existing ancillary relief proceedings (e.g. for a school fees order (CSA 1991, s.8(7)(a)) or by Form A specifically for child financial provision under MCA 1973, s.23(1)(d).

4.9.3 Variation of existing orders

It is possible to vary existing periodical payments orders whether made before or after April 1993 subject to (where the parent with care is on benefits) there being no application to the CMEC.

4.9.4 'Segal' orders

Following the principles of *Dorney-Kingdom* v. *Dorney-Kingdom* [2000] 2 FLR 855, the court can make an order for periodical payments for a parent which will later absorb any subsequent child maintenance calculation (a so-called 'Segal order'). This is a global order for the parent and the child(ren) but two conditions must be fulfilled:

(a)   the parent must follow up the order with an application to the CMEC; and
(b)   there must be a substantial element of spousal support in the order.

4.9.5 Supplementary maintenance

Under CSA 1991, s.8(6) the court will have jurisdiction if it concludes that maintenance should be paid in addition to that assessed by the CMEC. This will apply where the non-resident parent has a net income of more than £2,000 per week. This will rise to £3,000 per week once the appropriate provisions under the Child Maintenance and Other Payments Act 2008 are implemented

4.9.6 Educational expenses

Section 8(7) of CSA 1991 provides that the court may continue to exercise its jurisdiction if the child is in education and provision is required to meet some or all of the expenses connected with that education. This may include school fees which are not met from a maintenance calculation or payment for uniforms, books or other equipment.

4.9.7 Children with a disability

Section 8(8) of CSA 1991 enables the court to make an order supplementing the maintenance calculation to meet expenses attributable to a child's disability. Section 8(9) defines a child as disabled if the child is blind, deaf or dumb, or is substantially and permanently handicapped by illness, injury, mental disorder or congenital deformity, or such other disability as may be prescribed.

4.9.8 Consent orders

Section 8(3) of CSA 1991 restricts the jurisdiction of the court to determine maintenance but it is still possible to arrange maintenance payments without an application to the CMEC. Section 8(5) preserves the power of the court to make an order if:

(a)   a written agreement (whether or not enforceable) provides for the making or securing, by a non-resident parent of the child, of periodical payments to or for the benefit of the child; and

(b)   the maintenance order which the court makes is, in all material respects, in the same terms as that agreement.

All that is required therefore is a written agreement and is most usually incorporated into the recitals to a consent order.

Where a consent order was made before 3 March 2003, no application can be made to the CMEC under CSA 1991, s.4 for a period of 12 months. After a year it is therefore open to either parent to apply for a maintenance assessment. This may present a more attractive route than mounting an application to the court to vary an agreement, because of the cost and the fact that the entire ancillary relief procedure under Form A must be endured if an application to court is made. This is compared with the no-cost option of applying for a maintenance calculation through the CMEC.

4.9.9 Separating parents

There can be no application to the CMEC whilst the parents are still living together. Where an agreement has been reached between the parties under s.8(5) but the paying party reneges from the agreement, the court has no jurisdiction to make an order. If the residential parent cannot secure a Segal-type order (see **4.9.4**) because that parent has income of his or her own, providing the parents are still living together at the time, the court can make an order without the consent of the paying party. For the purposes of a CMEC assessment, there must be a parent with care and a non-resident parent, thus in these circumstances the CSA 1991 provisions do not apply and the court's jurisdiction is unfettered.

4.10   THE DUTY TO CONSIDER A CLEAN BREAK

Under MCA, s.25A the court has a duty to consider a clean break. The object of the clean break is to settle on a permanent basis, the parties' financial responsibility towards each other and to end any financial interdependence between them.

The duty to consider a clean break exists in every case and is a positive duty for the court after consideration of the s.25(2) factors. There are three elements to consider:

(a)   termination – whether it is appropriate to terminate the financial obligations as soon after the decree as is 'just and reasonable';
(b)   term – if there is to be a periodical payments order, whether an order should be made (or secured) only for such period as to allow adjustment without undue hardship to termination;
(c)   dismissal – if there is no continuing obligation for periodical payments, the court may dismiss the application with a direction of no future application for an order under s.23(1)(a) or (b).

Even where a clean break is not being sought by either party, the court has the power to impose a clean break without the consent of either party if the circumstances are appropriate.

Clean break orders may be inappropriate where there are dependent children and the parties have an ongoing responsibility to house and maintain them. In these circumstances it is usual for there to be a nominal periodical payments order to safeguard the position of the party caring for the children.

The same might apply in the case of an older spouse without substantial capital or significant earning capacity (*Flavell* v. *Flavell* [1997] 1 FLR 353 and *SRJ* v. *DWJ* [1999] 2 FLR 176).

A clean break may not be appropriate where there is insufficient capital to compensate a party for the loss of maintenance. For example, where assets were tied up in a family company, it was found to be proper for a husband to make periodical payments to his wife from the profits from the tied-up capital (*F* v. *F* [2003] 1 FLR 847).

4.10.1 Inheritance (Provision for Family and Dependants) Act 1975

It is important when drafting clean break orders, to ensure that all rights and liabilities that are intended to be dismissed are included in the order.

A former spouse is entitled by virtue of the Inheritance (Provision for Family and Dependants) Act 1975, s.1(1)(b) to apply for provision out of the deceased spouse's estate. Where a clean break order has been achieved it is most likely that the termination of any continuing financial obligations between the parties remains after death.

Section 15(1) of the 1975 Act provides that on the grant of an order for divorce or separation or a decree of nullity (or at any time thereafter) the court may order that the other party shall not be entitled on the death of the applicant to apply for an order for provision out of the other's estate. Whilst this may seem an obvious inclusion when drafting a clean break order, consideration should be given as to whether it is appropriate. For example, in a no-asset case, a clean break may be the only realistic solution at the time of the making of the order but it may be just and reasonable to keep open the possibility of a claim in the event of the death of the other party.

4.10.2 Clean break on variation

The duty of the court to consider a clean break applies on a variation application in the same way as it applies in any original application for periodical payments.

CHAPTER 5

Experts and valuations

Andrew Newbury

5.1 INTRODUCTION

The role of experts within ancillary relief proceedings has changed significantly in the last 10 years. Historically, the role of the expert was often the 'gun for hire' who acted for one party and assisted that party in running his or her case. Since the introduction of the CPR in 1998, the role of the expert has become that of an independent individual who provides an opinion or advice on an issue which is beyond the scope of the parties' own knowledge or expertise. It is an independent and objective role. Despite that, circumstances may still arise where either party requires his or her own expert.

5.2 INSTRUCTION OF EXPERTS

Although the purpose of this section is to consider the provisions of the pre-action protocol in respect of the instruction of the experts, the same principles apply where experts are instructed to prepare a report where the parties are attending mediation or are seeking to resolve matters within the collaborative process.

The pre-action protocol includes the following provision in respect of the instruction of experts. The paragraph numbering set out below refers to the relevant paragraphs in the protocol.

5.2.1 Paragraph 3.8

Expert valuation evidence is only necessary where the parties cannot agree or do not know the value of a significant asset. The cost of a valuation should be proportionate to the sums in dispute and, wherever possible, a valuation should be obtained from a single valuer instructed by both parties.

The following practical guidance is given:

1. The party wishing to instruct an expert should give the other party a list of names of experts whom that party considers suitable to instruct.

2. Within 14 days, the other party may indicate an objection to one or more of the named experts and, if so, should supply the names of one or more experts whom he or she considers suitable.

It is suggested that both parties provide the names of experts but this is, however, impractical and it can often lead to a polarisation of views. A more practical approach is for both parties to agree in advance that one party will provide a list of, say, three names and that the other party will pick one name from that list. When providing the names, it can be useful if the letter is accompanied by CVs from each of the suggested experts.

5.2.2 Paragraph 3.9

Where the identity of the expert is agreed, the party should agree the terms of a joint letter of instruction. See precedents at **Appendices 9, 10** and **11** for draft letters of instruction to an accountant, surveyor and pensions expert.

5.2.3 Paragraph 3.10

Where no agreement is reached as to the identity of the expert, each party should think carefully before instructing his or her own expert because of the costs implications. Disagreements about disclosure and the use of such experts' reports may be better managed by the court within ancillary relief proceedings. Indeed, if the parties cannot agree upon the identity of an expert, that does not bode well for negotiating a settlement and perhaps ancillary relief proceedings may be a better option in such circumstances.

5.2.4 Paragraph 3.11

Where a joint report is commissioned or the parties have chosen to instruct separate experts, it is important that the expert is prepared to answer reasonable questions raised by either party.

5.2.5 Paragraph 3.12

Where the experts' reports are commissioned pre-application, it should be explained to the experts that they may in due course be reporting to the court and should therefore consider themselves bound by CPR Part 35.

5.2.6 Paragraph 3.13

Where the parties propose to instruct a joint expert, there is a duty on both parties to disclose whether they have already consulted that expert about the assets in issue.

5.2.7 Paragraph 3.14

If the parties agree to instruct separate experts, they should be encouraged to agree in advance that the reports will be disclosed.

5.3 CIVIL PROCEDURE RULES 1998 PART 35

Part 35 deals with the provision of expert evidence within court proceedings. By virtue of FPR rule 2.61C, Part 35 relates to family proceedings with the exception of rules 35.5(2) and 35.8(4)(b).

It is essential that practitioners are familiar with the provisions of Part 35 as they will be the court's first point of reference in any disputes over the provision of expert evidence. The following is a summary of the principal provisions of Part 35:

1. Rule 35.1 – expert evidence shall be restricted to that which is reasonably required to resolve the proceedings. The court may therefore be disinclined to allow expert evidence where it is viewed as unnecessary or disproportionate.
2. Rule 35.2 – defines an expert as being somebody who has been instructed to give or prepare evidence for the purpose of the court proceedings.
3. Rule 35.3 – sets out the duty of an expert. The expert's overriding duty is to help the court on the matters within his or her expertise. The duty to the court overrides any obligation to the person from whom the expert has received instructions or by whom the expert is paid.
4. Rule 35.4 – this is an important provision as it sets out the court's power to restrict expert evidence. It is the first task of a court to decide whether it needs expert evidence at all. Expert evidence is only admissible where the court needs it because the matters in question fall outside the court's expertise. Also note:

   (a) Rule 35.4(1) states that no party may call an expert or put an expert's report in evidence without the court's permission.
   (b) Rule 35.4(2) states that when a party applies for permission, the party must identify the field in which he or she wishes to rely on expert evidence and, where practical, the expert in that field and on whose evidence the party wishes to rely. Where making such an application, in practical terms it is therefore sensible to attach a letter and CV from each of the proposed experts.
   (c) Rule 35.4(3) states that if the court does grant permission, it will only be in relation to the expert named or the field identified.
   (d) Rule 35.4(4) provides that the court may limit the amount of the expert's fees and expenses that one party may recover from any other party. This is, however, a power which is rarely exercised by the courts.

5. Rule 35.5 – paragraph (1) specifies that expert evidence is to be given in a written report, unless the court directs otherwise.
6. Rule 35.6 – either party may put written questions to an expert instructed by another party on that expert's report. If a single joint expert is appointed, then either party may put written questions to that expert about the report. Questions may be put once only and must be put within 28 days of service of the expert's report (rule 35.6(2)). Questions must also be for the purpose only of clarification of the report unless the court gives specific permission or the other party agrees. The expert's answers to the questions are treated as part of the original report (rule 35.6(3)).

   By virtue of rule 35.6(4), where a party has put a written question to the expert and the expert does not answer the question, the court may make one or both of the following orders in relation to the party who instructed the expert:

   (i) the party may not rely on the evidence of that report; or
   (ii) the party may not recover the fees and expenses of that expert from any other party (this provision pre-dates the new costs rules under FPR rule 2.71 and should now be read in that context).

   The general purpose of rule 35.6 is to provide a general procedure to replace cross-examination when an expert's evidence will be in written form only. In practice, it is exceedingly rare for a jointly instructed expert to be called to give evidence at court.
7. Rule 35.7 – sets out the court's power to direct that evidence is to be given by a single joint expert. Such a direction may be given where both parties wish to submit expert evidence on a particular issue. Where parties cannot agree who should be the expert, the court may select the expert from a list prepared or identified by the parties or the expert may be selected in such other manner as the court may direct.
8. Rule 35.8 – where the court has directed under rule 35.7 for there to be a single joint expert, each instructing party may give their own instructions to the expert. When doing so, a copy of the instructions must be sent to the other side. The practice of sending independent instructions is, however, discouraged and note should be had of the Family Law protocol and the President's Best Practice Guide for instructing a single joint expert – see **5.5**.

   When giving directions that a joint expert be instructed, the court may also give directions about payment of the expert's fees and expenses and any inspection or examination which the expert wishes to carry out (rule 35.8(3)). The court may also limit the amount that can be paid by way of fees and expenses to the expert. Unless the court directs otherwise, the instructing parties are jointly and severally liable for payment of the expert's fees and expenses.
9. Rule 35.9 – where one party has access to information which is not reasonably available to the other side, the court may direct the party who has

access to the information to prepare and file a document recording the information and serve a copy of that document on the other side. Such a direction may be used where, for example, the husband has access to company information which is not otherwise available to the wife.

10. Rule 35.10 – refers to Practice Direction 35 (see **5.4**). An expert's report must comply with the requirements in PD 35.

11. Rule 35.11 – where a party has disclosed an expert's report, any party may use that report as evidence at the trial.

12. Rule 35.12 – the court may at any stage direct that there be a discussion between the experts for the purpose of requiring them to identify the issues and, where possible, to reach agreement on the issues. The court may even specify the issues which the experts must discuss and, following a decision, the court may also direct that they must prepare a statement for the court showing the issues on which they agree and those on which they disagree and a summary of their reasons for disagreeing.

13. Rule 35.13 – a party who fails to disclose an expert's report may not use the report at the trial or call the expert to give evidence orally, unless the court gives permission.

14. Rule 35.14 – an expert may file a written request for directions to assist him in carrying out his function as an expert. The request may be done within giving notice to any party. When giving directions, the court may also direct that a party be served with a copy of the directions and a copy of the request for directions.

5.4 PRACTICE DIRECTION 35

Practice Direction 35 sets out the requirements for an expert's report as follows:

(a) The report should be addressed to the court and not to the party from whom the expert has received instructions.

(b) The report must be verified by a statement of truth.

(c) The expert must confirm their qualifications and they must also detail any literature or material that they have relied upon in the preparation of their report. When instructing an expert to prepare a report and to ensure that the report complies with Part 35, the following request should be included in the letter of instruction as follows:

The court rules provide that your report must obtain the following:

(i)   The report must be addressed to the court/Principal Registry and not to this firm or other side's solicitors.

(ii)   The report must contain details of your qualifications and also details of any literature or any other material which you have relied upon in making your report.

(iii) The report must contain a statement that you understand your duty to the court and that you have complied with that duty.

(iv) The report must also contain a statement setting out the substance of all material instructions which you will be given and must also set out the facts and the instructions given to you which are material to the opinions expressed in your report.

(v) The report must be verified by a statement of truth as follows:

'I confirm that insofar as the facts I have stated in my report are within my own knowledge, I have made clear which they are and I believe them to be true and that the opinions I have expressed represent my true and complete professional opinion.'

5.5 PRESIDENT'S BEST PRACTICE GUIDE

Note should be had of the *President's Ancillary Relief Advisory Group Best Practice Guide for Instructing a Single Joint Expert* which is set out at Appendix 14 of the Family Law protocol.

The Practice Guide refers to the President's Practice Direction dated 25 May 2000 ([2000] 1 FLR 997) which encouraged the appointment of single joint experts (see **Appendix 19**). Even where parties cannot agree on the identity of an expert, the Practice Direction states that the court will consider using its powers under Part 35 to appoint a single joint expert at the First Appointment.

The principal practical points of the Practice Guide are as follows:

1. The Guide sets out principles which should be applied either within ancillary relief proceedings or prior to the issue of such proceedings.
2. An expert instructed by one party separately will not usually be appointable later as a single joint expert and therefore parties should consider the costs implications of instructing their own expert at the outset.
3. Prior to appointing a single joint expert, information should be obtained from the expert including the following:

   (a) there is no conflict of interest;
   (b) the matter is within the range of expertise of the expert;
   (c) the expert is available to provide the report within a specified timescale including his or her availability for the attendance of any dates that are known to be relevant;
   (d) the expert's fee rate, basis of charging and other terms of business and a best estimate of the likely fee; and
   (e) if applicable, whether the expert will accept instructions on a publicly funded basis

4. Before the instruction of the single joint expert, the parties should agree in what proportion the fees are to be shared between them and, if applicable, have obtained agreement for public funding.
5. If the identity of the expert has not been agreed prior to the First Appointment, the information set out in (c) above should be obtained from all prospective experts prior to the First Appointment.

6. Where the court directs a report by a single joint expert, the order should:

   (a) if the single joint expert has already been instructed, adopt the instructions already given or make such amendment to the instructions as the court thinks fit;

   (b) identify the expert and specify the task he or she is to perform;

   (c) provide that the instructions are contained in a jointly agreed letter and specify the time within which that letter of instruction is to be sent and the date by which the report is to be produced;

   (d) provide for the date by which written questions may be put to the joint single expert and the date by which they must be answered; and

   (e) make any such provision as to the single joint expert's fees which the court thinks appropriate.

7. The joint instructions to the single joint expert should reflect the proportionality principle and include:

   (a) basic relevant information and any assumptions to be made;

   (b) the principal known issues;

   (c) specific questions to be answered;

   (d) arrangements for attendance at a property, business or accountant's office or other place;

   (e) a copy of paragraphs 1.1 to 1.6 of the Practice Direction to Part 35 and a copy of the President's Best Practice Guide;

   (f) a copy of the relevant parts of the court order;

   (g) documents necessary for the expert's consideration of the case, clearly legible, properly sorted, paginated and indexed.

8. Upon proceeding with the joint letter of instruction or at any time later should it become necessary, the single joint expert should raise with the solicitors any issues or questions which may arise, including proportionality, lack of clarity or completeness in the instructions and the possible impact on fees of complying with the instructions.

9. Should a party wish to give supplementary instructions to the single joint expert, full consideration must be given to proportionality and the possible effect on the timetable. Supplementary instructions should not be given to the single joint expert unless the other party has agreed or the court has sanctioned it.

10. All communications by the single joint expert should be addressed to both parties and correspondence must be copied in to each party.

11. Any meeting or conference attended by the single joint expert must be proportionate to the case and would normally be with both parties and their advisers.

12. The report should be served simultaneously on both parties.

13. If the joint expert feels that the proportionality principle cannot be complied with, the expert should give notice to the parties, identifying what is

perceived to be the problem. If the difficulty cannot be resolved by the parties and the expert, then the expert should file a written request to the court pursuant to rule 35.14.

14. As a last resort, the expert may resign the joint appointment. If that were to happen, the expert should serve a precise statement on both parties, and where the court has ordered the expert's appointment, the court should also be served with the statement.

5.6 PRACTICAL CONSIDERATIONS WHEN INSTRUCTING EXPERTS

The comments in this section should be read in the context of the rules and guidelines set out above. Some practical points to consider are as follows:

1. Although the court's inclination is strongly in favour of instructing single joint experts, this may not be appropriate in all cases. An example may be where there are serious issues about the husband's conduct of his business and/or disclosure issues in that regard. In such circumstances, an accountant may need to be instructed in the more traditional role of fully investigating the husband's business structure, potentially with a view to tracing hidden assets. The court may, however, require compelling arguments at the First Appointment to justify such an approach.

2. One of the inherent problems of the single joint expert is the lack of communication channels. It is not possible to simply pick up the phone to the accountant and openly discuss his or her views. Furthermore, when the single joint expert's report is received, how is the solicitor or client to know whether it is correct and whether the findings should be challenged? Neither will be experts in that area. In sufficiently high net worth divorces, it is increasingly common therefore to instruct a 'shadow expert' to advise upon the contents of the single joint expert's report and assist in formulating questions. The role of the shadow expert may be particularly important when acting for a wife who has no direct knowledge of a family business. By contrast, her husband who runs the business will usually have a clearer view as to whether the single joint expert's views are correct or not.

   Where shadow experts are being appointed in addition to single joint experts, ironically, it is often the case that the costs therefore become higher compared to parties having simply instructed their own experts at the outset.

3. One of the issues which a district judge must consider at the First Appointment is the instruction of expert witnesses (FPR rule 2.61D(2)(b)). Serious consideration needs to be given to the instruction of experts when preparing for the First Appointment. Accordingly, if the identity of a single joint expert cannot be readily agreed, then it is essential to take the following steps:

(a) Consider the identities of the possible experts to be instructed and obtain a letter and CV from them as well as the information set out in the President's Best Practice Guide.

(b) The aforementioned information should be served on the other side prior to the First Appointment with confirmation that an order is to be sought at the hearing that one of the selected experts be instructed.

(c) Ideally, a draft letter of instruction should also be prepared in advance of the First Appointment. If there may be a dispute as to the exact terms and nature of the instruction to the expert, then those issues can be addressed before the district judge and the final version of the letter of instruction can be appended to the First Appointment order.

Whilst the above may seem like substantial additional work in advance of the First Appointment, it will usually ensure that significant costs can be saved in the long run as well as avoiding a delay if there is a dispute as to the identity of the valuer and the terms of instruction after the First Appointment.

4. If problems arise regarding the instruction of a valuer after the First Appointment (for example, it is impossible to agree the identity of a valuer or the exact terms of instruction), there is much to be said for making an immediate application to the court for further directions in accordance with FPR rule 2.61D(4)(a). It is often the case that such disputes cannot be resolved promptly in correspondence and an early application to the court may save time and costs in the longer term.

5. When considering the listing of court timetables, careful thought should be given to realistic timescales. In accordance with the President's Best Practice Guide, experts should be asked for a realistic timescale of when their reports will be ready. Thereafter, time should be factored in for questions to be asked of the expert and those questions to be answered. Only after those questions have been addressed by either party will they be in a position to submit proposals for settlement. The listing of the FDR should therefore be realistic, taking into account the above steps.

5.7   INSTRUCTION OF ACCOUNTANTS

Careful thought should be given as to what exactly the accountant is being instructed to do. When faced with a limited company, partnership or any kind of business structure, the initial reaction is that a valuation of that business is required. The actual value of the business may, however, in fact be an academic point, or one of the least relevant issues to be addressed with the accountant.

Issues which an accountant may be instructed to cover include the following:

1. A value of the business as a whole.
2. More significantly, a valuation of either party's interests in the business. By way of example, the husband may own shares in a private limited company with one or more third parties. In such circumstances the value of the entire business may be academic and it is the value of the husband's shares which are relevant. Where valuing a minority interest in a limited company, a discount may have to be applied to the value of those shares.
3. CGT calculations. The family court is always interested in the true net value of any asset. Even though it is rarely anticipated that a party would be obliged to sell or transfer their shares, the impact of any CGT in calculating the true net value of shares needs to be taken into account.
4. An extremely important area for accountants to consider is liquidity. It may be necessary to consider how, for example, the husband might be able to raise a lump sum in favour of the wife to meet his obligations under any proposed final order. The accountant can therefore be instructed to advise upon how money can be withdrawn from the business by the husband and the tax implications of various approaches. The accountant may also be instructed to advise upon how much capital could be withdrawn immediately and how much could be raised in instalments over various fixed periods of time.
5. The level of income drawn from the business may be unclear and there may be a particular issue as to the potential future income which it will be possible to draw. An accountant could advise upon the realistic maintainable future earnings through the business. Such information can be useful in calculating both spousal maintenance and child maintenance.

In *D* v. *D and B Limited* [2007] 2 FLR 653, Charles J was critical of the cases put forward as he was of the view that they did not properly explore the viable alternatives concerning realising the value of business assets. Charles J set out the information which would normally be required in respect of companies as follows:

- a brief history and the benefits derived from the company during the marriage;
- a description of the business;
- audited accounts for a reasonable period, say, the last five years;
- up-to-date accounts in the form produced to auditors;
- up-to-date management accounts, or if they are not available, an up-to-date assessment by the spouse owning the company backed by appropriate records for the current position;
- an up-to-date account from that spouse of the prospects for the company, accompanied by appropriate records;
- up-to-date accounts from the spouse owning the company with his or her plans for the company, backed up by records;

- whether or not the plans include a sale and who might be interested in buying the business or part of it.

Furthermore, Charles J set out a list of questions which would generally require an answer in a case concerning the private company, mainly:

- Is there a market for the shares or any of the assets?
- If the shares or assets were to be sold, what would be the strategy that should be adopted?
- What is the appropriate method of valuation? If the valuation is on an earnings basis, what is the correct approach to determine the maintainable profits and what is the range of appropriate profit/earning ratios?
- How money could be raised and paid out to the shareholders or directors, to include an assessment of distributable profits and the tax consequences of any such distribution.
- What would be the likely impact on the company as a going concern and its valuation if money were taken out of the company as suggested?
- What structures could be used to share the benefits between the spouses by way of dividend or other methods and, in the interim, which would enable one spouse to continue to have the day-to-day control of the business, whilst at the same time protecting the other spouse?

5.8   INSTRUCTION OF SURVEYORS

5.8.1 Residential property

Undoubtedly, the most common form of expert evidence in ancillary relief proceedings is the instruction of a surveyor for the valuation of property. That will most commonly be a valuation of the former matrimonial home. It is usually unnecessary to formally instruct a surveyor to value any property prior to the exchange of Forms E. As stated at point 3 of **3.5.2**, when preparing Form E most clients will obtain informal written valuations from local estate agents in the hope that property valuations can be agreed.

Where there is a divergence of opinion or if both parties have obtained significantly different views from local estate agents, a surveyor will usually be instructed as a single joint expert at the First Appointment. In the majority of cases the surveyor will simply be asked to provide an opinion as to the open market value of the property on the basis that it has been marketed for a reasonable period of time and a sale takes place at arm's length between a willing seller and a willing buyer.

Practical issues to consider are as follows:

1. Where expert evidence is being sought under Part 35, the expert should be a qualified surveyor and not an estate agent. Some firms of estate agents will, however, include in-house surveyors.

2. Note should be had of the points made in this chapter: a check should be
    made with the surveyor that he or she has previous experience in provid-
    ing valuations for court proceedings and that he or she has not previously
    been contacted or instructed by either party. An estimate of costs should
    be obtained before the surveyor is asked to prepare the valuation.
3. A full structural survey is usually unnecessary; the surveyor is simply
    being asked to provide a valuation for court proceedings.
4. In certain unusual cases, the surveyor may be asked to give an opinion on
    issues such as the following:

    (a) Whether the value of the property/land could be enhanced with
         planning permission. If so, the surveyor could be asked to give an
         opinion as to the planning permission which should be sought.
    (b) If there is more than one building on the plot of land, the surveyor
         could be asked to provide an opinion as to sale prices which would
         be achieved if the plots were sold separately or as a whole.
    (c) Even if planning permission is not a relevant consideration, the
         surveyor could be asked how the value of the property could be
         enhanced by, for example, part of it being converted.
    (d) The surveyor could be asked to pass an opinion upon any repairs or
         remedial works that should be carried out to enhance the eventual
         sale price.

5.8.2 Commercial property

The same considerations apply in the valuation of commercial property as
they do for residential property; it is, however, clearly necessary to instruct
specialist commercial valuers.

It is often the case that valuations of commercial properties are based
upon their rental yields and, accordingly, the surveyor will require copies of
any existing leases or sub-leases.

Where commercial property is owned by a business owned by one of the
spouses, these premises will usually need to be valued prior to the accountant
preparing the business valuation.

Likewise, self-administered pension schemes (known as SASS) often own
business or commercial premises. A re-valuation of such business premises
will be required so that an up-to-date valuation of the pension fund can be
obtained.

5.9   INSTRUCTION OF PENSION EXPERTS

In cases where the pension provision is relatively modest, the costs of instructing an expert may be disproportionate to the sums involved; however, many

firms of actuaries or financial advisers will provide a basic report or information for £500 to £1,000 plus VAT or thereabouts.

5.9.1 Instruction of an actuary

The nature of the instructions to an actuary may vary from case to case, although the following may be common areas to seek expert evidence:

(a) The most common area is where a view is required upon the (CETV) produced by the pension provider. Particularly with final salary schemes (such as NHS, civil service or teachers' pensions), the true CETV calculated by an actuary may be significantly higher than that produced by the pension provider. This can particularly be the case with armed forces pensions. Ascertaining the true CETV may be less important if there is to be an equal share of that policy; however, where there is to be a set-off arrangement or an unequal share of the pension, an expert's view on the true CETV can be absolutely essential.

(b) Many solicitors, counsel and district judges are of the view that to achieve a fair division of the assets, it is necessary to look at equalising future pension income and benefits as opposed to equalising the present CETV. As women actuarially live longer than men, women may need a larger share of the CETV to provide them with the same income benefits upon retirement.

(c) Those spouses earning a high income or in good final salary schemes may be able easily to build up their lost benefits post-divorce. Particularly after a long marriage it could be argued that it is unfair to one spouse for pension benefits to be frozen at the time of divorce whereas the pension of the other spouse can be built up considerably post-separation. This is a further issue that could be addressed by an actuary.

5.9.2 Instructions to an independent financial adviser

Arguably, it is less likely that an independent financial adviser will be instructed to provide expert evidence to be submitted to the court under CPR Part 35. If there is to be a pension sharing order, however, the financial adviser's input may be crucial, particularly with regard to where a pension credit should be invested and the sums which could be received by either spouse upon retirement.

Independent financial advisers can also be used to advise on the following:

(a) Available mortgages and maximising the client's mortgage potential if there is an issue as to meeting the cost of future housing. An independent financial adviser could prepare a report either for your own client or for the other spouse to illustrate how they could afford a property of a certain standard and afford a mortgage secured on such a property.

(b) If your client is to receive a capital payment by way of a clean break, it is preferable for the client to receive advice as to how to maximise investment income and how to invest that money for the future. The *Duxbury* tables provide a relatively modest rate of return of 3.75%, although many good independent financial advisers will help to ensure that your client will receive a greater rate of return in the future.

(c) Financial advisers can also advise upon such products as life insurance or illness protection, which may be necessary to protect ongoing periodical payments orders.

CHAPTER 6

Agreements between the spouses

Ann Corrigan

6.1 PRE-NUPTIAL AGREEMENTS

An increasing number of couples enter into pre-nuptial agreements. A pre-nuptial agreement is a formal written agreement between engaged couples setting out what is to happen in the event that the couple separate or divorce.

The important starting point is to remember that the court's jurisdiction cannot be ousted and any agreement will be considered along with all the circumstances of the case when the court carries out the MCA 1973, s.25 exercise.

It should also be borne in mind that the agreement must be a valid agreement by complying with general principles of contract law.

6.1.1 The court's approach

Traditionally, the courts have been reluctant to attach much weight to pre-nuptial agreements but it is becoming more common for couples to enter into such agreements and expect notice to be taken of them. Recent cases demonstrate a shift in the court's approach and clear principles are beginning to emerge.

In *M* v. *M* [2002] 1 FLR 654 it was held that a pre-nuptial agreement did not oust the jurisdiction of the court and it was for the court to decide in the particular circumstances of the case, what weight should be attached to it. The parties had been married for five years and there was one child of the marriage. The couple entered into a pre-nuptial agreement that provided for a payment of £275,000 to the wife but in ancillary relief proceedings she claimed a one-off payment of £1,300,000 contending that she had been under pressure to enter into the agreement at a time when she was pregnant and already committed to the wedding ceremony. The husband's position was that after such a short marriage, the wife should be bound by the agreement and the lump sum of £275,000 paid to her. The court held that the agreement had to be looked at as one of the circumstances of the case and to receive a just result, consider what weight (if any) should be attached to it. Also, that it would be unfair to the wife to hold her to the terms of the agreement, and unfair to the husband to ignore it. The wife was awarded considerably more than provided for in the agreement but the court had taken the agreement on board stating that it 'tended to guide the court to a more modest award than might have been made without it'.

In *K* v. *K* [2003] 1 FLR 120 the pre-nuptial agreement provided that if the parties separated or divorced within five years, the husband would pay to the wife a lump sum of £100,000 increased by 10 per cent for every year of the marriage that had elapsed. It also contained a clause that the parties did not intend the agreement to affect any order that might be made for a child but was silent on the question of spousal maintenance. The marriage lasted just 14 months and there was one child. The wife claimed a lump sum of £1,600,000 to re-house herself and spousal maintenance of £57,000 per annum. The judge awarded neither but instead awarded the wife £15,000 per annum during the child's minority and £1,200,000 for housing but any property to be held on trust for the husband, reverting to him when the child finished full-time education. The court considered that the wife had been properly advised and had not been under pressure to sign the agreement notwithstanding that she had been five months' pregnant at the time and that by adhering to the capital provision contained in the agreement, the outcome was not unjust.

The increasing importance of pre-nuptial agreements and the approach the courts were now taking was again emphasised in *Crossley* v. *Crossley* [2008] 1 FLR 1467. Again, this was a marriage that lasted just 14 months and the effect of the pre-nuptial agreement was that each should walk away from the marriage with whatever they brought into it. In this case the Court of Appeal held that the agreement was so compelling a factor in the particular circumstances of the case, the wife should have to explain why the terms of the agreement should not be implemented. Thorpe LJ described the facts as 'a paradigm case' where the existence of the pre-nuptial agreement was a factor of 'magnetic importance'. He went on to say that the approach of the lower court was in accordance with a developing view that pre-nuptial agreements were growing in importance.

In 2008 the Privy Council dealt with a husband's appeal that a pre-nuptial agreement, later varied in a post-nuptial agreement, should be valid and binding. It was held that it was not open to the Board to reverse the long-standing rule that pre-nuptial agreements were contrary to public policy and thus not valid or binding in the contractual sense and that the validity and effect of such agreements were matters of legislative and not judicial development (*MacLeod* v. *MacLeod* [2009] 1 FLR 641).

Despite the Privy Council ruling in *MacLeod*, in 2009 the issue was once again before the Court of Appeal in *Radmacher* v. *Granatino* [2009] EWCA Civ 649.

In this case the Court of Appeal set out its views on the law regarding pre-nuptial agreements for the purposes of MCA 1973, s.25. In this case, the husband was French and the wife German. The parties had lived for most of their married life in England and there were two children. The parties had entered into a pre-nuptial agreement at the wife's request. The pre-nuptial agreement was valid under German and French law but the parties divorced in the UK. Some of the key points that emerge from the decision in *Radmacher* are that:

(a) although the public policy objections remain in principle, their practical consequences have diminished and such agreements are likely to be given substantial weight provided they cannot be impugned on contractual grounds;

(b) to the extent that an agreement makes inadequate provision for a spouse as parent, this can be resolved by making an award for the duration of a child's needs;

(c) neither a lack of independent legal advice nor absence of financial disclosure will necessarily devalue the agreement (particularly if where there has been advice and/or disclosure, the result would not have been different).

In the lead judgment, Thorpe LJ stated:

> in future cases broadly in line with the present case on the facts, the judge should give due weight to the marital property regime into which the parties freely entered. This is not to apply foreign law, nor is it to give effect to a contract foreign to English tradition. It is, in my judgment, a legitimate exercise of the very wide discretion that is conferred on the judges to achieve fairness to the parties to the ancillary relief proceedings.

It seems therefore that pre-nuptial agreements will be treated as binding unless there are very compelling reasons to disregard them.

6.1.2 Reform

A draft parliamentary Bill is expected from the Law Commission in 2012 but until then the courts will retain the power to ignore or vary any agreement. However, it does seem likely, given the decision in *Radmacher,* that pre-nuptial agreements will become more important and more than ever before, where an agreement exists, the parties will be bound by its terms.

6.1.3 Advising on and drafting pre-nuptial agreements

In considering a pre-nuptial agreement, the court must consider whether the terms of the agreement are fair and in particular whether the agreement favours one party over the other. Although not an exhaustive list, the following must be borne in mind when advising a client seeking an agreement as to whether or not it will satisfy the court if either party later seeks to rely upon it:

1. Are both parties taking independent legal advice? The extent to which the agreement has been the subject of negotiation between the parties and their lawyers is likely to be relevant if proceedings arise as to the validity and enforceability of any agreement.
2. How long in advance of the wedding is the agreement to be signed? If the wedding is imminent, consider instead whether the agreement should be a post-nuptial agreement.
3. Have both parties had the benefit of full and open financial disclosure? There should be a statement in the agreement that both parties have entered into the agreement on the basis of such disclosure.
4. Do both parties understand the nature and effect of the agreement and the financial position it will leave them in if implemented?
5. Did either party exert pressure against the other to enter into the agreement?
6. Is either party under pressure from any other source (e.g. parents) to enter into the agreement?
7. Is either party taking advantage of a dominant financial position?
8. Does the agreement make provision for any change in circumstances – particularly does the agreement deal with any variation in the event of the arrival of any children? This may be of particular importance if the agreement is made at a time when the parties already know there is to be a child.
9. Is provision being made in respect of the matrimonial home? Is it necessary to draft a separate declaration of trust or enter any restriction at the Land Registry?
10. Should there be a review clause in the event of the birth of a child, serious illness or disability, unemployment of either party or after the lapse of a specified number of years?
11. Is it necessary for there to be a 'mirror' agreement in any other jurisdiction?

Pre-acquired assets

The practitioner may advise clients who are planning to marry later in life or for a second time and have already amassed wealth in their own right which they wish to protect. A careful schedule of any such assets must be clearly set out in the agreement to afford as much protection as possible if the intention is for the assets to remain with/revert to the person who owns them.

Relevance of the agreement

If parties entering into a pre-nuptial agreement wish its terms to influence (or be binding upon) a court in the event of divorce, it is important to advise a client that if their circumstances are wholly different from those which existed at the time of the agreement, the court may disregard the agreement. This would be particularly important, for example, if the agreement did not include variation when any children arrive or in the event of illness, disability or unemployment. However, the length of the marriage may in itself be a determining factor that renders an agreement unfair and this should be borne in mind when advising at the outset.

6.2 POST-NUPTIAL AGREEMENTS

There is no specific provision in MCA 1973, s.25 that directs the court to have regard to agreements reached between the parties but any agreement will fall to be considered along with all the circumstances of the case.

Section 35(1) provides:

> where a maintenance agreement is for the time being subsisting and each of the parties to the agreement is for the time being either domiciled in England and Wales, then ... either party may apply to the court ... for an order under this section.

A 'maintenance agreement' is defined in s.34(2) as being:

(a) an agreement containing financial arrangements, whether made during the continuance or after the dissolution or annulment of the marriage; or
(b) a separation agreement which contains no financial arrangements in a case where no other agreement in writing between the same parties contains such arrangements.

If the parties agree any variation to an agreement, this can be done without any application to the court and in the absence of agreement, either party can apply to the court.

Any separation agreement must be formed in accordance with normal contract principles and any agreement reached as a result of undue influence, duress, mistake or misrepresentation cannot be binding and it has long been the case that the courts will be slow to upset an agreement freely reached between the parties.

6.2.1 *Edgar* v. *Edgar*

In *Edgar* v. *Edgar* [1980] 3 All ER 887, a separation deed which had been prepared for the parties with the benefit of legal advice and full financial disclosure was ignored by the trial judge who made financial provision for the wife over and above what was contained in the separation agreement. The husband appealed and the Court of Appeal had to consider to what extent the deed of separation, which had been prepared with the benefit of legal advice and made provision for the wife, barred the wife from seeking ancillary relief and if this was not the case, did it affect the outcome? Ormrod LJ in his leading judgment stated that 'formal agreements, properly and fairly arrived at with competent legal advice, should not be displaced unless there are good and substantial grounds for concluding that an injustice will be done by holding the parties to the terms of their agreement'. He also highlighted that the circumstances that existed at the time the agreement was entered into were relevant, as were any important changes of circumstances that were unforeseen or overlooked at the time the agreement was made.

Consideration must also be given when drafting a separation agreement (in the same way as with pre-nuptial agreements above) to whether the client is under any pressure from the other party to enter into the agreement and whether the client has sufficient knowledge of the overall financial position to reach agreement.

6.2.2 Contents of a separation agreement

The contents of a separation deed will, naturally, vary depending on the circumstances of the parties but there are certain issues that may be common to all separation agreements.

Agreement to separate

The parties may wish to include the date of separation. This is useful in preventing either party being in desertion and is evidence that the parties are treating the marriage as being over. A date also provides evidence where the intention is for one or other party to petition for divorce based on MCA 1973, s.1(2)(d) and for the purposes of establishing how transfers of property between the spouses may be treated for tax purposes.

Periodical payments

The agreement can set out agreed provision either for a spouse or for children of the family. Providing the payer complies with this clause, it is good evidence if a claim is mounted under MCA 1973, s.27 which enables applications to the court where one party has neglected to maintain the other party or a child. Consider also, within any provision for maintenance, whether provision for variation of the amount is needed or whether the paying party may be required to produce evidence of increased income to bring about any such variation.

The family home

Consideration should be given as to the occupation of the home, how the outgoings are to be met (both in the short and long term), whose responsibility it is to maintain the property and how the property is to be held in the event that a sale is not imminent. If it has been agreed that the occupying spouse may move to an alternative property, a clause should be included setting out upon what terms the substitute property is to be held, paid for and disposed of in due course.

If a transfer of the property from the joint names of the parties into the sole name of one party is agreed, this should be dealt with as soon as consent has been obtained from the mortgagee (if appropriate) to avoid any supervening event that may prove impossible or detrimental.

The family company

Particular care should be taken when drafting a separation deed that deals with either the transfer or sale of company assets. In *N* v. *N* [2001] 2 FLR 69, an equal division of the assets could only be achieved by the sale of a company owned by the husband and the court gave him several years to organise this to preserve, as far as possible, the value of the company. The court was careful to ensure that the order did not damage the family's financial security and adopted a creative and sensitive approach to achieve an 'orderly' redistribution of wealth between the parties. The question of any CGT must be considered as must the way in which one party is compensated. For example, consider whether a client is protected during the transfer process by a shareholders' agreement which can regulate how the company is managed and how dividends are paid during the transfer.

In cases involving a shareholding in a private company, Charles J in the leading case of *A* v. *A* [2004] EWHC 2818 (Fam), emphasised the need to search for a viable and pragmatic solution informed by a general knowledge of company law. He said this:

> it seems to me that in ancillary relief proceedings it is important for the parties and their advisers to look at issues concerning private companies through the eyes of both (a) persons with experience in and of matrimonial litigation and (b) persons with experience in and of business and business litigation. For example if this is done it may quickly become apparent (a) that there is a wide bracket of valuation and (b) that there may be a viable and pragmatic business solution which would avoid either or both of the uncertainties and difficulties of valuation and the raising of finance, albeit that it may not involve a clean break.

This should be borne in mind to the same extent in drafting a separation deed as when agreeing terms of settlement in a consent order and suitable advice should be sought from company law and employment colleagues.

Bank accounts and credit cards

Given that parties who operate a joint account have a joint and several liability in respect of that account, it is wise to consider whether the account should be closed to avoid one party incurring debt for which the other remains liable. Similarly, consideration should be given as to responsibility for any income tax that may be payable and who should be responsible for generating any documentation needed to give effect to the closure of an account and a suitable clause inserted into the agreement to give effect to the agreed arrangement and protection for each party.

Children

Although both parents do, of course, retain parental responsibility for the children, it may be appropriate to record any agreement relating to where the children will live and what arrangements have been agreed for the non-resident parent's contact. Notwithstanding any provision in the separation agreement, either parent remains at liberty to make an application to the court in respect of the children at any stage.

Advantages of a separation agreement

The parties may decide to enter into a separation agreement as all matters are agreed and both parties wish to avoid court proceedings.

A separation deed can be prepared (subject to the safeguards outlined above) quickly and at less cost than embarking upon court proceedings and can provide a more flexible vehicle for parties to deal with practical issues at an early stage.

Disadvantages of a separation agreement

A separation agreement is not enforceable although as outlined above, and in the light of *Edgar* and more recently, *MacLeod*, it carries considerable weight if it comes to be considered in the context of an application for ancillary relief. Difficulties may arise, however, if one party does not comply with parts of the agreement making an application to the court necessary involving delay and cost.

In addition a separation deed cannot provide the client with any guarantee that its terms will be upheld by the court as discussed above. In deciding what weight to attach to an agreement the court will ask how the agreement came to be made, did the parties themselves attach importance to it and have the parties themselves acted upon it?

When drafting a separation agreement, the client must be advised that its terms are binding and will not be varied unless:

(a) there is a change in circumstances making the agreed financial arrangements manifestly unjust; or

(b) it did not contain financial provision for a child; or

(c)   it is contrary to public policy (e.g. the financial responsibility falls on the state).

6.3   '*XYDHIAS* AGREEMENTS'

Most ancillary relief cases settle by agreement. This may be after an application to the court has been made in Form A and often as a result of negotiation at the FDR. Once agreement has been reached, heads of agreement should be drawn up and signed to evidence the necessary consensus.

It must be remembered that even where agreement has been reached and the terms of the agreement reduced to a proposed order, the agreement is not enforceable until approved by the court.

In *Xydhias* v. *Xydhias* [1999] 1 FLR 683 the Court of Appeal confirmed the *Edgar* principles but went on to say that the existence of a financial agreement between the parties does not avoid the need for the court to exercise its discretionary powers under MCA 1973, s.25 and normal contractual principles do not apply. The only way an ancillary relief agreement can be enforced is to convert it into an order and generally any 'without prejudice' negotiations are not admissible. The Court of Appeal went on to say that there were two lessons for family practitioners. First, there is a need to distinguish clearly between the two stages of negotiation. The first stage establishes what the applicant is to receive and has to be expressed in simple terms in heads of agreement signed by both parties and their representatives, and the second stage is to express the heads of agreement in the language of an order of the court.

Where an agreement is reached at the FDR and the terms approved by the judge but not incorporated immediately into a consent order, the court will uphold the approved agreement as an order. In *Rose* v. *Rose* [2002] 2 FLR 978, an FDR resulted in an agreement but heads of agreement were not drawn up between the parties. The husband sought to resile from the agreement on the basis that the judge had treated the FDR as a preliminary trial, that the court had not had the full picture and that he, the husband, was not in a fit state to compromise. On appeal Coleridge J rejected the husband's arguments and found that the whole purpose and effect of the FDR would be lost or compromised if parties were free to analyse and re-evaluate a previous crucial decision.

In the event of a dispute as to whether or not agreement has been reached, for example, where a draft consent order has been submitted and one party does not wish to be bound by its terms, the full ancillary relief procedure can be avoided and the following steps should be taken:

1.   File an application in Form A.
2.   Seek immediate directions:

    (a)   to stay the requirement of Forms E;

    (b)   to vacate the First Appointment;

    (c)   for trial of the preliminary issue as to whether or not there is an agreement on the face of any documents produced which settles financial issues between the parties subject to the subsequent consideration of the agreement in the light of s.25;

    (d)   as to what evidence should be filed. This is an important direction as much of the evidence will comprise without prejudice correspondence.

3.   List for hearing. If the judge dealing with the preliminary issue finds that there is no agreement, the case will be listed before a different judge in the usual way.

6.4   CONSENT ORDERS

6.4.1 FPR 2.61 and Form M1

Tips on drafting consent orders can be found in **Chapter 8** and the usefulness of the Resolution Precedents for Consent Orders cannot be overstated.

Once the proposed order is signed and ready to be sent to the court, it is worth remembering that where Forms E have not been filed, the judge is seeing the facts for the first time. To avoid a proposed order being sent back it is essential that the court has sufficient information to enable the judge to carry out his discretionary s.25 exercise.

The statement of information required by FPR rule 2.61 must include those matters set out at FPR rule 2.61(1)(a)–(f) and contained in Form M1, but rule 2.61 specifically states that the statement of information may be made in more than one document.

It follows that if the circumstances require further clarification, additional information should be supplied to the court. This will not only avoid orders being returned, thus incurring delay and further cost to your client but also prevent the court listing the matter for a hearing requiring the parties to come along and explain anything that has prevented the court making the order.

In some cases, it may be worth setting out the background to the proposed order and the result that is to be achieved by it in a side letter accompanying the order. This may prove particularly useful evidence if one party seeks to vary the order at a later date.

6.4.2 Undertakings

An undertaking given to the court is, in practical terms, as effective as an order. Any non-compliance of an undertaking is punishable as a contempt of court. Careful consideration must always be given to the wording of undertakings and whether, in fact, the parties would be better protected by dealing with such matters by way of agreements in the recital to the order.

6.4.3 Recitals

Whilst most factual issues will have been dealt with in the statement of information, it may be useful to include recitals in the preamble to the order itself. A common example of this is where the family home has already been sold and the proceeds have already been divided by agreement. Another example is where the parties have reached agreement as to the level of child support payments and the parties wish to invoke the provisions of CSA 1991, s.8(5).

CHAPTER 7

Unusual considerations

Shona Alexander

7.1 INTRODUCTION

This chapter will look at some of the exceptional issues that may arise in some cases. Whilst practitioners cannot be expected to be 'experts' in all matters, it is essential to have basic knowledge and to know when expert advice needs to be taken.

7.2 CAPITAL GAINS TAX

Some families may have second homes, business assets and/or investments. If they do, there may be CGT to be paid upon transfer or disposal and advice will need to be taken at an early stage so that tax liabilities can be taken into account in negotiations and included in Form E.

7.2.1 Tax year of separation

Couples are able to transfer assets without incurring CGT if transfers are made in the tax year of separation.

If spouses/civil partners are living together they can transfer assets between them on a 'no gain no loss' basis under the Taxation of Chargeable Gains Act (TCGA) 1992, s.58(1).

A couple are 'living together' unless:

(a) they are separated under a court order; or
(b) they are separated by a formal deed of separation executed under seal; or
(c) they are separated in such circumstances that separation is likely to be permanent (this will be the case where divorce proceedings have commenced and/or the parties are living separately).

It is important to be aware that it is the tax year that is relevant, not the 12-month period from which the parties first separated. Therefore, if there are considerable assets and the parties are considering separation, if the date is

94

close to 5 April it may be financially advantageous to them both to delay final separation until the new tax year.

If it is judged by HM Revenue & Customs (HMRC) that the couple have separated, then any transfers that take place between them after the tax year of separation are liable for CGT, even if the parties are still married at the time of the transfer. It is therefore essential, if possible, that if there are to be transfers between spouses/civil partners that these take place in the tax year of separation. These may necessitate interim agreements to be made to allow for transfers to take place and to save an immediate tax charge.

7.2.2 Current levels

From 6 April 2008 there is a flat CGT rate of 18 per cent on all disposals. Every individual has an annual exemption which can be set against any gains made; for the year to 5 April 2010 this is £10,100.

Dealing with CGT is a complicated issue and accountancy advice and guidance should be sought at an early stage. There may be CGT to be paid when the asset is later disposed of and this should be considered.

7.2.3 Matrimonial home

In most cases the main asset will be the former matrimonial home. Under the principal private residence exemption, the sale or transfer of the family home will not usually trigger a charge to CGT.

However, a person can only have one principal private residence at any time so if the parties own two or more homes they must elect which will be the matrimonial home, as that property will qualify for relief. They cannot both elect different properties in order to attempt to avoid CGT.

The exemption covers the house and up to 0.5 hectares of land, but only if the land is required for the reasonable enjoyment of the property (which it will be in practically all cases). Tax may, however, be payable upon the sale or disposal of properties with very large gardens or with adjoining paddocks and land.

Principal private residence relief continues for three years after nomination, even if the person has vacated the property that was nominated (TCGA 1992, s.223(1)).

There is an additional concession for divorcing couples (Extra Strategy Concession D6) which allows the exemption to be extended beyond the three years on the basis that:

1. the matrimonial home remains the principal private residence of the former spouse; and
2. during this time, the transferring party does not acquire a residence on which he or she seeks to claim principal private residence relief; and
3. the property must be transferred between the spouses, not to a third party.

7.2.4 Transferring properties

If there are transfers of a property, which is not the matrimonial home, after the tax year of separation, then there may be a CGT charge upon that transfer.

The CGT should have been calculated prior to any agreement/court order as it is a liability that will need to be taken into account.

This is likely to necessitate accountancy advice, preferably by joint instruction. If tax is going to be paid then provision should be made in the order for an indemnity to be given and, if necessary, a lump sum order included within the order for the payment of this.

7.2.5 Business assets

Some couples will have run businesses together or held shares in the family business and these may need to be transferred as part of the settlement.

Where there are business assets being transferred hold-over relief may apply. In order for this to be applicable the transfer of shares or qualifying business assets must take place pursuant to a court order or consent order. Therefore the best approach is to include a property adjustment order relating to the transfer of that particular asset. It would also be wise for there to be a recital stating that the husband and wife will co-operate and will both undertake to apply for hold-over relief. In the situation where there is a transfer of business assets taking place, following Coleridge J in *G* v. *G* [2002] EWCH 1339, HMRC will now allow there to be hold-over relief.

7.2.6 Properties being sold

If properties (not the matrimonial home) are sold these could trigger a CGT charge. Whilst practitioners are used to dealing with the net proceeds of sale once a deduction of the mortgage, costs of sale, etc. are discharged, often no consideration is given to the amount of CGT that will be payable. If there is to be an equal division of the net proceeds of sale then it may be fair and equitable for each party to meet his or her own CGT liability. It is more difficult when the proceeds are being divided in unequal shares as it may be unfair for the tax to be borne equally. This will be a negotiation issue. The couple will also need to consider that as the CGT may not be payable until many months after the sale has taken place, they will be required to co-operate in the future and there may well need to be sharing of information.

7.3 OVERSEAS ASSETS

In recent years, it has become more common for families to have acquired or inherited assets overseas. These assets need to be considered within the

English proceedings and this can lead to various problems which need to be addressed at an early stage.

7.3.1 Valuations

Property valuations will be required and, depending on where the property is situated, this may be difficult to arrange. The instruction should be on a joint basis, if possible, and the report should comply with CPR (if possible). The valuers chosen should be members of the appropriate professional body (the equivalent of the RICS).

When valuing properties, it is essential that the letter of joint instruction is agreed and sets out clearly the basis on which the joint instruction is to be conducted. In particular, the fee that will be charged and the basis on which it is charged should be stated, as in some foreign jurisdictions the amount charged will not be a fixed fee but will be based upon a percentage of the property value itself, which could lead to disputes. It is also important to ensure that the letter of instruction makes it clear that if there is any dispute with regard to the instruction, or the contract generally, then the dispute is to be governed by the laws of England and Wales and not the other jurisdiction.

7.3.2 Tax/sale

If the assets involved are significant then it would be prudent to engage the services of either an accountant with overseas expertise or an accountant in the relevant jurisdiction so that they can advise on possible tax charges, etc. which will arise on the transfer or the sale of the foreign property. Their input should be sought at an early stage so the potential liability can be included in Form E. It would also be wise to consider engaging the services of a family lawyer in the jurisdiction to advise on the conditions that need to be satisfied in respect of a sale or transfer of properties in so far as the drafting of a consent order is concerned. There may well be charges that will have to be paid by, say, the transferor regardless of what the English court order says, and it is better that the parties have this information before any agreements are reached.

7.4 TRACING INFORMATION

In many cases the parties will be suspicious of each other and may allege that there are 'hidden assets'. In order to make such an allegation there would need to be evidence to substantiate such details.

It may be possible to identify undisclosed accounts, etc. by careful and detailed analysis of financial disclosure and a forensic accountant may be able to assist if it is judged that the case warrants such expense. For some clients this may not be enough and they will wish to retain the services of an enquiry agent.

If an enquiry agent is to be used to trace information and locate undisclosed assets, then it is essential that the agent used is experienced and qualified to provide a report that can be used in court proceedings. Careful consideration must be given to ensuring that any information received is obtained in accordance with data protection legislation. Practitioners should consider the Computer Misuse Act 1990 and the Data Protection Act 1998 particularly where computers are involved (see *L* v. *L* [2007] EWHC 140 (QB) and *White* v. *Withers* [2008] EWHC 2821 (QB)).

7.5   COMPANY PENSION SCHEMES

Final salary pension schemes are no longer as prevalent as they were previously. However, they do still exist and special consideration needs to be given to them. The first step is to ascertain what type of scheme it is.

An occupational pension scheme describes any scheme which is provided by an employer for employees. The member will have been provided with the rules of the scheme, and this should be requested in the disclosure process.

The scheme may be a final pay scheme/defined benefit scheme. The benefits will be dependent on years of service and the employee's final salary. These schemes may have additional discretionary benefits such as early retirement benefits, ill-health benefits, etc. and it may not be clear whether these have been included in a valuation. To 'share' the benefits under these schemes can prove very costly with considerable benefits and value lost, so offsetting may be more appropriate. Advice will be required from a pensions expert and a joint report sought.

Some companies, instead of an occupational scheme, now offer group personal pension arrangements. These are, in effect, personal pension plans but with reduced costs and are paid for by the employer. These are easier to value.

Careful consideration needs to be given to the pension benefits as they may, depending on the case, be a sizeable asset and depending on the nature of the scheme, advice should be sought at an early stage.

CHAPTER 8

The route to settlement

Andrew Newbury

8.1 APPROACHES TO NEGOTIATIONS

8.1.1 When to start negotiating

Before any settlement discussions can take place, there must first be full and frank disclosure of the parties' financial circumstances. Solicitors cannot advise upon, nor consider, any proposals for settlement until all of the relevant financial and other circumstances are known. Indeed, under the old costs rules, a *Calderbank* letter (see **8.1.4**) would not bite or have any impact until there had been prior disclosure (*Gojkovic* v. *Gojkovic (No.2)* [1992] Fam 40). The level of disclosure required prior to negotiations taking place will vary from case to case. At one end of the spectrum, in straightforward cases where both parties are fully aware of the financial circumstances, negotiations can proceed after only modest disclosure. By contrast, in more complex or big money cases, extensive disclosure and often expert evidence will be needed before parties can be advised upon submitting proposals or considering a settlement. For example, where there is a family business, the value of that business will need to be ascertained and issues of liquidity addressed before any realistic offers can be made.

The bottom line is that negotiations should start as soon as practicably possible. The sooner negotiations start, the sooner matters can be brought to a conclusion. Unfortunately, a common area of frustration within ancillary relief proceedings is that one party may be unwilling either to make an offer or to respond to an offer. Unfortunately, within the FPR, the court cannot compel parties to submit proposals for settlement. Whilst rule 2.61E provides for proposals to be filed with the court not less than seven days before the FDR, it does not compel the parties to make proposals. Under the rules, the earliest stage a party can be compelled to submit an offer is by way of open proposals for settlement prior to the final hearing in accordance with rule 2.69E.

8.1.2 Who makes the first offer?

There are no hard and fast rules stating how and when an offer should be made and by whom. Conventional practice stems from *Gojkovic* whereby the onus is placed upon the respondent to the application to submit an offer in response to that application. The applicant is then compelled to either accept or reject that offer. In practice, this has led to the convention that it is usually the husband who is expected to submit the first proposals for settlement. Although this is the conventional approach, it is not cast in stone. It should also be borne in mind that the decision in *Gojkovic* of course pre-dates the existing costs rules contained in FPR rule 2.69 (subsequently amended with the introduction of FPR rule 2.71 which came into force in April 2006).

8.1.3 How the proposals should be made

Where proposals for settlement are to be submitted via the solicitor, it is sensible and prudent for those proposals to be made in writing. Whether the offer should be 'open' or 'without prejudice' is considered further at **8.1.4**. An offer should be made in writing so that its terms are clear and unequivocal. Where proposals for settlement are made over the telephone, there is often the risk of misunderstanding at a later date as the parties are reliant upon the attendance notes made by the solicitors at the time.

The other principal benefit of an offer being in writing is that it gives a clear opportunity to explain the reasoning behind the offer and its rationale. A draft offer for settlement is included at **Appendix 17**. It can be seen that before setting out the terms of settlement, time has been spent in justifying the reasoning for the offer. For example, if it is being proposed that the family home be sold, then that should be explained. Likewise, justification should be given for the proposed division of the proceeds of sale. Arguments can also be put forward regarding the term and quantum of spousal maintenance as well as the calculation of child maintenance.

It is also important to ensure that any offer in writing deals with all of the aspects of the proposal to avoid any uncertainty or arguments at a later date. For example, if there are still joint accounts in existence, reference should be made to how they are to be dealt with. Likewise, if the wife is a director of the family business, reference may be made to her resigning her position. One of the benefits of a detailed offer is that it can then be used as a checklist when negotiating or when preparing a draft consent order at a later date.

8.1.4 Open or without prejudice proposals for settlement

Prior to the implementation of the new costs rules on 3 April 2006, the conventional approach for many years had been to submit *Calderbank* proposals marked 'without prejudice save as to costs'. Such offers would potentially give the parties protection on costs should the matter go to a final hearing and would allow parties to negotiate freely, knowing that a district judge would not see the proposals at a final hearing until after their decision had been made.

The position in respect of proceedings issued on or after 3 April 2006 is not so clear cut. When considering whether to make a costs order or not, the court can only take into account open proposals for settlement (FPR rule 2.71(5)(b)). Accordingly, a letter marked without prejudice would provide no protection on costs. The new rule does not preclude the parties from submitting without prejudice proposals, but simply means that they would not give any costs protection. Thus since April 2006, practitioners have taken different approaches. Some practitioners adopt a cautious position and carry out negotiations on a without prejudice basis, often until the FDR. If the matter does not settle at the FDR and if a clear view has been given by the district judge at that hearing, it is only thereafter that they submit open proposals for settlement.

By contrast, other practitioners adopt a more robust approach. The view is that if an offer is being made which is sensible and fair and if the client clearly wishes to stand by that offer, then making an open offer sends a clear message to the other side and puts pressure upon them to negotiate sensibly.

Although open offers may provide some protection on costs under the post-April 2006 costs rules, costs orders are now exceedingly rare in ancillary relief proceedings and clients should be warned that the prospect of securing a costs order at a final hearing is slim. By contrast, the danger in making an open offer is that it can be produced to the court at a final hearing and it is difficult to reduce or review that offer at a later stage. Clients should always be given clear advice in writing about making an open offer before any such offer is submitted to the other side.

8.1.5 Negotiations on the telephone

For the reasons set out at **8.1.3**, it is usually sensible if initial proposals for settlement are clearly set out in writing. Once detailed proposals have been made in writing, the negotiation process can therefore be accelerated by picking up the telephone. That is often the case if there is a good rapport between the solicitors and/or if they are both members of Resolution. Resolution is the largest organisation of solicitors in England and Wales outside of the Law Society. Its members subscribe to the Code of Practice and adopt a conciliatory approach to family work. Details of Resolution can be found on its website (**www.resolution.org.uk**).

Whilst written proposals for settlement are often a useful tool in clearly setting out a case, if ongoing negotiations are carried out in correspondence, such letters can have a tendency to polarise the positions of the parties. By contrast, a frank discussion between solicitors on a without prejudice basis on the telephone can often save weeks or even months of time. It is often not clear where the priorities of the two parties lie. For example, the wife may have a particular desire to remain in the family home, whereas the husband may have a particular desire to secure a clean break. By discussing the issues and priorities on the telephone, constructive discussions may often open up.

Practitioners should, however, always take care on the telephone not to give assurances regarding their client's position, nor to make assumptions about the client's position without having clear instructions from the client first. It must also be made clear whether any conversation on the telephone is open or without prejudice.

8.2 NEGOTIATIONS BETWEEN THE PARTIES

8.2.1 Kitchen table agreements

The ideal scenario for many separating couples is to reach an agreement as quickly and as painlessly as possible and with minimum legal cost. As long as one spouse does not have an undue advantage over the other (e.g. by virtue of a domineering personality, or by being in possession of all of the financial information), it can be eminently suitable for a couple to agree a settlement between the two of them. That is particularly the case where their financial situation is straightforward. Prior to entering into such discussions, couples may individually choose to see solicitors to obtain advice on the powers of the court and parameters of settlement, before attempting to resolve matters directly with their spouse.

Solicitors are therefore often instructed to prepare separation agreements and/or consent orders following on from kitchen table agreements. In such circumstances, solicitors are often asked to walk a fine line between protecting the client and giving proper advice yet are specifically instructed not to interfere with agreements entered into between couples at arm's length. In such circumstances, it is not at all unreasonable to comment upon the fairness of the agreement reached. If a solicitor believes that the proposed agreement is unfair, advice should be given to the client in writing. Where a solicitor is being asked to prepare a consent order to reflect such an agreement and if the solicitor does have concerns, it may be appropriate to ask the client to sign a disclaimer letter before the matter is taken any further forward.

8.2.2 Mediation

The next step down from a kitchen table agreement is where a settlement is agreed directly between the parties following on from mediation. The mediator's role is to help the parties reach an agreement, but they cannot advise the parties upon legal issues. The mediator's position is entirely neutral. Mediation sessions take place without the parties having their own solicitors in attendance, although they are, of course, able to seek advice from their solicitors between sessions should they wish. Mediation can be an excellent alternative to the traditional approach of negotiating via solicitors. It is usually a cheaper option; however, it is not suitable for everyone. Where one party is in a stronger bargaining position or where the financial affairs are particularly complex, mediation may not be suitable. Furthermore, financial disclosure within mediation is usually limited to the production of schedules of assets. If there are concerns about full and frank disclosure being provided, mediation may not be an appropriate option.

To some extent solicitors are gatekeepers of the mediation process as they will advise clients of the option of mediation at their first meeting. Where a solicitor feels that mediation is not an appropriate option, such advice should be given to the client.

8.2.3 Collaborative law

Collaborative law is a relatively new concept which has come to the country from the United States. It is to an extent a hybrid between mediation and traditional negotiation through solicitors. At the outset of the collaborative process, the husband, wife and their solicitors will all sign a participation agreement which sets out the ground rules for the collaborative process. One of the basic underlying principles is that the parties contract not to issue court proceedings. They are therefore committed to the collaborative process. If the process does break down, then the solicitors involved cannot continue to act and the parties will need to instruct new solicitors to represent them within contested proceedings.

The collaborative process takes place by way of a series of 'four-way' meetings which are attended by the solicitors and the parties. The meetings are similar to mediation in the sense that the parties will discuss their positions and will aim to agree a settlement. Solicitors themselves adopt a hybrid role between mediating and representing their clients. The underlying idea is that negotiations take place on a frank and open basis and are led by the client's wishes as opposed to legal advice.

As with mediation, collaborative law is not suitable for everyone. On the one hand it can be an expensive process for relatively straightforward cases. On the other hand, it may be unsuitable for couples where there is an imbalance of power in the relationship. Accordingly, solicitors must adopt a screening process whereby they assess whether clients are suitable for the collaborative process or not.

8.3 ROUNDTABLE MEETINGS

Loved by some practitioners and loathed by others – everybody has strong views about roundtable meetings. They can be an effective method for achieving a prompt settlement in a case, but they can also do more harm than good and lead to increased bitterness between the parties.

Some practitioners are keen to set up a roundtable meeting as soon as a divorce petition has been issued. However, this is usually far too early in the process, for the following reasons:

1. Emotions are often very raw at the beginning and people are simply not ready to discuss matters constructively.
2. As was said at **8.1.1**, negotiation cannot take place until there has been full and frank disclosure in advance.
3. It is usually sensible for proposals for settlement to be submitted by both sides prior to lining up a roundtable meeting. It is only once proposals for settlement have been submitted can solicitors then gauge whether a roundtable meeting will have a reasonable prospect of reaching a settlement. Where there is a significant divergence in views, or if there is a fundamental disagreement as to an issue of principle, then a roundtable meeting may simply be an expensive but ultimately pointless exercise at that stage in the proceedings.

Another issue to consider is the format of the roundtable meeting. They can be approached in two very different ways as follows:

1. **Three separate rooms**. A conventional approach is where the husband and his solicitor are based in one room, the wife and her solicitor in another room and in the third room the solicitors will meet to discuss proposals before going back to their clients. Whilst this may appear to be a cumbersome form of negotiation, it often proves to be effective. It is particularly suitable where one party may feel particularly vulnerable or anxious about meeting his or her spouse. Furthermore, where solicitors are not negotiating in front of their clients, it can lead to free and frank discussions taking place and avoid posturing. The negative side of such an approach, however, is that the clients feel that they are not part of the negotiation progress and can feel isolated.
2. **One room meeting**. This is where solicitors and the clients meet in one room and discuss matters around a table. Where both spouses feel comfortable, such an arrangement can be successful; however, such meetings can have a tendency to break down as emotional issues are more likely to be raised within the discussions.

8.4 NEGOTIATING TACTICS

On the whole it is difficult to advise on this issue as tactics in negotiations tend to be a very personal matter for the individual. The following are simply points which may be of some use:

1. There is often a tendency for clients to make extreme offers at the outset, for example, a husband to make the lowest possible offer and the wife to

seek the highest possible offer. The problem with such an approach is that it often leads to polarised positions and protracted negotiations. Clients should be encouraged to make opening offers which are realistic, but which will still allow them some leeway in negotiations.

2. One school of thought finds little favour with making an initial high or low offer and then proceeding to horse trade and finding a compromise in the middle. A preferred approach may be to make an excellent and extremely realistic offer at the outset which then gives little or no scope for further negotiation, save for dealing with relatively minor points. Whilst this may be viewed as a risky approach, it can be highly effective, particularly in those divorces where the ultimate solution is relatively clear cut.

3. Never assume anything in discussions. If in doubt, you must check with your opponent or your client.

4. An inexperienced negotiator will never concede any points whatsoever. By contrast, experienced negotiators will know what can be conceded and what cannot be conceded. When considering proposals for settlement with your client, you should have a clear picture from them of what are the important issues and the issues which are relatively peripheral. An offer can contain built-in issues which the client may be willing to concede in negotiations further down the road.

5. Make sure that you always do your maths. Any offer that is made should be workable and the figures must stack up. Also ensure that any offer can be complied with, for example, if a client is proposing to assume responsibility for a mortgage, the client must ensure that he or she can take over that mortgage and release the other spouse from the covenants. Likewise, always bear in mind tax issues and any taxation implications of a proposed settlement.

6. Silence is golden. Sometimes in negotiating, it is better to listen, rather than talk. As solicitors, we all have a tendency to talk too much.

7. Give consideration to the timing and speed of negotiations. At the beginning of this chapter it was stated that the aim should always be to try and resolve matters as soon as possible. Where ongoing negotiations are taking place, consideration should be given to how promptly a response should be made to an offer. A counter-offer made the same day as an offer may give the impression of a desperation to settle. Some clients may need to be encouraged to sleep on an offer or think about it over the weekend.

8. In some cases it is worthwhile giving consideration to offers being made in the alternative, for example, when acting for a husband a clean break settlement could be offered with a lump sum of £X, or in the alternative, spousal maintenance at a rate of £Y. Such an approach can be useful to get an indication of the other spouse's preference, or an offer in the alternative could be phrased in such a way to try and make one option more attractive than the other.

105

8.5 TIPS ON DRAFTING CONSENT ORDERS

Every practitioner must have a copy of the Resolution Precedents for Consent Orders (**www.resolution.org.uk**). They are used by family law practitioners across the country and by district judges, and are absolutely indispensable.

The following are mentioned as a few practical points to consider in the preparation of draft consent orders:

1. Try and make the document as user-friendly as possible, which will be helpful when it needs to be read in the future. For example, group the recitals together in categories as opposed to giving an endless list of individual recitals. The following is an example:

   Upon the husband undertaking to the court and agreeing with the wife that:

   (a) He will use his best endeavours to procure the release of the wife from the covenants under the mortgage with Halifax Plc secured on 1 High Street.

   (b) He will indemnify the wife and keep her indemnified in respect of all utility bills and outgoings in respect of 1 High Street.

2. It is usually more 'user friendly' to refer to the parties as husband and wife or by their names within the order as opposed to using 'Petitioner' and 'Respondent'. The latter can be confusing, particularly where the respondent within the main suit is the applicant within the ancillary relief proceedings.

3. Undertakings often prove to be a thorny problem for many reasons. Many courts will accept undertakings from the parties to the court, whereas some courts will only accept undertakings between the parties, unless they attend before the district judge when the order is approved so that they can give a formal undertaking. The position should be checked with the court before the order is lodged. Consider also whether issues which have been drafted as undertakings can be included in the body of the order or whether they can be implemented prior to the order being made as that will avoid the potential problem of trying to enforce an undertaking. For example, the transfer of assets including bank accounts, cars, etc. can be included in the body of the order as a property adjustment order.

4. When dealing with bank accounts, shares or any investments, always provide full account details so that they can easily be identified and to avoid any misunderstanding. Furthermore, the order will also be a useful point of reference in the future.

5. Orders of a capital nature only take effect from decree absolute. Care should therefore be taken in how the order is drafted. Accordingly, where the order is being made before pronouncement of decree absolute, the timing of payment of, for example, a lump sum or transfer of property

should take effect from the date of decree absolute. By contrast, where the decree absolute has already been pronounced and the order is being made at a later date, timescales for payment run from the date of the order itself.

6. Give careful thought to the interaction between the timing of lump sum payments and the transfer of property. Which is to take place first or are they to be simultaneous? Does there need to be provision that one party will vacate the family home in conjunction with transferring the property or making the lump sum payment? If so, provision must be included.

7. Where interest is to be paid on a lump sum, clients must be advised that the recipient of that interest will be liable to pay tax on the interest payment. It is just the same as receiving an interest payment from a bank or building society. An alternative approach is for the interest to be phrased as periodical payments so they are tax free in the recipient's hands. A periodical payments order is, of course, contrary to a clean break and may not therefore be suitable in every case.

8. Where there is to be a series of capital payments, think carefully whether it is to be drafted as a lump sum in instalments or a series of lump sums. A lump sum in instalments can be varied under MCA 1973, s.31 and in extreme cases some of the instalments can even be extinguished (note the negligence case of *Westbury* v. *Sampson* [2001] EWCA Civ 407). By contrast, the court can order a series of lump sums at the time of making the final order and they are not capable of variation under s.31, although note should be had of the comments of Coleridge J in the unreported decision of *Lamont* v. *Lamont* (where he questioned whether mere drafting should be able to exclude the court's power under s.31). His view was that regardless of how the order was drafted, it should be capable of variation under s.31. He did acknowledge that in some cases there may be a true series of lump sums, for example, a payment being made forthwith upon the making of the order and then a further lump sum being paid upon a future event, such as the death of a parent of one of the parties or the sale of the family business.

9. Where the order includes a provision for spousal maintenance to be paid over a fixed term (e.g. five years), it must have been resolved in negotiations whether that term would be subject to a bar under MCA 1973, s.28(1A). Where no such bar exists, the recipient can apply to the court before the end of the original term to seek an extension (note, however, the Court of Appeal's decision in *Fleming* v. *Fleming* [2004] 1 FLR 667), whereas no such application is possible where there is a s.28(1A) bar. 'Exceptional circumstances' would need to be shown to justify an extension of the original term.

10. Note that under the wording of MCA 1973, s.24A, an order for sale of the property can only be made upon the court making a secured periodical

payments order, an order for the payment of a lump sum or a property adjustment order. Care should be taken in the drafting.

11. It is absolutely necessary to ensure that the terms of the order are consistent with one another. If there are ongoing periodical payments, then there cannot be a dismissal of the recipient's claims under s.23(1)(a) and (b). Conversely, where there is a clean break order, a clear dismissal of all claims must be included in the order.

CHAPTER 9

Interim applications and orders

Andrew Newbury

9.1 INTRODUCTION

Interim applications of a purely procedural nature, such as applications for further disclosure, inspection appointments, etc. are dealt with in **Chapter 3** in the context of ancillary relief procedure. This chapter deals with substantive interim applications as follows:

1. Applications for maintenance pending suit/interim periodical payments.
2. Applications for injunctions to secure the preservation of assets.

9.2 NO POWER TO ORDER INTERIM LUMP SUMS

It should be made clear that the court does not have the power to make interim orders of a capital nature. Although provision for interim capital sums was included in the Family Law Act 1996, it was never enacted.

The leading decision is *Wicks* v. *Wicks* [1998] 1 FLR 470. In theory it is possible to bring a claim for interim capital provision under the Married Women's Property Act 1882, s.17, although the position has not been tested by the court since the decision in *Wicks.* The prevailing view, however, is that claims arising from the breakdown of a marriage should only be brought in the context of MCA 1973 (*Tee* v. *Tee and Hillman* [1999] 3 FCR 409, [1999] 2 FLR 613).

9.3 APPLICATIONS FOR MAINTENANCE PENDING SUIT

The court's power to order maintenance pending suit is set out in MCA 1973, s.22. The wording of the section itself gives little guidance as to the approach the court will take upon an application. The key phrases in the section are as follows: '. . . the court may make an order for maintenance pending suit, that is to say, an order requiring either party to the marriage to make to the other such periodical payments for his or her maintenance . . . as the court thinks reasonable'.

The provision therefore grants district judges a wide discretion upon making maintenance pending suit orders. The following are considerations that should be borne in mind when advising a client upon making an application:

1. Different district judges take very different approaches to maintenance pending suit applications. Some judges are simply concerned with ensuring that the applicant's basic needs are met pending settlement. Others will look more closely at the overall standard of living during the marriage and may take a more generous approach.

2. Issues of proportionality of costs must be taken into account. Contested maintenance pending suit applications can be expensive and also emotionally quite draining for the parties. If the difference between the parties is only several hundred pounds a month, that figure should be considered in the context of the time left to the conclusion of ancillary relief proceedings. By way of example, if the parties are arguing over £500 a month and there are six months left to the end of the ancillary relief timetable, that is a sum in dispute of only £3,000. The total costs of a fully contested maintenance pending suit hearing would usually be far greater than that.

3. Although the courts are often keen to emphasise that an order made at a maintenance pending suit hearing should not be viewed as indicative of the final level of periodical payments, it is often the case that solicitors or the parties will use it as a yardstick. An application for maintenance pending suit can therefore set a low benchmark for future maintenance.

4. An applicant should be advised of the alternative of borrowing money as opposed to incurring the costs of a contested maintenance pending suit application. At the conclusion of the case the applicant could contend that the borrowing was reasonably incurred and needed to be taken into account in the final settlement. Maintenance pending suit applications are usually dealt with solely upon submissions by counsel or solicitors and without evidence being given by the parties. Often, district judges do not wish to look at the minutiae of expenditure budgets and they therefore take a broad-brush approach.

Although there is relatively little case law on contested maintenance pending suit hearings, the comments of Nicholas Mostyn QC sitting as a Deputy High Court Judge in *TL* v. *ML* [2005] EWHC 2860 (Fam) are certainly worthy of note. The guidelines given include the following:

1. The sole criterion to be applied is 'reasonableness' in accordance with s.22, which is synonymous with fairness.

2. A very important factor in determining fairness is the marital standard of living, although that is not to say that the exercise on a maintenance pending suit application is merely to replicate that standard.

3. In every maintenance pending suit application, there should be a specific budget for that application which excludes capital or long-term expenditure

which should be considered at a final ancillary relief hearing. The budget should be examined critically in every case so as to exclude forensic exaggeration.

4. Where the affidavit or Form E disclosed by the paying party is deficient, the court should not hesitate to make any robust assumptions about the ability to pay. The court is not confined to the mere say-so of the payer as to the extent of any income or resources. In such circumstances, the court should err in favour of the payee.

5. Where the paying party has historically been supported by an outsider (e.g. parents or the trustees of a settlement) and where the payer is asserting that that third party has curtailed the financial support, but where the position of that third party is ambiguous or unclear, then the court is justified in assuming that the third party will continue to supply the financial support, at least until the final hearing.

9.4 PROVISION FOR LEGAL FEES

Since the decision in *A* v. *A (Maintenance Pending Suit: Provision for Legal Fees)* [2001] 1 FLR 377, upon making an order for maintenance pending suit, the court has been able to include an element for the applicant's ongoing costs in the substantive proceedings. In 2005 and 2006 there was a series of cases in which the court considered the circumstances in which it would be appropriate to include an element for legal costs.

In *Moses-Taiga* v. *Taiga* [2005] EWCA Civ 1013, the Court of Appeal held that such an award should only be made in 'exceptional circumstances'. In *TL* v. *ML* [2005] EWHC 2860 (Fam), Nicholas Mostyn QC sitting as a Deputy High Court Judge suggested that to satisfy that test, a wife would need to show that she had no assets, could not raise a litigation loan and that she could not persuade her solicitors to enter into a *Sears-Tooth* v. *Payne Hicks Beach* agreement (i.e. an agreement that the wife would assign part of her settlement received upon her divorce to her solicitors in settlement of outstanding legal fees, see **10.2**).

In *C* v. *C (Maintenance Pending Suit: Legal Costs)* [2004] 2 FLR 1207, Headley J suggested the test in *TL* v. *ML* was illustrative in defining a case as exceptional, but was not definitive. All big money cases were, by their nature, exceptional and in the present case the wife's need to investigate the husband's assets made the case exceptional. The Court of Appeal in *Currey* v. *Currey* [2006] EWCA Civ 1338 held that the word 'exceptional' was obstructing the proper exercise of the court's jurisdiction to include a costs allowance. The initial, over-arching enquiry should be whether the applicant could demonstrate that she cannot reasonably procure legal advice and representation by any other means.

111

9.5   PROCEDURE FOR MAKING AN APPLICATION

The procedure for making any application for an interim order is set out in FPR rule 2.69F. The following practical points should be noted:

1. An application can only be made within ancillary relief proceedings. Accordingly, if there are no existing ancillary relief proceedings ongoing, then a full application for ancillary relief also needs to be made in Form A at the same time.

2. The application for maintenance pending suit itself is made by way of notice of application. The rules do not say that the application should be made in Form A. The writer is of the view that as rule 2.69F(2) specifically refers to 'Notice of Application', then that is the format of the application and the requisite fee of £80 is payable. Practice does, however, appear to vary around the country.

3. The date fixed for the application of the hearing must be not less than 14 days after the date the notice of application is issued. Care should be taken in time estimates as contested maintenance pending suit applications often take longer than anticipated. A general approach is that at least two to three hours will be required.

4. Where the application for maintenance pending suit is made before a party has filed Form E, then that party must file with the application and serve on the party a draft of the order requested together with a 'short sworn statement' explaining why the order is necessary and giving necessary information about his or her means. Solicitors often fail to take notice of the requirement that the sworn statement should be 'short'. Where a statement is required, it must be concise and limited to the basic issues: the applicant's income and any other relevant means, a breakdown of the applicant's outgoings and a statement of why the application is necessary. It is also useful to give details about the respondent's income and lifestyle, so far as they are known to the applicant. Also see **9.6**.

5. Not less than seven days before the date fixed for the hearing, the respondent must file with the court and serve on the other party a short sworn statement about his or her own means. Such a statement must be filed unless the respondent has filed Form E. Again, note should be had of the requirement that the statement is short. Respondents should provide details of their own outgoings and often it is a good idea to include a Scott Schedule setting out the respondent's comments upon the applicant's stated income requirements.

The precedent statement of issues included at **Appendix 8** has been prepared in the form of a Scott Schedule. It is a useful tool when setting out the respective positions of both parties. A Scott Schedule prepared for a maintenance pending suit application may appear in the following format.

Item of Expenditure	Wife's Figure	Husband's Suggested Figure	Husband's Comments
Food/supermarket bill:	£600	£400	£400 represented the expenditure by my wife before we separated
Cleaner:	£100	Nil	We have never previously had a cleaner

9.6   GUIDANCE ON SWORN STATEMENTS

In accordance with FPR rule 2.69F, there is no requirement to file statements once Forms E have been filed, although many courts now expect maintenance pending suit statements in all applications, regardless of whether Forms E have been filed or not. Most courts will deal with maintenance pending suit applications by way of submissions and without hearing any oral evidence. Statements sworn in advance therefore mean that the application can be disposed of more efficiently by the court. Note should also be had of the comments of Nicholas Mostyn QC in *TL* v. *ML* referred to at **9.3**. He suggested that in every maintenance pending suit application, there should be a specific budget for that application and that can usually be dealt with in the form of a sworn statement.

The following is intended as useful guidance when preparing maintenance pending suit statements.

9.6.1 Applicant's sworn statement

1. Rule 2.69F specifically directs that a 'short' statement should be filed. The statement should therefore only cover issues directly relevant to the application and should not dwell upon extraneous issues.
2. The main element of the statement should be a budget setting out realistic interim needs. Many firms prepare pro-forma schedules of outgoings which can be sent to clients in advance to enable them to prepare a comprehensive breakdown. Long-term expenditure which would not be covered by a maintenance pending suit application should obviously be excluded and therefore the breakdown should not include such items as redecorating the home (unless, for example, it is necessary for the house to be marketed for sale), purchasing furnishings or a car replacement fund. Depending upon when the application was made and the antici-pated period to the conclusion of the proceedings, it may, however, be perfectly reasonable to include the expenses of a summer holiday or Christmas expenditure.

3. Full details should be provided of income from all sources. Where there is an investment income, a breakdown should be given. An important area, which is often overlooked, is the means tested benefits which may become available when the parties have separated. Post-separation a wife may be entitled to claim for child tax credits or working tax credits, the level of which can be significant and which may have a profound impact upon the level of maintenance pending suit which is ultimately ordered.

4. Where an application is made at an early stage in the proceedings, it can be difficult to advise the client upon what is an appropriate level of expenditure or an appropriate claim where there are little or no details available of the respondent's income. Where any details are known by the client, these should be included in the statement. If the client does not have details of the other party's income, then perhaps a brief indication of the standard of living enjoyed during the marriage could be included in the statement.

9.6.2 Respondent's statement

1. The respondent's statement should usually cover four main issues: the respondent's own income, the applicant's income/earning capacity, the respondent's own outgoings and also comments upon the applicant's outgoings.

2. Ideally, the statement should exhibit evidence of the respondent's income. In straightforward cases, the last three payslips and a P60 would be sufficient, although where the respondent is self-employed, the most recent tax return, bank statements and/or company accounts may be more appropriate.

3. If the respondent is asserting there has been a reduction in income since that last tax return or accounts, this statement should be corroborated with evidence in support. Unless clear evidence can be given in support of the contention of reduced income, a district judge is likely to be sceptical about such statements.

4. If the applicant has not produced evidence of benefits available, such as tax credits, an estimate can usually be obtained online and a copy of the calculation can be exhibited to the sworn statement. A district judge may be less likely to consider arguments about earning capacity, but where there are no young dependent children and if work is available to the applicant, then evidence of obtainable local jobs can be exhibited to the statement.

5. A realistic budget of the respondent's own expenditure needs to be provided, although the respondent should be careful not to submit a budget which is far in excess of the applicant's budget, which the respondent is seeking to argue downwards.

6. When providing a critique of the applicant's budget, that should be done by way of a Scott Schedule. The schedule is broken down into four columns: the specific item of expenditure, the applicant's figure, the respondent's suggested adjusted figure and a final column for the respondent's comments and justification for the reduced figure.

9.7 INJUNCTIONS TO SECURE THE PRESERVATION OF ASSETS

There are a number of routes which can be taken to secure the preservation of assets pending the conclusion of an ancillary relief application. Although the most common approach is to make an application under MCA 1973, s.37, it is also possible to seek a freezing injunction or an order under the inherent jurisdiction of the court.

9.7.1 Orders under the Matrimonial Causes Act 1973, s.37

Practical issues

A few practical points must be noted as follows:

1. An application for an order under s.37 can only be made within ancillary relief proceedings. Therefore, an application for ancillary relief in Form A must be made either prior to or at the same time as bringing an application under s.37.
2. There are two forms of remedy under s.37. The first is contained in s.37(2)(a) and is to prevent the other party to the proceedings making any disposition or to transfer out of the jurisdiction or otherwise deal with any property. It is therefore an application that would be made to stop a transaction taking place in the future. To secure an order under s.37(2)(a), it is fundamentally necessary to be able to prove to the court that such a transaction was going to be made 'with the intention of defeating the claim for financial relief'.
3. The second power is contained in s.37(2)(b) and that is to set aside a disposition or transaction which has already taken place. To secure such an order from the court, the applicant needs to satisfy not only that it was made with the intention of defeating the claim for financial relief, but also that if the transaction were set aside, financial relief or different financial relief would be granted to the applicant.
4. When seeking an order for a previous disposition or transfer to be set aside, it has to be a 'reviewable' disposition. By virtue of s.37(4), it is reviewable unless it was made for valuable consideration to a person who, at the time of the disposition, acted in relation to it in good faith and without notice of any intention on the part of the other party to defeat the applicant's claim for financial relief.

5. By virtue of s.37(5), where an application is made under s.37 to set aside a reviewable disposition, where the disposition took place less than three years before the date of the application under s.37, there is a presumption, unless the contrary is shown, that the disposition took place with the intention of defeating the claim for financial relief. The same presumption applies where an application is made to prevent a future transaction where the effect of such an application would be to defeat the applicant's claim for financial relief.

It should be noted that even where applicants satisfy the test under s.37 for an order to be made in their favour, the ultimate decision as to whether an order should be made rests with the discretion of the court, as under s.37 the court 'may' make an order.

Practical considerations should also be taken into account before making an application to the court under s.37. The size and the value of the asset in question must be considered in the context of the overall value of matrimonial assets. Even if that asset were disposed of by the respondent, consideration should be given as to the value of the remaining assets and whether they are sufficient to meet the applicant's claims. An application to prevent the disposal of an asset worth, say, £50,000 may be wholly unnecessary where the entire net worth of the marriage is, say, £1 million. Consideration should, however, be given to the nature of the remaining assets. If the asset being disposed of represents a significant proportion of the liquid assets of the marriage and the remaining assets are either tied up in the business or are located abroad, injunctive relief may be more appropriate. Following on from the decision in *Hamlin* v. *Hamlin* [1986] 1 FLR 61, an order under s.37 can be granted in respect of assets abroad, although the court may still be slow to grant the order requested if the order of the English court were unenforceable in the country in question.

Procedure

An application is made by way of notice of application with an affidavit in support. It is good practice to prepare a draft of the order sought.

In certain circumstances, it may be necessary to make an urgent without notice application for a s.37 injunction. Whether an application should be made without notice or not will depend upon the circumstances of the case. The most common scenario will be if the applicant has evidence to show that the respondent intends to dispose of an asset imminently and therefore urgent injunctive relief is required. Likewise, applicants may wish to urgently set aside a reviewable disposition if they have only just become aware of the transaction having taken place and if there is evidence to suggest that the third party may then transfer the asset on to another person.

Where an application is made urgently, the following must be prepared:

1. The solicitor with conduct of the matter, or preferably the partner in charge of the matter, must prepare a certificate of urgency summarising the reasons why the matter needs to be listed urgently.
2. A draft of the order being sought should be filed at the same time as the application and sworn statement in support.
3. The sworn statement must address not only substantive issues, but also why the application needs to be heard urgently.

Where an order is granted on an urgent without notice basis, it is necessary to arrange personal service of the order and accompanying application and sworn statement upon the respondent. The court will also fix a return date and the respondent must be served with notice of that return date.

Where the assets in question are held by a third party, for example, monies in a bank account or investments, the order must also be served upon those third parties immediately by fax. As a matter of good practice, it should be ensured that the third parties acknowledge receipt of the order and provide confirmation that they will comply with it.

Where the without notice order is in respect of a reviewable disposition which is to be set aside, the third party who has received the asset in question must also be personally served with the order and supporting documents. They, too, must be notified of the return date of the hearing and given the opportunity to attend with representatives.

9.7.2 Freezing injunctions

Freezing injunctions used to be known as *Mareva* injunctions (*Mareva Cia Naviera SA* v. *Internacional Bulkcarriers SA, The Mareva* [1980] 1 All ER 213).

The power to grant such injunctions is contained in the Supreme Court Act 1981, s.37 and this is applied to the county courts by the County Courts Act 1984, s.38. Although strictly speaking the county courts have the jurisdiction to make such orders, generally, such applications are dealt with in the High Court.

Although clearly a case must be made to the court to justify the granting of a freezing injunction, the requirements are not as strict as MCA 1973, s.37, for example, it is not necessary to have to show that the respondent intends to defeat the applicant's claims. In certain circumstances this may therefore be a more appropriate option.

The freezing injunction may be granted on a worldwide basis and may be more appropriate in big money cases where the respondent has assets outside of the jurisdiction.

In terms of the procedure for making an application for a freezing order, note should be had of CPR Part 25 and the associated Practice Direction.

9.7.3 Freezing orders under the inherent jurisdiction of the court

There is a debate amongst some family practitioners as to whether the court has the power to order an injunction under its inherent jurisdiction as opposed to under s.37. The county court may grant injunctions to preserve assets under its inherent jurisdiction by virtue of the County Court Remedies Regulations 1991, SI 1991/1222.

Case law would suggest that the courts do have such a power (*Shipman* v. *Shipman* [1991] 1 FLR 250 and *Poon* v. *Poon* [1994] 2 FLR 857) although the reported cases pre-date *Wicks* v. *Wicks* [1998] 1 FLR 470 in which there was a detailed consideration of the limitation of the court's powers under its inherent jurisdiction.

Such applications remain uncommon and it may be that practitioners find, in practice, that the High Court is more likely to grant an injunction under its inherent jurisdiction as opposed to a district judge in the county court.

CHAPTER 10

Costs

Andrew Newbury

10.1 COSTS INFORMATION TO BE GIVEN TO THE CLIENT

10.1.1 Solicitors' Code of Conduct 2007

The Solicitors' Code of Conduct replaced the old professional conduct rules and came into effect on 1 July 2007. Rule 2 deals with solicitor/client relations. Of particular note is Rule 2.03 which deals with information that must be given to the client in respect of costs. Important points to note are as follows:

1. At the outset and, where appropriate, as the matter progresses, the client must be given the best information possible about the likely overall cost of a matter.
2. Such information includes advising the client as to the basis and terms of charges, charging rates and whether they are likely to be increased, likely payments which may need to be made by way of disbursements, eligibility for public funding, the circumstances in which a lien can be exercised in respect of unpaid costs and the potential liability to pay the other party's costs.

There is also additional guidance to Rule 2 in the Solicitors' Code of Conduct. Paragraph 36 of the guidance states:

> It is often impossible to tell at the outset what the overall cost will be. Subrule 2.03 allows for this and requires that you provide the client with as much information as possible at the start and you keep the client updated. If a precise figure cannot be given at the outset, you should explain the reason to the client and agree a ceiling figure or review dates.

10.1.2 Relevant case law

Practitioners should be aware of cases where insufficient information has been given to clients in respect of costs and where the solicitors in question have therefore been unable to recover their costs from the client.

(a) *Mastercigars Direct Limited* v. *Withers LLP* [2009] EWHC 651 (Ch)

Although this is a civil litigation matter, and the applicable rules are the old Solicitors' Guide to Professional Conduct, the principles are of general application. In the present case the costs rendered by the solicitors were far in excess of the original estimate.

It was not the proper function of the court to punish the solicitor for providing a wrong estimate or for failing to keep it up to date. The ultimate question was as to the sum which it was reasonable for the client to pay, having regard to the estimate and any other relevant matter.

(b) *David Truex (A Firm)* v. *Simone Kitchen* [2007] EWCA Civ 618

The Court of Appeal held that the solicitor had not done enough to check the true position of the parties' finances. A solicitor is also bound at the outset to consider the question of whether a client might be eligible for public funding. Firstly, because it would be wrong to incur substantial expenditure chargeable privately if public funding were available. Secondly, a client would have greater difficulty changing firms of solicitors if work had been done and the relationship built up before advice was given that a different firm who carried out publicly funded work could become involved. The Court of Appeal therefore upheld the decision of the lower court to deny the solicitors their fees and awarded the client the bulk of the money she had paid on account.

(c) *Reynolds* v. *Stone Rowe Brewer* [2008] EWHC 497 (QB)

This is also a civil litigation matter. The solicitors provided their client with an original costs estimate to trial of £10,000 to £18,000 plus VAT. Throughout the proceedings the solicitors advised the client of revised costs estimates. The final estimate was for up to £60,000 plus VAT.

When the client disputed the final fees, it was held at first instance that the solicitors should be bound by the original estimate they had given, plus a 15 per cent margin. The first instance decision was appealed by the solicitors. On appeal, Tugendhat J held that before the court considered the reasonableness of the costs themselves, it must consider what, in all circumstances, it is reasonable for the client to pay. The judge considered that the solicitors' reasons for the revised costs estimates were inadequate to explain the 'very large discrepancies'. He upheld the first instance decision and held that the solicitors' original estimate was a significant underestimate upon which the client had relied and that the revised estimates were merely attempts to correct the original underestimate and were not attributable to any change in facts.

10.1.3 Practical costs considerations

In light of the Solicitors' Code of Conduct 2007 and the above judgments, the following are some practical considerations to avoid problems arising in respect of costs:

1. It is clear from the *Reynolds* v. *Stone Rowe Brewer* case that the costs estimate given at the outset is of vital importance, regardless of revised costs estimates given subsequently in proceedings. Accordingly, it is crucial to give very careful consideration to the costs estimates set out in the Rule 2 letter which must be sent to the client at the outset. In most ancillary relief cases it is clearly impossible to know what the ultimate costs will be as much depends upon how quickly a settlement can be reached and the issues which may arise during the proceedings. In those circumstances, it may be appropriate to give various costs estimates depending upon when an agreement is reached. For example, an estimate could be given for the costs of resolving matters via voluntary disclosure and further estimates given for the estimated costs up to and including FDR and, say, final hearing.
2. A clear note should be kept on the file, ideally on the front of the section containing bills, with a running total of the costs together with a note of any costs estimate given. Accordingly, where it becomes apparent that the costs estimate given may be exceeded or needs to be revised, the information is readily available.
3. Revised costs estimates should always be provided before any previous costs estimate is exceeded. Any costs estimate should be given in writing and, where possible, an explanation given for why it is being revised. Revising costs estimates is, however, no real substitute for providing an accurate and realistic costs estimate at the outset.
4. At the first meeting, careful consideration should be given to whether the client is eligible for legal funding. Any view taken should clearly be recorded in the initial attendance note and also in the first letter to the client. If the client is potentially eligible for legal funding, but expressly stated that he or she wishes to instruct solicitors on a privately paying basis, that wish should also be recorded in the attendance note and in correspondence. Ideally, the client's written instructions to that effect should be obtained.

10.2 FUNDING OF LITIGATION

For some clients funding litigation is not an issue as either they are eligible for public funding or they have sufficient income or savings to meet the costs of ongoing matrimonial litigation. Many clients, and in particular applicant wives, fall between two stools. Whilst they may have a reasonable expectation of a good or substantial capital settlement at the conclusion of the proceedings, in the meantime they may not have the funds to meet the costs of litigation.

The following are funding options which can be considered with the client in such circumstances.

10.2.1 Sears Tooth agreements

A so-called 'Sears Tooth agreement' would be entered into between the client and his or her solicitors, in which the client agrees to assign to the solicitors his or her rights to any capital settlement so as to discharge fees owing to the solicitors. The validity of such agreements was first considered by Wilson J (as he then was) in *Sears Tooth (A Firm)* v. *Payne Hicks Beach (A Firm) and Others* [1997] 2 FLR 116. Wilson J held that such agreements were a valid contract and did not constitute a conditional fee agreement. The following should, however, be borne in mind:

1. The client must be given the opportunity to seek independent legal advice before entering into such a deed.
2. Such a deed is a discoverable document within divorce proceedings and therefore could be disclosed to the solicitors acting for the other party and the court.
3. Solicitors entering into such agreements should perhaps consider them as a last resort option, as payment will not be received until the final order is implemented.

10.2.2 Litigation loans

Certain high street banks are now specialising in loan agreements specifically tailored for matrimonial litigation. Hallmarks of the schemes are generally as follows:

1. A firm of solicitors will become a member of the bank's scheme and will therefore recommend individual clients to the bank where appropriate.
2. The loan arrangement is entered into directly between the client and the bank, with arrangements being put in place by the solicitor.
3. As and when the solicitor renders a bill to the client, upon approval of that bill the solicitor seeks payment from the bank and payment of each individual bill is added to the loan total.
4. At the outset, the client sets up a direct debit with the bank to pay interest on the outstanding balance on a monthly basis; however, repayment of the capital only takes place at the conclusion of the proceedings and once the client receives the eventual settlement.

5. The loan will also become immediately re-payable by the client if the client defaults on the direct debit payments or if the solicitors stop acting for the client.
6. The principal problem for solicitors with these schemes is that effectively the loans are underwritten by the solicitors. Although ostensibly the loan is between the client and the bank, if the client defaults and will not or cannot repay the loan, then the solicitors are liable to the bank to discharge the loan. Care must therefore be taken in recommending suitable clients to the bank.

An alternative to a formal litigation loan would be for the client to take out their own loan either with their bank or another financial institution. A better rate of interest may be secured compared to a litigation loan; however, under most conventional loan arrangements, capital and interest become repayable immediately on a monthly basis and it may therefore be difficult for the client to meet the costs of the loan. Furthermore, such arrangements do not usually have the flexibility of a litigation loan which entails the client being able to draw down sums upon receipt of an invoice.

10.2.3 Loan from friends or family

Although this may be an option for the client to consider, caution should be exercised. Loans between clients and family or friends are often viewed as 'soft loans' by the court and are therefore at risk of not being treated as a liability within the ancillary relief proceedings. If, however, a client does borrow money from friends or family to pay legal costs, the client should be advised to enter into a formal loan agreement and to pay interest to the lender on a monthly basis, preferably by standing order.

10.2.4 Provision for legal costs within maintenance pending suit orders

The court's power to include a provision for legal costs within a maintenance pending suit order was established in *A* v. *A (Maintenance Pending Suit: Payment of Legal Fees)* [2001] 1 FLR 377. Since that decision, there has been a string of cases in which the court has considered the circumstances where it would be appropriate for a court to order provision for legal fees.

Thorpe LJ in the Court of Appeal's decision in *Moses-Taiga* v. *Taiga* [2005] EWCA Civ 1013 expressed the view that such orders should only be made in exceptional circumstances. The test for 'exceptional circumstances' as endorsed by Nicholas Mostyn QC sitting as a Deputy High Court Judge in *TL* v. *ML and Others (Ancillary Relief: Claim against assets of extended family)* [2005] EWHC 2860 (Fam) was that the applicant needed to prove the following:

(a)   she had no assets; and
(b)   she could not raise a litigation loan (to prove that he suggested her solicitors should produce correspondence between them and two banks showing a negative response); and
(c)   she could not persuade her solicitors to enter into a Sears Tooth agreement. A statement from her solicitors confirming that to be the case would be sufficient.

The rigidity of the test was subsequently considered by Headley J in *C* v. *C* (*Maintenance Pending Suit: Legal Costs*) [2006] 2 FLR 1207 and by Wilson LJ in the Court of Appeal in *Currey* v. *Currey* [2006] EWCA Civ 1338. The following principles have therefore been established:

1.   The test laid down in *Moses-Taiga* and *TL* v. *ML* was illustrative as opposed to definitive. In *C* v. *C*, the case was viewed as 'exceptional' as the husband was a wealthy man who owned the bulk of the assets of the marriage and those assets needed investigation.
2.   Apart from having no facility to fund the litigation, the applicant did not otherwise need to show that his or her case was exceptional.
3.   The initial enquiry of the court was whether the applicant could demonstrate that he or she could not reasonably procure legal advice and representation by any other means.
4.   The word 'exceptional' was obstructing the proper exercise of the court's jurisdiction.
5.   There is no public funding available to the applicant as would provide him or her with legal advice and representation at a level of expertise apt to the proceedings.

In the majority of cases, the court may certainly be unwilling to include a provision for legal fees in view of the relatively limited income of the paying party. In practical terms there will be insufficient income to cover legal costs in addition to meeting day-to-day expenditure. By contrast, in big money cases where the paying party is a high earner, and following on from the approach in *C* v. *C* as adopted by Headley J, there may be a more compelling reason for the court to include a provision for legal fees within a maintenance pending suit order. Such cases by their very nature may also be viewed by the courts as 'exceptional'.

10.2.5 Interim lump sum for costs

Although the court does not have the power to order payment of an interim lump sum there is nothing to prevent the parties agreeing such an arrangement between them. By way of illustration, if a paying husband may be at risk of being ordered to pay towards his wife's costs by way of a maintenance pending suit order, any such funds paid by him will certainly not be taken into account in a final settlement. By contrast, if an interim lump sum is paid during the course of the proceedings, it could be agreed that any lump sum should be taken into account as part of the final settlement.

10.3   COSTS ORDERS WITHIN FAMILY PROCEEDINGS

Costs orders within family proceedings are governed by FPR rule 2.71. The existing Family Proceedings Rules were amended by virtue of the Family Proceedings (Amendment) Rules 2006, SI 2006/352. They apply to ancillary relief applications (including a prayer in a petition or answer for ancillary relief) issued on or after 3 April 2006.

10.3.1   President's Practice Direction dated 20 February 2006

The Practice Direction was issued to coincide with the 2006 costs rules. It makes two important practical points as follows:

1.   A maintenance pending suit order which includes an element for legal fees is not to be viewed as a 'costs order' under the 2006 rules. Such provision can therefore continue to be made.
2.   Where a party intends to seek a costs order, such a claim should usually be made in open correspondence or in a skeleton argument prior to the hearing. Clearly, such arguments will focus upon a litigation conduct issue as set out below. The purpose of this approach is to enable the court to rule on the issue of costs at the conclusion of the substantive hearing, rather than having to adjourn the costs issue to a later date.

10.3.2   The 'no order' principle and litigation conduct

By virtue of rule 2.71(4)(a), the general rule is that the court will not make an order requiring one party to pay the costs of another party.

The court, however, retains the power to make a costs order at any stage of the proceedings where it considers it appropriate to do so because of the conduct of a party in relation to the proceedings (whether before or during them) (rule 2.71(4)(b)).

When considering conduct issues and deciding what order, if any, to make by virtue of para. (4)(b), the court must have regard to the following in accordance with rule 2.71(5):

1.   Any failure by a party to comply with the FPR, or any order of the court or any practice direction which the court considers relevant.
2.   Any open offer to settle made by a party.
3.   Whether it was reasonable for a party to raise, pursue or contest a particular allegation or issue.

125

4. The manner in which a party has pursued or responded to the application or a particular allegation or issue.
5. Any other aspect of the party's conduct in relation to the proceedings which the court considers relevant.
6. The financial effect on the parties of any costs order.

As at the time of writing, there has been no substantive guidance from the court regarding the application of the 2006 rules. Although there remains the prospect of the court making costs orders at the conclusion of proceedings, such orders are exceedingly rare. When the new rules were introduced, it had been anticipated that there could be a substantial amount of satellite litigation on the issue of costs with arguments being pursued in respect of the relevance of the conduct of the party within proceedings. To date, that has not happened.

In practice, it would, however, seem that interlocutory costs orders remain relatively commonplace where either party has failed to comply with the FPR or the court timetable.

10.3.3 Open offers and without prejudice offers

As can be seen from rule 2.71(5)(b), only an 'open offer to settle' can be taken into account as relevant litigation conduct when the court is considering whether to make a costs order. Even where a party fails to beat an open offer at a final hearing, the court is still not compelled to make a costs order in light of the new rules.

The new rules do not prevent either party making 'without prejudice' offers, although it is simply the case that they will not have any protection on costs. Without prejudice offers may still be filed with the court in advance of an FDR in accordance with FPR rule 2.61E.

Many family practitioners still see without prejudice correspondence as a useful negotiating tool which can be an aid to settlement. On that note, the following are practical points to consider:

1. Some family practitioners prefer to only make offers on a without prejudice basis prior to the FDR. If the FDR hearing then fails, offers may then be made on an open basis in anticipation of a contested final hearing.
2. Some practitioners advise clients to make without prejudice proposals in conjunction with open proposals. For example, a detailed offer may be set out in open correspondence, but at the same time that offer is accompanied by an alternative proposal which may be more attractive to the other party. One possibility may be for an open offer to include provision for spousal maintenance, whereas the without prejudice offer may offer capitalised maintenance on a clean break. The latter may be a concession that the paying party may not wish to make on an open basis at that stage in the proceedings.

3. Clients should be advised that the principal purpose of making a good open offer is therefore with a view to encouraging settlement as opposed to providing protection on costs. Whilst a costs order at the conclusion of the proceedings may still be a possibility under the new rules if 'litigation conduct' under FPR rule 2.71(4)(b) can be established (see **10.3.2**), the client should be advised that such costs orders are unlikely in view of the no order principle.
4. Unless the case in question falls under the old rules, there is no scope for *Calderbank* correspondence within proceedings and therefore correspondence should no longer be marked 'without prejudice save as to costs'.

10.4 INTERACTION WITH THE CIVIL PROCEDURE RULES 1998

Rule 2.71 of the FPR specifically deals with the interaction between the CPR and the FPR. Rule 2.71(1) states that CPR rule 44.3(1) to (5) shall not apply to ancillary relief proceedings, yet rule 44.3(6) to (9) does apply to costs orders made under rule 2.71.

Practical points to note under CPR rule 44.3 are as follows:

1. Rule 44.3(6) – the court may make an order that a party only pays a proportion of the other party's costs, a stated fixed amount of costs, costs only from or until a specified date, costs incurred before the proceedings were issued, or costs relating to particular steps or in respect of a discrete part of the proceedings. The court also has the power to order interest on costs from or until a specified date.
2. Rule 44.3(8) – the court has the power to order a payment on account of costs and this may be done pending a detailed assessment of the costs in the future.
3. Rule 44.3(9) – the costs due to the receiving party may be set-off against any costs owed by that party to the paying party. For example, the receiving party may be liable to pay the paying party's costs under an earlier interlocutory order.

A useful practical provision to note is rule 44.8, which deals with the time for payment of costs. It provides that costs orders must be complied with within 14 days of the date of the judgment (where the costs have been specifically stated) or within 14 days of the date of the costs certificate (where the costs have been fixed at a later date). The 14-day time limit will apply unless the court orders an alternative date.

CPR Rule 47 deals with the detailed assessment of costs (summary assessment is dealt with at **10.6**). The detailed assessment of costs can arise following on from a costs order having been made and therefore on a party/party basis. Likewise, if there is a dispute between solicitors and their own clients over costs, a detailed assessment may arise on a solicitor/client basis.

The procedure for a detailed assessment of costs is set out in rule 47.

An important issue which arises on the assessment of costs is whether those costs should be assessed on either the standard or the indemnity basis. On a party/party basis, costs can be assessed on either the standard or indemnity basis: where the order is silent, the costs will be assessed on the standard basis. An indemnity costs order is relatively rare.

When assessing costs on the standard basis, CPR rule 44.4(2) states that the court will only allow costs which are proportionate to the matters in issue. Where there is any doubt as to the reasonableness of costs, this will be resolved in favour of the paying party. By contrast, under rule 44.4(3), any such doubts would be resolved in favour of the receiving party.

10.5 FORM H

In accordance with FPR rule 2.61F at every hearing or appointment each party must produce to the court an estimate in Form H of the costs incurred up to the date of that hearing or appointment. It should be noted that there is no requirement to serve Form H in advance of the hearing.

Rule 2.61F refers to Form H being produced at 'every hearing or appointment' and therefore presumably extends to any directions hearing or any interlocutory hearing, although general practice is that Forms H tend to be produced at First Appointments and FDRs.

As part of keeping clients informed of costs, it is good practice at each hearing to ensure that the client is given a copy of Form H and is advised as to the breakdown of costs. Note that in respect of proceedings issued on or after 3 April 2006, the revised Form H must be used, in which more information must be given.

In accordance with FPR rule 2.61F(2), not less than 14 days before the final hearing each party must file with the court and serve on each other party Form H1 which must provide full particulars of all costs in respect of the proceedings that have been incurred or will be incurred.

10.6 DRAFTING STATEMENTS OF COSTS

With the 'no order' principle of FPR rule 2.71 in mind, on occasions it may still be appropriate to seek a costs order, particularly on an interlocutory hearing where there are compelling arguments regarding litigation misconduct. A common example would be an application for a penal notice where the other party has failed to file and serve Form E.

Where a costs order is to be sought on behalf of a client, clearly, it is beneficial to the client if those costs can be summarily assessed immediately which would entail the costs being fixed and a time made for payment. Such an approach saves time and cost in the future.

In accordance with the Costs Practice Direction to the CPR, there is a general rule that there should be a summary assessment of costs at the conclusion of any hearing which lasts for one day or less. Accordingly, a summary assessment of costs can follow on from an interlocutory hearing or even a final ancillary relief hearing which does not last for more than a day.

Where a party intends to seek a costs order and wishes for that order to be subject to a summary assessment, a written statement of costs must be filed and served at least 24 hours before the hearing in accordance with paragraph 13.5 of the Practice Direction. Some district judges take a very rigid view of the 24-hour deadline and will not allow a summary assessment of costs where that deadline has not been met; however, other district judges take a far more flexible approach. Also note the decision in *McDonald* v. *Taree Holdings Limited* [2001] CPLR 329 where a summary assessment was allowed even though the 24-hour deadline was missed.

The statement of costs should follow the form set out in Form N260 and should deal with the following issues:

(a) The hourly rate and grade of each fee earner involved in the conduct of the case should be set out. See below regarding 'grades' of fee earners.

(b) The work is then broken down into the appropriate categories by reference to the individual fee earners. The categories include attendance upon the client, attendance upon the other party, preparation of documents, attendance at court, etc.

(c) Counsel's fee, name and year of call should also be included.

(d) Details of any other disbursements to be claimed likewise must be included.

(e) The statement must conclude with a certificate to the effect that the costs being sought from the other party do not exceed those which the client is liable to pay, i.e. confirmation that there is no breach of the indemnity rule.

Practitioners should also be aware that court areas will have standard hourly rates which will allow for different grades of fee earner. When making an inter partes order, some district judges may not be willing to make costs orders in excess of those standard hourly rates, particularly where costs are being assessed on the standard basis. The four grades are as follows:

- solicitors with over eight years' PQE (regardless of whether the solicitor is a partner);
- solicitors and legal executives (who are Fellows of the Institute of Legal Executives) with over four years' PQE;
- other solicitors and legal executives and fee earners who have equivalent experience to solicitors and legal executives;
- trainees, paralegals and other fee earners.

129

In the event that a costs order is made at the conclusion of the hearing and the judge is willing to provide a summary assessment, the following issues are likely to be addressed by the paying party in an assessment:

1. The grade of fee earner involved with the case; for example, it could be contended that specific items of work could have been conducted by a more junior fee earner.
2. The individual charging rates applied. In defence of such issues, it is always worth noting the charging rates applied by the other party's solicitors and how they compare with your own.
3. The amount of time spent on individual tasks, such as the preparation or perusal of documents. One area which can often be open to criticism is time spent attending your own client, particularly if the client needs a great deal of 'hand holding'.
4. There may even be arguments about refusal to negotiate or unreasonableness within negotiations.
5. There may also be issues about the reasonableness of using counsel at that hearing and whether that was an appropriately incurred disbursement.

As detailed arguments may arise over the reasonableness of the fees, the fee earner with day-to-day conduct of the matter should be in attendance at the hearing. It is often useful to be armed with a full billing guide or other print out with details as to the time recorded as well as the file itself together with attendance notes.

10.7 PROPORTIONALITY OF COSTS

10.7.1 The overriding objective

When advising clients and engaging in litigation, practitioners should always bear in mind the overriding objective set out in FPR rule 2.51D. The whole of rule 2.51D focuses on issues of proportionality. Rule 2.51D(1) confirms that the ancillary relief rules are a procedural code with the overriding objective of enabling the court to deal with cases justly. Dealing with a case justly includes the following:

1. Ensuring the parties are on an equal footing.
2. Saving expense.
3. Dealing with the case in ways which are proportionate to the amount of money involved, the importance of the case, the complexity of the issues and the financial position of each party.
4. Ensuring that it is dealt with expeditiously and fairly.

The parties are required to help the court to further the overriding objective and the court must likewise further the overriding objective by actively managing cases. Active case management includes the following:

1. Encouraging the parties to co-operate with each other in the conduct of the proceedings.
2. Encouraging the parties to settle their disputes through mediation, where appropriate.
3. Identifying the issues at an early date.
4. Regulating the extent of disclosure of documents and expert evidence so that they are proportionate to the issues in question.
5. Helping the parties to settle.
6. Fixing timetables or otherwise controlling the progress of the case.
7. Making use of technology.
8. Giving directions to ensure a case proceeds quickly and efficiently.

10.7.2 Family Law protocol

Section 4.17 of the Family Law protocol deals with the issue of costs and the statutory charge. Paragraph 4.17.1 specifically states that solicitors must keep in mind at all times the principle of proportionality between the amount at stake and the amount which it is appropriate to spend on resolving the dispute.

Although much of the protocol relates to the pre-April 2006 costs rules, the general underlying principles remain.

CHAPTER 11

Future applications

Shona Alexander

This chapter will focus on the applications that can be made at a later stage, after the final order has been made.

11.1 VARIATION

People's circumstances change and often clients (new or old) will seek advice as to whether financial orders can be varied to reflect these changes.

As always, it is essential to go back to MCA 1973 to consider whether or not the order is capable of variation. Generally, the orders made under MCA 1973 are divided into two types:

1. Final orders – cannot be reconsidered.
2. Variable orders – reconsideration is possible.

The relevant section of MCA 1973 relating to variation is s.31. For ease of reference parts of the section are set out below. Those orders which can be varied are set out in s.31(2).

> (1)   Where the court has made an order to which this section applies, then, subject to the provisions of this section and of section 28(1A) above, the court shall have power to vary or discharge the order or to suspend any provision thereof temporarily and to revive the operation of any provision so suspended.
>
> (2)   This section applies to the following orders, that is to say –
>
> > (a)   any order for maintenance pending suit and any interim order for maintenance;
> > (b)   any periodical payments order;
> > (c)   any secured periodical payments orders;
> > (d)   any order made by virtue of section 23(3)(c) or 27(7)(b) above (provision for payment of a lump sum by instalments);
> > (dd) any deferred order made by virtue of section 21(1)(c) (lump sums) which includes provision made by virtue of –
> >
> > > (i)   section 25B(4); or
> > > (ii) section 25C,
> >
> > (provision in respect of pension rights);

(e) any order for a settlement of property under section 24(1)(b) or for a variation of settlement under section 24(1)(c) or (d) above, being an order made on or after the grant of a decree of judicial separation;

(f) any order made under section 24A(1) above for the sale of property;

(g) a pension sharing order under section 24B above which is made at a time before the decree has been made absolute.

Unsurprisingly, maintenance is clearly variable (either upwards or downwards) but the maintenance may be for a fixed term, which affects its variability. Section 31(1) makes specific reference to s.28(1A) as this is the section which makes it clear to the court (and the parties) that no further applications can be made in relation to that maintenance once the term has come to an end – all future applications are barred. The most likely application would be for the term to be extended. Therefore, should there be a s.28(1A) bar upon the maintenance term it is essential that any application for variation (be it for extension or increase/decrease) is made in good time before the termination of the term.

Section 31(2) makes no reference to lump sum orders and property adjustment orders. These are intended to be final orders and therefore are not capable of variation. This needs to be made clear to clients when advising on the terms of a consent order. Clients need to be aware that, even if there is a subsequent change in circumstances (unless it is a *Barder* event which is dealt with at **11.10.2**), these orders will not be varied.

11.2   PERIODICAL PAYMENTS AND MAINTENANCE PENDING SUIT

Given the ongoing nature of maintenance claims, most variation cases will be applications to vary, in whatever form, periodical payments orders. It is possible under MCA 1973, s.31(2) to seek the variation of any order for maintenance pending suit and a periodical payments order. The court also has the power, under MCA 1973, s.31(2A), to order the payment of any arrears due under the order or any part thereof. The court can vary the order in whatever way it considers appropriate – it could increase/decrease the amount paid, change the order (i.e. lump sum to be paid) or, in fact, discharge the order altogether. When considering what order should be made, the court must have reference to MCA 1973, s.31, which states as follows:

(7) In exercising the powers conferred by this section the court shall have regard to all the circumstances of the case, first consideration being given to the welfare while a minor of any child of the family who has not attained the age of eighteen and under the circumstances of the case shall include any change in any of the matters to which the court was required to have regard when making the order to which the application relates, and –

(a) in the case of a periodical payments or secured periodical payments order made on or after the grant of a decree of divorce or nullity of marriage, the court shall consider whether in all the circumstances and after having regard to any such change, it would be appropriate to vary the order so that payments under the order are required to be made or secured only for such further period as will in the opinion of the court be sufficient (in the light of any proposed exercise by the court, where the marriage has been dissolved, of its powers under subsection 7B below) to enable the party in whose favour the order was made to adjust without undue hardship to the termination of those payments;

(b) ...

(7A) Subsection 7B below applies where, after the dissolution of a marriage, the court –

(a) discharges a periodical payments order or secured periodical payments order made in favour of a party to the marriage; or

(b) varies such an order so that payments under the order are required to be made or secured only for such further period as is determined by the court.

(7B) The court has power, in addition to any power it has from this subsection, to make supplemental provision consisting of any of –

(a) an order for the payment of a lump sum in favour of a party to the marriage;

(b) one or more property adjustment orders in favour of a party to the marriage;

(ba) one or more pension sharing orders;

(bb) a pension compensation sharing order;

(c) a direction that the party in whose favour the original order discharged or varied was made is not entitled to make any further application for –

(i) a periodical payments or secured periodical payments order; or

(ii) an extension of the period to which the original order is limited by any variation made by the court.

This means that the court can, if it considers it appropriate, 'capitalise' the maintenance payable: it can order a lump sum order, a pension sharing order or property adjustment order in place of the maintenance order. This can come as a surprise to clients who had believed that the opportunity for those orders to be made had passed when the original order had been made. Clients need to be aware of this when agreeing to maintenance orders because if they are going to receive substantial bonus payments/pension lump sums, etc. in the future, then capitalisation and a clean break may be the court's preferred option upon a subsequent variation application.

The court does not just look at the maintenance being paid and then use the *Duxbury* tables to calculate how much should be paid but will consider what lump sum, if appropriate, would be fair in all the circumstances: see Charles J in *Cornick* v. *Cornick (No.3)* [2001] 2 FLR 1240. This was considered again in *Pearce* v. *Pearce* [2003] 2 FLR 1144 where Thorpe LJ clearly stated the following:

1. The clean break is to be considered; however, the court should not re-open capital claims but should substitute for the maintenance 'such

other order or orders as will fairly compensate the payee and at the same time complete the clean break'.

2. Pension sharing should be considered as a first option, if possible, to take the place of a periodical payments order.

11.3 WHAT DOES THE COURT CONSIDER?

When a variation application is made, under s.31 the court has to consider all circumstances of the case and, in particular, it has to consider any changes in any of the specific issues that were considered when the original order was made. The court should not seek to reconsider the case from the starting point of before the order was actually made. It is not a rehearing of the case but in many ways a review. As the s.25 factors will have been considered previously, with some being more relevant than others, they will have to be reconsidered in the light of the change in circumstances. The s.25 factors have, of course, to be considered in the light of the recent case law and in particular *Miller, Macfarlane* as Baron J held in *Lauder* v. *Lauder* [2007] 2 FLR 802 that she considered 'the proper approach in this type of application is to apply the precise terms of the statute in light of the factual matrix and give proper consideration to the recent guidance given by the House of Lords in the case of *Miller* v. *MacFarlane*'. This view was also taken in *VB* v. *JP* [2008] EWHC 112 (Fam).

The effect of this is that the court may, if appropriate, consider compensation arguments and that can be an ongoing consideration rather than just being dealt with at the time that the marriage comes to an end when the original order is made. 'Reasonable requirements', which used to be a limiting factor as it was then the benchmark, is no longer determinative. How much consideration the court will give to specific factors will depend on the individual circumstances of the case but it is useful to refer the client to the s.25 factors at the outset. The court will look to achieve a fair result, see Thorpe LJ, *North* v. *North* [2007] EWCA Civ 760.

11.4 SITUATION UPON DEATH

Normally, maintenance is made on the basis of a joint lives order so ends upon the death of the payer. However, in some cases, it may be appropriate for maintenance to continue and so you will have secured periodical payments. Where maintenance has been made on a secured periodical payments basis the order survives the death of the paying party. The paying party will have to provide security for those payments during his or her lifetime and that obligation continues after death. Upon their death it is possible, under MCA 1973, s.31, for the person entitled to the payments, or the personal representatives of the deceased, to apply to the court for variation as another order may be more appropriate, such as capitalisation or property adjustment. Under MCA 1973, s.31(8), that application must be made before six months has expired from the date that the representation was first taken out, as the estate needs to be administered within a reasonable timeframe. It may make sense for all involved for the maintenance claim to be capitalised upon funds from the estate being realised and, if possible, for such a variation to be negotiated and agreed.

11.5 PENSIONS

The court can also vary any deferred order under s.31(2)(dd) in respect of pension attachment orders in relation to orders under s.25B(4) and s.25C. It has to be noted that, of course, these orders will cease with the death of either of the parties.

11.6 TERMINATION OF PAYMENT

Section 31 makes it clear that the court must consider whether or not it is appropriate for there to be a clean break by termination of payment, as in *Fleming* v. *Fleming* [2004] 1 FLR 667.

11.7 PROCEDURE

An application to vary falls clearly within the definition of ancillary relief as set out at FPR rule 1.2(1). It therefore complies with the normal rules applicable to ancillary relief and thus considerable costs can be incurred as, effectively, it can be the whole financial procedure again with a similar costs bill at the end. Clients need to be made aware of this at the outset when considering the likely change in the monthly amount compared to legal fees they may incur. It may take many years for the reduction in monthly maintenance to be a benefit when comparing it to the capital outlay of legal costs. Forms E must be completed in full as the court has wide discretion as to the orders it can make, so all financial details are relevant, and full disclosure will have to be provided. Before embarking on an application, and engaging the court timetable, practitioners should provide as much disclosure as possible to the other side, on a voluntary basis, explaining why the application is required/appropriate, to see if variation can be agreed by negotiation thus saving considerable time and expense.

11.8 VARIATION OF LUMP SUM ORDERS

Earlier in this chapter it was stated that the majority of lump sum orders could not be varied. However, under MCA 1973, s.31(2), the court can vary a lump sum order when that lump sum order is due to be paid by instalments.

Whilst this appears relatively straightforward, this is an area where often a problem will arise – do you have a situation where there is a lump sum payable by instalments or is it, in fact, a series of lump sums? This should be easily identifiable from the face of the order (if correctly drafted) but there will, undoubtedly, be cases where it is not as clear-cut as it should be. This may particularly be the case where there is a *Rose* agreement (see **11.10.1**) following a day of long discussions at court.

If it is a lump sum payable by instalments then what can actually be varied by the courts?

In *Westbury* v. *Sampson* [2002] 1 FLR 166 the court held both timing and quantum could be varied. In this case it was held that the quantum in respect of both the amount of an individual lump sum and the amount of the principal lump sum itself were capable of variation. This was further confirmed by Wilson J in *R* v. *R (Lump Sum Repayment)* [2004] 1 FLR 928.

It is essential that practitioners draft recitals to clearly set out what the parties intend, to ensure that the position is clear to all involved.

When considering the provisions of MCA 1973, s.31(2)(d), the court will look in each case whether or not the reality of an agreement was a lump sum payable by instalments rather than there being some clever drafting so as to have the instalments appearing as separate lump sums in order to avoid variation applications. Coleridge J considered this in *Lamont* v. *Lamont* (13 October 2006) (unreported) where he made it clear that where an order provided for a series of lump sum payments but was, in fact, a lump sum in instalments, the parties should not be allowed to avoid s.31.

11.9 APPEALS

Cases do not always go as expected, and hoped, and it may be necessary to consider the appeal process which, by its very nature, is complicated and expensive. The assistance of Counsel will be needed to determine whether an application should be made. Given their nature, a decision will have to be made quickly as to whether or not to proceed with an appeal as significant further costs will be incurred.

The appeal process is very complicated and does not have one unified system. However, since 6 April 2009 due to various amendments to the magistrates' courts' procedures and the FPR, all magistrates' courts' 'family proceedings' appeals will now go to the county court.

In civil proceedings, all appeals at all levels are governed by CPR Part 52. Appeals to the Court of Appeal in family proceedings are also governed by CPR Part 52. However, appeals to the county court under FPR remain family proceedings and, as such, CPR do not apply.

In this chapter we will look at the situation with the most likely appeals – from the district judge of a county court to a judge of the county court and from a district judge of the High Court to a judge of the High Court. From there would lie the appeal from a judge of the county court or High Court to the Court of Appeal and from there it would be to the Supreme Court. However, given the complexity and the rarity of such appeals, these have not been addressed in this chapter, as specialist advice will need to be taken when considering making such an appeal.

It is important that clients are aware that all appeals are dealt with as a review (see FPR rule 8.1(3)(a)), not as a re-hearing of the issues unless that is considered to be absolutely necessary in the 'interest of justice'. The guidance which was given in *Piglowska* v. *Piglowski* [1999] 2 FLR 763 should be considered.

11.9.1 Appeal from a district judge (county court) to a judge (county court)

This appeal will lie to a judge of the same court. The procedure will be governed by FPR rule 8.1 and CCR Ord. 37 rule 1.

Procedure

Application by way of notice of appeal which must be served within 14 days of the decision (FPR rule 8.1(2) and CCR Ord. 37 rule 6(2)).

Documents

It is necessary for the appellant to file and serve the notice of appeal/a copy of the summons or application and order appealed against and the reasons given for the decision. It is also useful for the appellant to have obtained a transcript of the hearing so that that can also be submitted. This should be ordered as soon as the hearing is over as it will assist in determining whether an appeal should be made and will be useful at the appeal hearing itself.

The judge is limited to a review of the first instance decision unless the judge considers that it would be in the interests of justice to hold a re-hearing. Regardless of this, it is possible for fresh evidence to be admitted if it is in the interest of justice to do so.

The appeal from such a decision would be to the Court of Appeal under the County Courts Act 1984, s.77.

11.9.2 Appeal from a district judge (High Court) to a judge (High Court)

In this case, an appeal to the High Court 'in family proceedings' does not fall within the definition of 'civil proceedings' under CPR rule 2.1 and therefore the old rules have not been repealed. Accordingly, the Rules of the Supreme Court (commonly known as 'The White Book') apply.

Under these rules, the notice of appeal must be issued within five days of the decision and served within five days thereafter in relation to an appeal in the Principal Registry (RSC Ord. 58, rule 1) and within seven days of the decision and served within seven days thereafter in respect of any other court (RSC Ord. 58 rule 3).

The appellant is to file and serve the notice of appeal, a copy of the summons or application order appealed against, notes of evidence and reasons given for the decision. If this case is appealed the appeal would lie to the Court of Appeal unless the appeal lies to the Supreme Court (if leave has been given).

It has to be noted that appeals are very expensive and before the appeal is lodged Counsel's advice as to the chances and likelihood of success must be taken as a priority.

11.10   APPLICATIONS TO SET ASIDE

The courts are, quite rightly, encouraged to bring an end to litigation. Ongoing litigation is expensive and difficult for families to deal with, and has a monetary and emotional cost. The court has made it clear that there will only be a small number of cases in which it is right to reopen litigation; see Thorpe LJ in *Shaw* v. *Shaw* [2002] EWCA Civ 1298 when he stated:

> the residual right to reopen litigation is clearly established by the decisions in *Livesey* v. *Jenkins* and *Barder* v. *Calouri*. But the number of cases that properly fall into either category is exceptionally small. The public interest in finality of litigation in this field must always be emphasised.

There are two ways in which the court can be asked to set aside a final order: material non-disclosure and intervening events. They should not be used in conjunction; the choice is either one or the other.

11.10.1 Non-disclosure

In many cases, a party will be convinced that there has been material non-disclosure by the other throughout the court proceedings; it is a common accusation made. Practitioners have to make decisions as to how far these 'beliefs' should be pursued, as fishing expeditions for disclosure are rightly dissuaded and expensive. The costs of seeking the 'pot of gold' can often outweigh, by many times, the amounts found, if any. Clients' expectations need to be carefully managed.

In many cases, there may well have been instances of non-disclosure but in order for the court to re-open the final order that has been made, it must be proven that the non-disclosure is material. This was clearly dealt with in *Livesey* v. *Jenkins* [1985] 1 All ER 106, HL. For the court to reopen the case, it had to be considered that the order made was 'substantially different from the order which it would have made if such disclosure had taken place'. The non-disclosure has to be such that it would have made a considerable difference to the order that was made.

In some cases, clients will choose not to pursue disclosure even if they have suspicions. If they choose to do this then they cannot rely on that non-disclosure at a later date. In *Rose* v. *Rose* [2003] 2 FLR 197, Bennett J relied upon both *Shaw* and *Livesey* when striking out the husband's application in which he had sought to withdraw from an agreement reached at the FDR. The fact that the husband decided at the FDR stage not to pursue his belief that the wife was cohabiting was held against him. He could have pursued his suspicions and he could have taken the matter to final hearing, but he did not. Therefore, he could not rely upon this non-disclosure as a basis of setting aside the agreement that had been reached.

Practitioners will always advise clients that they are under an ongoing duty to make full and frank disclosure and in *Burns* v. *Burns* [2004] 3 FCR 263 Thorpe LJ made it clear that the 'duty of candour must clearly continue beyond the making of a substantive order' in certain circumstances. He also reiterated that it would be possible to say that there had been a breach of disclosure duties in a case where somebody had actively presented 'a false case or passively failed to reveal relevant facts and circumstances'.

It is essential that practitioners note that *Burns* made it very clear that the duty of disclosure is an ongoing duty and it has to be full and frank disclosure.

If there has been a material non-disclosure it is very important that the party seeking to set aside the order applies to do so quickly. The courts may take a more lenient view on how long the delay can be, depending on the circumstances of the case. In *Den Heyer* v. *Newby* [2006] 1 FLR 1114, the applicant became aware of a sale of her former husband's business in February 2003. In June 2003, she changed solicitors and there was an eventual exchange of Forms E in December 2003. She did not actually issue her application until January 2004 (after Counsel's advice) yet the court said that she had dealt with the matter promptly and her case was allowed.

Sale of business interests

The duty of full and frank disclosure is particularly pertinent in the sale of businesses and was considered in *T* v. *T* [1996] 2 FLR 640 and *Vicary* v. *Vicary* [1992] 2 FLR 271.

It is essential when dealing with a case where there are business assets and interests that the questionnaire includes questions as to whether or not there have been any approaches or negotiations in respect of that business, so that the matter can be dealt with clearly and with as much certainty as possible before the FDR and any possible settlement. The questions asked need to be clear and unambiguous. If it is likely that a valuation will be needed, the questions should be formulated with the assistance of an accountant (if appropriate).

11.10.2 An intervening event – *Barder* appeals

The intervening events which can give rise to an application to be set aside are often referred to as '*Barder* events' as the main case in this area is *Barder* v. *Calouri* [1987] 2 FLR 480. In this case, sadly, weeks after the consent order was made in which the wife was to receive the former matrimonial home, she killed both herself and the children of the family. This led to the '*Barder* test'; which can be summarised as follows:

1. a new event must have occurred since the making of the order;
2. the event invalidates the basis or the fundamental assumption upon which the order was made;
3. (a) if leave to appeal out of time was given the appeal would be certainly or very likely to succeed;
    (b) the new event should have occurred within a relatively short space of time of the order having been made;
    (c) the application for leave to appeal out of time should be made promptly;
    (d) there should be no prejudice to third parties.

There is no particular guidance as to the length of time between the order and the new event but it is generally considered that it is unlikely that it could be considered as long as a year and, in most cases, it will only be a few months.

Many of the cases which have now sought to use this principle have been in relation to business assets and the valuations of private companies such as in *A* v. *A* [2006] 2 FLR 115. This was also looked at in *Cornick* v. *Cornick* [1994] 2 FLR 530 in which Charles J made clear the following:

1. If the matter is correctly valued and taken account of at the time of the order but changes in value due to price fluctuation, that is not within the *Barder* doctrine.
2. A wrong value attributed at the time of order which would have led to a different order may come within the *Barder* doctrine.
3. Something unforeseen and unforeseeable happening since the date of order, which has altered a value dramatically, may be within the *Barder* doctrine, but this will not be the case where it is natural market fluctuation. However it is essential to remember that a party cannot seek to use this if they have failed to properly investigate the situation as in *Edmonds* v. *Edmonds* [1990] 2 FLR 202.

In *Cornick*, the husband's shares increased dramatically in value. In *Myerson* v. *Myerson* [2009] EWCA Civ 282 the converse was true. In *Myerson* Thorpe LJ stated, '. . . the natural processes of price fluctuation, whether in houses, shares, or any other property, and however dramatic, do not satisfy the *Barder* test'. Clients need to be aware that if they chose to take high-risk assets, which could potentially soar in value or decrease, then they cannot seek to use such a decrease as a *Barder* event.

The test in *Cornick* has, however, been modified slightly in light of the Court of Appeal's decision in *Walkden* v. *Walkden* [2009] EWCA Civ 627. Mistake as to value, which previously fell into the second category under *Cornick*, as set out above, should no longer be seen as a *Barder* event. Following on from the decision in *Walkden*, the following test should be applied:

1. The first question was whether a contract or consent order had been vitiated by misrepresentation, mistake, fraud, undue influence or breach of the duty of full and frank disclosure.
2. If such a vitiating element is established, then the contract or order is no longer binding.
3. If no such vitiating element was established, then the parties to a contract or order may be relieved of their obligation as a result of a supervening event under the doctrine of frustration. A *Barder* event is akin to frustration.
4. Accordingly, if a party seeks to set aside an ancillary relief order on alternative grounds of a *Barder* event and/or vitiating element, the judge should rule first on the alleged vitiating element. If that ground fails, the court would then proceed to rule on the *Barder* event.

11.10.3 Procedure

Appeals and re-hearings are both governed by CCR Ord. 37 rule 1. If it is considered that the court made the wrong decision on the basis of the evidence in front of it, then this will be an appeal. However, if the court is wrong due to concealed evidence and material non-disclosure, then there should be a re-hearing.

First meeting checklist

CLIENT'S DETAILS	
1. Full name:	
2. Address:	
3. Correspondence address (if different):	
4. Email:	

5. Telephone:
    Home:
    Work:
    Mobile:	

6. Date of birth:	
7. Job title:	
8. Any relevant health issues?	
9. Any plans to cohabit or remarry?	
SPOUSE'S DETAILS	
1. Full name:	
2. Address:	
6. Date of birth:	
7. Job title:	
8. Any relevant health issues?	
9. Any plans to cohabit or remarry?	

DATE OF MARRIAGE, ETC	
1. Date of marriage:	
2. Date of commencement of cohabitation (check any periods of separation):	
3. Date of separation:	
CHILDREN	
1. Children of the marriage:	
(a) Full name:	
(b) Date of birth:	
(c) Name of school:	
(d) Fee paying? If so, how much?	
2. Any other children from previous relationships?	
(a) Full name:	
(b) Date of birth:	
(c) Name of school (if applicable):	
(d) Treated as child of the marriage?	
REASONS FOR BREAKDOWN OF MARRIAGE/GROUNDS FOR DIVORCE	
FINANCIAL CHECKLIST	
1. Property:	
(a) Matrimonial home:	
• Address:	
• Approximate value:	
• Outstanding mortgage(s):	
• Description – no. of bedrooms, etc:	

(b) Other properties: • Address: • Approximate value: • Outstanding mortgage(s): • Description – no. of bedrooms, etc:	
2. Assets, savings and investments:	
(a) Joint investments – seek approximate balance of each: • Bank and building society accounts: • Shares: • ISAs/PEPs: • Endowment policies: • Life insurance policies:	
(b) The client's own investments – seek approximate balance of each: • Bank and building society accounts: • Shares: • ISAs/PEPs: • Endowment policies: • Life insurance policies:	
(c) Spouse's own investments – seek approximate balance of each: • Bank and building society accounts: • Shares: • ISAs/PEPs: • Endowment policies: • Life insurance policies:	
3. Liabilities:	
(a) Joint liabilities – seek confirmation of approximate outstanding balances:	

• Loans:	
• Credit cards/store cards:	
• Hire purchase agreements:	
(b) The client's own liabilities:	
• Loans:	
• Credit cards/store cards:	
• Hire purchase agreements:	
(c) Spouse's own liabilities:	
• Loans:	
• Credit cards/store cards:	
• Hire purchase agreements:	
4. Cars and other chattels:	
Seek details of cars, boats, furniture, art, antiques, etc which may be of value	
5. Miscellaneous other interests:	
• Interests under family trusts – seek details of the trusts and history of any capital or income distributions:	
• Sharesave schemes or similar:	
• Share options:	
• Offshore assets or investments:	
• Tax deferment schemes:	
6. Business interests:	
Seek details of the following:	
• Name(s) of the business(es):	
• Names of partners/shareholders and percentage interests in the business(es):	
• Names of directors:	
• Details, including approximate value, of any property or other significant assets owned by the business(es):	
• An outline of the business's activities together with details of any trends upwards or downwards:	

• Details of the company's recent and projected profit: • Directors loan account balance?	
7. Pensions:	
Seek approximate details of the value of any pension provision: • Seek details of pension providers: • Seek details of any unusual schemes such as a SASS or **SIPP**:	
8. Income:	
• For those in employment, seek details of gross annual salary, net monthly income together with any additional benefits or bonuses: • For those who are self-employed, seek details of their total income and whether paid as salary, dividend or bonus: • Details of any investment income from shares, savings, etc: • Details of any income from properties: • Details of any state benefits: • Details of any maintenance payments, for example, from a previous divorce:	
9. Contributions:	
• Details of any inherited monies received. Seek details of how much received and when and how that money was utilised: • Details of any pre-marriage contributions or any assets built up post-separation:	
ADVICE GIVEN	
1. Jurisdictional issues:	
2. Advice with regards to divorce – grounds for divorce and procedure:	

3. Advice with regards to general terms of financial settlement, including overview of s.25 principles:	
4. Advice with regards to routes to achieving a financial settlement including the following: • Parties seeking to agree a settlement themselves: • Mediation: • Collaborative law: • Voluntarily disclosure and negotiations through solicitors: • Ancillary relief proceedings:	
5. Childcare arrangements including the following: • Residence: • Contact: • General principles under the Children Act 1989 including the 'no-order' principle: • Any particular considerations, such as schooling, leave to remove issues, etc?:	
6. Interim arrangements to address including the following: • Occupation of family home – need for application under FLA 1996?: • Injunctive relief with regards to disposal of assets?: • Use of joint accounts and credit cards: • Interim financial support: • Application for tax credits and other benefits: • Reduction in council tax due to single person occupancy:	

OTHER ISSUES TO ADDRESS	
1. Making a new will:	
2. Severing joint tenancy:	
3. Eligibility for public funding?:	
4. Advice given on costs, including hourly rates, frequency of billing and costs estimates. Will there be an issue as to funding?:	
NEXT STEPS	
1. Send terms of business/Rule 2 letter to client:	
2. Obtain marriage certificate or certified copy. Particularly important if parties were married abroad:	
3. Send letters of authority for client to sign if required for obtaining financial information such as pension valuations, duplicate bank account statements, etc:	
4. Send BR19 and B20 to client to sign for state pension illustrations:	
5. Conflict check carried out?:	
6. Money laundering regulations complied with? ID obtained from client?:	
7. Any other risk assessment issues to address?	

Ancillary relief checklist

Case Name ....

File No ....

ACTION	TASK COMPLETED?			DATE/OTHER COMMENTS
A. UPON ISSUE OF FORM A				
1. The client notified of dates set out in Form C?	Yes		No	
2. Draft Form E sent to client?	Yes		No	
3. Office copy entries obtained for all properties?	Yes		No	
4. Any properties in sole name of other spouse? If so, register notice or restriction?	Yes	No	N/A	
5. Letters of authority sent to client for information, such as pension transfer values?	Yes	No	N/A	
6. Form A served on mortgagee(s)?	Yes	No	N/A	
7. Form A served on pension trustees?	Yes	No	N/A	
8. Form A served in accordance with FPR 1991 (r.2.59(3) (variation of settlement/ s.37))?	Yes	No	N/A	
9. Application needed under MCA 1973, s.37?	Yes		No	
10. Application for maintenance pending suit required?	Yes		No	
11. Form P1 served upon pension trustees?	Yes	No	N/A	
12. Due date for filing and serving of Forms E:				

13. Form E served:		
14. Form E filed with the court:		
15. Due date for filing and service of questionnaire, statement of issues, chronology and Form G:		
16. Questionnaire, statement of issues, chronology, Form G and statement re: service of Form A filed?		
17. Questionnaire, statement of issues, chronology, Form G served?		
18. Has other party complied with pre-First Appointment requirements? If not, is application for penal notice required?	Yes	No

B. PREPARATION FOR FIRST APPOINTMENT

1. Client's instructions taken on other party's questionnaire?	Yes	No	
2. Do they object to answering any of the questions raised?	Yes	No	
3. Will valuations of any properties be required?	Yes	No	N/A
4. If so, have details of possible valuers been obtained (including CV, costs estimates, etc) and served on other side?	Yes	No	N/A
5. Draft letter of instruction to single joint expert sent to other side?	Yes	No	N/A
6. Is any other expert evidence required (e.g. accountancy evidence in respect of business or actuary in respect of pension?	Yes	No	N/A
7. If so, have details of possible accountants or actuaries been obtained (including CV, costs estimates, etc) and served on other side?	Yes	No	N/A

8. Form H prepared:				
9. If costs order sought at First Appointment, was it filed and served 24 hours before First Appointment?	Yes	No	N/A	
10. Counsel's availability for FDR obtained?	Yes	No	N/A	
C. POST-FIRST APPOINTMENT STEPS				
1. Replies to questionnaire due:				
2. Date for instructing experts as follows:- (a) Residential property: (b) Commercial property: (c) Business interests: (d) Pensions:				
3. Date joint expert reports are due: (a) Residential property: (b) Commercial property: (c) Business interests: (d) Pensions:				
4. Deadline for questions to be raised with joint expert: (a) Residential property: (b) Commercial property: (c) Business interests: (d) Pensions:				
5. Deadline for expert to respond to questions: (a) Residential property: (b) Commercial property: (c) Business interests: (d) Pensions:				
6. Replies to questionnaire filed and served?	Yes	No	N/A	
7. Replies to own questionnaire received from other side?	Yes	No	N/A	
8. Date of FDR hearing:				

9. Client notified of FDR hearing?	Yes		No		
10. Counsel reserved for FDR hearing?	Yes	No	N/A		
11. Client's instructions received to instruct counsel?	Yes		No		
12. Conference arranged with counsel prior to FDR hearing?	Yes	No	N/A		
D. PREPARATION FOR FDR HEARING					
1. Replies to questionnaire: (a) Have we fully replied to other side's questionnaire?	Yes		No		
(b) Has other spouse fully responded to our questionnaire?	Yes	No	N/A		
• Has application been made to court for penal notice?	Yes	No	N/A		
• Schedule of deficiencies/ supplemental questionnaire required?	Yes	No	N/A		
2. Expert evidence: (a) All reports received?	Yes	No	N/A		
(b) Questions raised with expert(s)?	Yes	No	N/A		
(c) Expert(s) responded to questions?	Yes	No	N/A		
3. Updating disclosure requested from client for FDR hearing?	Yes		No		
4. Updating disclosure requested from other spouse?	Yes		No		
5. Has client provided property particulars from local estate agents showing properties which are suitable for him/her and their spouse?	Yes	No	N/A		
6. Has client or his/her spouse provided evidence of borrowing capacity?	Yes	No	N/A		

7. Decree nisi pronounced?	Yes		No	
8. Double check Form A served upon pension trustees and/or mortgagees:	Yes	No	N/A	
9. Does respondent need to cross-apply in Form A if the applicant's Form A does not include a claim for pension sharing orders and has not been served upon pension trustees?	Yes	No	N/A	
10. If acting for applicant, have proposals for settlement been filed with the court at least seven days prior to FDR?	Yes	No	N/A	
11. Has bundle been prepared for the court for FDR in accordance with the President's Direction, FDA order or local practice?	Yes	No	N/A	
12. Counsel instructed for FDR?	Yes	No	N/A	
13. Form H prepared for FDR?				
14. Details of counsel's availability obtained for final hearing?	Yes	No	N/A	
E. PREPARATION FOR FINAL HEARING				
1. Once hearing date fixed: (a) Client advised of hearing date?	Yes		No	
(b) Counsel reserved for final hearing?	Yes	No	N/A	
2. FDR directions orders complied with? [list as applicable]				
3. Check decree nisi pronounced?	Yes		No	
4. Check Form A served upon pension trustees and mortgage trustees?	Yes	No	N/A	
5. Attendance of witnesses? Need to secure?	Yes	No	N/A	

6. Updating disclosure requested from client?	Yes		No	
7. Updating disclosure provided to spouse's solicitors?	Yes		No	
8. Updating disclosure requested from spouse's solicitors?	Yes		No	
9. Updating disclosure obtained from spouse's solicitors?	Yes		No	
10. Property particulars obtained in respect of suitable properties for client and his/her spouse?	Yes		No	
11. Draft trial index bundle agreed in accordance with President's Direction?	Yes		No	
12. Up-to-date schedule of assets, liabilities and income prepared and agreed?	Yes		No	
13. Pre-trial conference arranged with counsel?	Yes	No	N/A	
14. Counsel briefed and counsel's fees agreed with client? Payment on account of counsel's fees received?	Yes	No	N/A	
15. Applicant filed and served open proposals for settlement 14 days before hearing in accordance with FPR?	Yes		No	
16. Respondent filed and served open proposals in response seven days thereafter?	Yes		No	
17. Trial bundle filed with court?	Yes		No	
18. Form H1?				
19. If appropriate, has a template for the timing of witnesses and experts been prepared and agreed?	Yes	No	N/A	

F. POST-FINAL ORDER AND FILE CLOSING				
1. Has decree absolute been pronounced?	Yes		No	
2. Have the costs of the main suit been paid?	Yes		No	
3. Has final ancillary relief order been fully implemented?	Yes		No	
4. Have all notices/restrictions been removed in respect of properties?	Yes	No	N/A	
5. Have all disbursements been billed to client and paid?	Yes	No	N/A	
• Counsel				
• Accountant				
• Actuary				
• Surveyor – domestic property				
• Surveyor – commercial property				
• Other expert				
• Other disbursements (such as court fees, Land Registry fees, etc)				
6. Has client been billed in respect of all outstanding costs?	Yes		No	
7. Has final letter been sent to client, advising of closure of file and file destruction date, etc?	Yes		No	

First letter to client following first meeting

[*Address*]

Our Ref:

Your Ref:

Date:

Family Direct Fax

Dear [*name*],

It was a pleasure to meet you at our meeting on [*date*].

As agreed at our meeting, I am writing to you to confirm the advice that I gave at our meeting. Should you have any further questions about the advice set out in this letter, please contact me.

1. Divorce

You confirmed that you felt that your marriage had irretrievably broken down and that you wished to issue divorce proceedings. You did not feel that there was any realistic prospect of a reconciliation.

I am of the view that you have grounds to commence divorce proceedings on the basis of your [husband's/wife's] [unreasonable behaviour/adultery]. On the basis that you would wish to issue divorce proceedings yourself, would you please let me have the following:

(a) Some examples of your [husband's/wife's] [unreasonable behaviour/adultery]. They will need including in the petition for divorce. May I suggest that you provide me with some details of some recent examples as well as some general statements about your [husband's/wife's] [behaviour/adultery]. I can then incorporate them into a draft divorce petition.

[(b) I enclose a document called a statement of arrangements for children. This needs to be filed with the court at the same time as the petition. I suggest that you complete the form as far as you are able and return it to me in the envelope provided. If you would like some guidance upon completing the form, would you please let me know.]

(c) Would you please let me have a cheque for £[300] made payable to this firm to cover the court fee payable upon issuing the petition.

(d) Please also let me have your original marriage certificate as that needs to be lodged with the court at the same time as the petition. If you cannot find your original marriage certificate, please let me know and I can arrange for a certified copy to be obtained on your behalf.

Prior to issuing the petition, I would suggest that we first write to your [husband/wife] notifying them that you feel that the marriage has broken down and that you would wish for there to be a divorce. I therefore attach a draft letter for your approval. Please confirm that you are happy for it to be sent out as drafted.

[2. **Arrangements for the Children**

I would hope that you and your [husband/wife] are able to agree arrangements for the children without the involvement of the court. As you and your [husband/wife] both have parental responsibility for the children, you should consult each other in respect of major decisions regarding their upbringing.

In accordance with the principles under the Children Act, the court will not automatically make any orders regarding arrangements for the children unless either you or your [husband/wife] make a specific application to the court at any time. The most common form of application under the Children Act is for a contact order if an agreement cannot be reached over arrangements for how often the children see [you/your husband/ your wife].]

3. **Financial Consequences of Divorce**

As I explained at our meeting, one of the most difficult aspects of divorce is resolving financial matters arising. The law is one of discretion and therefore it is impossible to say at the outset what the eventual settlement will be. All a solicitor can do at this stage is to advise upon the range of potential outcomes.

Before I can provide you with specific advice, I will need financial disclosure from you and from your [husband/wife]. Once we have dealt with the issue of divorce proceedings, I will write to you further on the issue of financial disclosure.

The law governing the division of assets on divorce is set out in Section 25 Matrimonial Causes Act 1973. It is a checklist under which the court will first consider the children's welfare. Thereafter, the court will take into account such factors as your available assets, income, resources and earning capacities and they are balanced against your respective needs. The court will also take into account your ages, the length of the marriage, the standard of living you enjoyed during the marriage and your contributions. In only extreme cases will the court take into account any bad behaviour or 'conduct'.

Following on from the landmark divorce case of *White* v. *White* in 2000, the court also has to consider issues of fairness and the 'yardstick of equality'. Following on from subsequent important cases, the court also takes into account issues of needs, compensation and sharing.

I appreciate that it may be difficult to apply those rather uncertain principles to your own circumstances; however, once I have further financial information from you and your [husband/wife], I would hope to be in a position to provide you with some more specific advice.

There are various ways in which we can try and negotiate a financial settlement with your [husband/wife]. We discussed these at our meeting, but to assist you in considering the options I enclose leaflets in respect of mediation and collaborative law. I would welcome discussing these options with you again, although if you feel uncomfortable discussing matters directly with your [husband/wife], we can deal with matters in a more traditional manner through solicitors.

4. **Interim Arrangements**

We may need to give early consideration to the level of support that you are providing for your wife/the level of support being provided for you by your [husband/wife]. Once I have details of your respective incomes, I will then be able to provide you with some advice regarding an appropriate level of interim support [that you should be paying to your [husband/wife] [and children]/that you should be receiving from your [husband/wife] [for you and the children]].

I would hope that we can agree an appropriate level of interim support. If an agreement cannot be reached, then your [[husband/wife] may make an application to the court for maintenance pending suit/you may need to consider an application to the court for maintenance pending suit]. I do, however, hope that is unnecessary.

5. Making a Will/Severing the Joint Tenancy

You may wish to consider reviewing your will now that you and your [wife/husband] have separated. I should, however, explain that if you prepare a new will which excludes your [husband/wife], then they could potentially bring a claim against your estate under the Inheritance Act. In those circumstances, you may prefer to delay making a new will until you have finalised your financial settlement arising upon your divorce. I would welcome discussing the pros and cons of this issue with you in due course.

[At present you own your family home as joint tenants with your [husband/wife]. Accordingly, if you were to pre-decease your husband/wife, your share would automatically pass to your [husband/wife], regardless of any contrary provision in your will. You may wish to consider severing the joint tenancy so that you hold the property as tenants in common. If that were to happen, your half share in the property would pass in accordance with any provision in your will.

Again, you need to consider the pros and cons of severing the joint tenancy. If you sever the joint tenancy and if your [husband/wife] pre-deceased you, then their share would not automatically pass to you but would rather pass in accordance with their will.]

6. Terms of Business

Finally, I enclose the firm's terms of business. I would ask that you read the letter carefully as it sets out an agreement between you and this firm regarding our terms of business and in particular in respect of fees.

I should be grateful if you would acknowledge your acceptance of our terms of business by signing the enclosed form of acceptance and returning it to me in the enclosed envelope.

Yours sincerely,

APPENDIX 4

First letter to other spouse following first meeting

[*Address*]   **Our Ref:**

Your Ref:

Date:

Family Direct Fax

Dear [*name*],

I have been instructed by your [husband/wife] in respect of your marriage. [*name*] has sadly come to the conclusion that your marriage has irretrievably broken down and [he/she] would wish to seek a divorce.

It is [*name*]'s wish that the divorce can be dealt with as quickly and as amicably as possible and with minimum legal cost. In view of the contents of this letter, I would ask that you instruct a solicitor as soon as possible. Would they please contact me so that we can discuss how best to progress matters.

[*name*] would wish to issue a petition for divorce and this is an issue that I would welcome discussing with your solicitor. Likewise, [*name*] has asked that I raise the issue of [*issues here can be listed if they are particularly pressing, such as contact, interim support, occupation of the family home, etc*].

I would ask that either you or your solicitor contact me within 14 days of the date of this letter. I also enclose a copy of this letter for you to pass on to your solicitor.

Yours sincerely,

Disclosure schedule (voluntary disclosure)

IN THE [*name*] COUNTY COURT

No. of matter: [*number*]

BETWEEN

[*name*]

Petitioner

and

[*name*]

Respondent

[HUSBAND/WIFE]'S DISCLOSURE SCHEDULE
AS AT [*date*]

A. PROPERTY

1. **[*address of property*] (owned in joint names of Husband and Wife)**

   Approximate value based upon estate agents' valuations **(exhibit 1)**: £[*amount*]

   Less:

   Outstanding mortgage with [*lender*], account no. [*number*] **(exhibit 2)**

   Outstanding balance as at [*date*]: (£[*amount*])

   Costs of sale estimated at [2]%: (£[*amount*])

TOTAL NET EQUITY: £[*amount*]

B. BANK ACCOUNTS AND INVESTMENTS

1. Current account with [*bank/building society*], account no. [*number*].

   Balance as at [*date*]: £[*amount*]

   Statements for [*date*] to [*date*] **(exhibit 3)**

2. Savings account with [*bank/building society*], account no. [*number*].

   Balance as at [*date*]: £[*amount*]

   Copy passbook attached **(exhibit 4)**

3. [*number*] shares in [*company*].

    Based on price of £[*amount*] per share as at [*date*] :   £[*amount*]

    See latest dividend counterfoil attached **(exhibit 5)**

4. Endowment policy with [*insurer*], policy no. [*number*].

    Held in the sole name of [*husband's/wife's name*], but written on the lives of [*husband's* and *wife's names*].

    Surrender value as at [*date*]:   £[*amount*]

    See surrender value statement from [*insurer*] dated [*date*] **(exhibit 6)**

C. PENSION PROVISION

Pension policy held with [*pension provider*], policy no. [*number*].

Cash equivalent transfer value as at [*date*]:   £[*amount*]

See CETV statement from [*pension provider*] dated [*date*] **(exhibit 6)**

D. INCOME

[*Husband/wife*] is employed by [*company*] and earns a gross annual salary of £[*amount*].

He does not receive any other benefits.

His net monthly salary after tax and national insurance is: £[*amount*]

See P60 for year to 5 April [*year*] together with last three payslips for [*month*], [*month*] and [*month*] [*year*]**(exhibit 7)**

Form A

Notice of intention to proceed with an Application for Ancillary Relief

IN THE [*name*] COUNTY COURT	

Case No. *Always quote this*	[*number*]
Applicant's Solicitor's reference	[*reference*]
Respondent's Solicitor's reference	[*reference*]

(*delete as appropriate)

Respondents (Solicitor(s)) name and address

Respondent's Solicitors' Details Postcode (Name and address of Respondent(s)/Respondent(s) Solicitors)

Between

[*name*]   **(Petitioner)**

[*name*]   **(Respondent)**

TAKE NOTICE that the Applicant intends **to apply** to the Court for

☐ an order for maintenance pending suit or outcome of proceedings

☑ a periodical payments order

☑ a secured provision order

☑ a lump sum order

☑ a property adjustment order *(please provide address)*

☑ A pension sharing order or a pension attachment order

[*address*] [*further address if appropriate*]

The Respondent's pensions with [*company*], policy number [*number*] and [*company*], policy number [*number*]

If an application is made for any periodical payments or secured periodical payments for children:

• and there is a written agreement made before 5 April 1993 about maintenance for the benefit of children,
tick this box   ☐

- and there is a written agreement made on or after 5 April 1993 about maintenance for the benefit of children,

  tick this box ☐

- but there is no agreement, tick any of the boxes below to show if you are applying for payment:

  ☐ for a stepchild or stepchildren

  ☐ in addition to child support maintenance already paid under a Child Support Agency assessment

  ☐ to meet expenses arising from a child's disability

  ☑ to meet expenses incurred by a child in being educated or training for work

  ☐ when either the child **or** the person with care of the child **or** the absent parent of the child is not habitually resident in the United Kingdom

  ☐ Other (please state)

Signed: Dated:

[Applicant/Solicitor for the Applicant]

The court office at [*name*] County Court is open between 10:00am and 4:00pm Monday to Friday. When corresponding with the court, please address forms or letters to the Court Manager and quote the case number. If you do not do so, your correspondence may be returned.

Schedule of expenditure

ITEM OF EXPENDITURE	MONTHLY	ANNUAL
A. HOUSING		
Mortgage/rent:		
Council tax:		
Buildings insurance:		
Contents insurance:		
Repairing/replacing furniture and electrical goods:		
Gas:		
Electricity:		
Oil:		
Water rates:		
Home telephone:		
TV licence:		
Broadband:		
Sky/digital TV:		
B. OTHER HOUSEHOLD EXPENSES		
Mobile telephone:		
Dry cleaning:		
Cleaner:		
Window cleaner:		
Gardener:		
Food/supermarket shopping:		
Lunches at work:		
C. TRANSPORTATION		
Car tax:		
Car insurance:		
Petrol and oil:		
Maintenance, servicing and MOT:		

AA/RAC:		
Car loan/finance/lease/hire purchase payments:		
Depreciation:		
D. PERSONAL EXPENDITURE AND LEISURE		
Clothes:		
Shoes:		
Accessories		
Hairdressing:		
Beautician:		
Cosmetics and toiletries:		
Opticians:		
Dentistry:		
Medical insurance:		
Entertainment (meals out, theatre, cinema, etc):		
Books/CDs/DVDs:		
Gym:		
Holidays:		
Christmas expenses:		
Pension contributions:		
Endowment premiums/savings plans:		
E. EXPENSES FOR CHILDREN		
School fees:		
Nanny:		
Babysitting:		
Clothes:		
Shoes:		
Sports kit:		
School uniform:		
School trips:		
Extra tuition:		
Private health:		
Holidays:		
Entertainment:		
Pocket money:		

Statement of issues

Case No.[*number*]

IN THE [*name*] COUNTY COURT

BETWEEN:

[*name*]

Applicant

and

[*name*]

Respondent

APPLICANT'S STATEMENT OF ISSUES
FOR FIRST APPOINTMENT

[Text below used by way of example – complete details as appropriate]

	APPLICANT WIFE'S POSITION	**RESPONDENT HUSBAND'S POSITION**
A. MATRIMONIAL HOME		
1. Sale or Transfer	The wife seeks a transfer of the property into her sole name. She believes that the property is appropriate for her and children. She also seeks a discharge of the mortgage by the husband.	The husband seeks a sale of the property with an equal division of the net proceeds of sale between the parties. The husband states that the property is far too large for the wife's needs.
2. Value of the Property	The wife estimates the property to be worth £300,000, but accepts that a valuation will be required if the value cannot be agreed.	The husband believes that the property is worth £350,000, but suggests that a valuation is unnecessary if the property is to be sold.
B. INCOME AND PERIODICAL PAYMENTS		
1. Husband's Income	The wife believes that the husband's income should	The husband believes that he will not receive a bonus this

	be calculated by reference to his historical bonus payments. She believes that his historical income will be maintained and may increase in the future.	year, nor does he anticipate receiving any bonuses in the foreseeable future. His future income should be calculated by reference to his base salary.
2. The Wife's Earning Capacity	The wife states that she does not have an earning capacity which she can exercise at the moment as she has the care of young children of the family. In any event, the wife does not have any relevant qualifications which she could use in generating an income.	The husband's position is that the children are now of an age which means the wife can at least work part time or re-train with a view to working full time within the next two to three years. The husband believes that the wife could be financially self-sufficient within a maximum of five years.
3. Term and Quantum of Maintenance	In view of the length of the marriage, the ages of the children, the husband's historical income and the wife's lack of earning capacity, the wife maintains that it is a suitable case for joint lives periodical payments. Maintenance should be calculated by reference to the husband's historical income.	The husband's position is that the wife will be able to be fully self-sufficient in the foreseeable future. Furthermore, in light of the husband's dramatically reduced income, periodical payments can only be made at a modest level. The husband would propose that such maintenance is paid for a term of three years and that there should be a s.28(1A) bar.
C. PENSION PROVISION	The wife would propose that the pension provision is shared equally to provide equality of income from age 60 onwards.	The husband's position is that pension provision should be shared equally to provide equality of transfer values based upon the latest valuations obtained.
D. CONTRIBUTIONS	The wife inherited £30,000 from her grandfather five years ago. The wife's position is that this money should be ringfenced and excluded from any calculation of the overall assets of the marriage.	The husband believes that it is inappropriate for the wife's inherited monies to be ringfenced. Such money should be utilised by the wife towards meeting her future housing needs.

Letter instructing accountant to value a family business

[*Address*]   **Our Ref:**

                                               Your Ref:

                                               Date:

                                               Family Direct Fax

Dear Sirs,

Re: [*name of husband*] and [*name of wife*]
          [*name*] County Court – Case No. [*number*]

You are instructed to prepare a report as a single joint expert for divorce proceedings ongoing in [*name*] County Court.

[*firm*] solicitors act for [*name*] and our details are as follows:

[*name and address of firm*]

[*firm*] solicitors act for [*name*] and their details are as follows:

[*name and address of firm*]

Nature of your Instructions

[You are being instructed pursuant to an order of District Judge [*name*] sitting at [*name*] County Court on [*date*]. The order provides as follows:

[*insert wording of order of the court*]]

or

[Although there are ongoing divorce proceedings, neither Mr and Mrs [*name*] have issued ancillary relief proceedings. Accordingly, you are being instructed to prepare your report to assist the parties in negotiating a settlement.

   In your report, you are specifically asked to deal with the following:]

[NOTE: *The exact questions to be put to the accountant will vary from case to case. The questions will depend upon whether one or both parties have an interest in the business and whether it is a limited company, partnership, LLP or sole trader. The following questions assume that the business is a limited company and both parties have shares in that business. Where the terms of the order made by the court do not specify what is to be addressed by the accountant, then the following details should be included in the letter of instruction*]

(a)   Please provide your opinion of the value of [*company*] Limited.
(b)   Please provide your opinion as to the value of the interests of Mr and Mrs [*name*] in [*company*] Limited.

(c)   To enable us to ascertain the net value of the interests of Mr and Mrs [*name*] in [*company*] Limited, please provide your opinion of the capital gains tax which would be payable by them if they were to sell their shares in the business during the present financial year. You are to assume that neither of them has used their capital gains tax allowances.

(d)   Please provide your views on liquidity as follows:

   (i)   Please confirm the various routes by which money can be withdrawn from the business, to include the taxation consequences of each route.

   (ii)   In each case, please confirm the maximum sum which could be withdrawn within the next six months.

   (iii)   Please also provide your opinion of the maximum sum or sums which could be withdrawn from the company over the next five years.

   (iv)   Please provide your opinion as to the maintainable future income which Mr [*name*] could draw from the business, assuming Mrs [*name*] were to have no further involvement with the business.

   (v)   Please also address any other issues in respect of any of the businesses which you may feel are relevant to the present proceedings.

Background Information

(a)   Mr [*name*] was born on [*date*].

(b)   Mrs [*name*] was born on [*date*].

(c)   The parties married on [*name*] and a petition for divorce was issued by [Mr/Mrs] [*name*] on [*date*]. Decree nisi was pronounced on [*date*]. Decree absolute has not yet been pronounced.

(d)   Mr and Mrs [*name*] run a business called [*company*] which specialises in [*provide brief description*].

(e)   The shares in [*company*] are held as follows:
        [*List shareholders, number of shares they hold and percentage shareholding. If there are different categories/classes of share, provide details*]

(f)   The directors of the company are as follows:
        [*List names*]

(g)   The company secretary is [*name*].

Enclosures

The following documents are enclosed:

(a)   [*List documents to be enclosed with the letter – may simply be limited to company accounts*]

Requests for Further Information

We would suggest that requests for information should be made as follows:

(a)   To Mr [*name*] direct whose contact details are as follows: [*provide details*]

(b)   To the company's accountant, whose contact details are as follows: [*provide details*]

(c)   To the company's financial director, whose contact details are as follows: [*provide details*]

(d)   As Mrs [*name*] is involved in the business, we would suggest that you would wish to discuss matters with her. Her contact details are as follows: [*provide details*]

As you are being instructed as a single joint expert, we would, however, ask that any request for information is copied in to both sets of instructing solicitors.

Civil Procedure Rules 1998

The court rules provide that your report must contain the following:

(a) The report must be addressed to the [*name*] County Court and not to [*name of solicitors*] or [*name of other solicitors*].

(b) The report must contain details of your qualifications and also details of any literature or any other material which you have relied upon in making your report.

(c) The report must contain a statement that you understand your duty to the court and that you have complied with that duty.

(d) The report must also contain a statement setting out the substance of all material instructions which you will be given and must also set out the facts and the instructions given to you which are material to the opinions expressed in your report.

(e) The report must be verified by a statement of truth as follows:

> 'I confirm that insofar as the facts I have stated in my report are within my own knowledge, I have made clear which they are and I believe them to be true and that the opinions I have expressed represent my true and complete professional opinion.'

Costs

Prior to the preparation of your report or carrying out any preliminary work, we should be grateful if you would provide us with an estimate of your costs. Once they are agreed, we would ask that you prepare your report.

Upon completion of your report, would you please invoice both [*name of solicitors*] and [*name of other solicitors*] for one half of your costs respectively.

Yours faithfully,   Yours faithfully,

[*Name of Solicitors*]   [*Name of Solicitors*]
Solicitors for Mr [*name*]   Solicitors for Mrs [*name*]

Letter instructing pensions expert

[*Address*]   **Our Ref:**

                                                      Your Ref:

                                                      Date:

                                                      Family Direct Fax

Dear Sirs,

Re: **[*Name of husband*] and [*Name of wife*]**
       [*name*] County Court – Case No. [*number*]

You are instructed to prepare a report as a single joint expert for divorce proceedings ongoing in [*name*] County Court.

[*firm*] solicitors act for [*name*] and our details are as follows:
[*name and address of firm*]

[*firm*] solicitors act for [*name*] and their details are as follows:
[*name and address of firm*]

Nature of your Instructions
[You are being instructed pursuant to an order of District Judge [*name*] sitting at [*name*] County Court on [*date*]. The order provides as follows:
[*insert wording of order of the court*]]

or

[Although there are ongoing divorce proceedings, ancillary relief proceedings have not been issued by either party. Accordingly, you are being instructed to prepare a report to assist the parties in reaching a negotiated settlement. We would ask that you provide your report by [*date*]. If you cannot produce your report by that date, would you please let both sets of instructing solicitors know as soon as possible.]

   In your report, you are specifically being instructed to advise upon the following:

(a)   Please provide your view as to how Mr [*name*]'s pension provision is to be shared to achieve equality of pension income for Mr and Mrs [*name*] assuming retirement at each of the following ages:

- 55
- 60
- 65

(b)   You are asked to provide your answer to question (a) above based upon the up-to date-cash equivalent transfer values of Mr and Mrs [*name*]'s pension provision and assuming no further contributions are made to the respective pensions.

(c)   In the alternative, you are asked to provide your answer to question (a) above assuming contributions continue to be made to Mr and Mrs [*name*]'s pensions at the present rate and based upon assumed inflationary increases and/or continued years of service up until each of the ages set out above.

(d) In each case, please provide your opinion assuming either the maximum tax free lump sum is drawn down upon retirement, or assuming no tax free lump sum is drawn upon retirement.

(e) Please confirm the earliest stage at which either Mr or Mrs [*name*] will be able to draw benefits under each of the respective pensions.

(f) Please provide your opinion as to whether the cash equivalent transfer values provided in respect of each of the pensions provides a realistic and accurate statement of each pension fund. If you feel that any of the cash equivalent transfer values are inaccurate, would you please explain your reasoning and provide your estimate of the realistic present transfer value.

Background Information

(a) Mr [*name*] was born on [*date*] and is employed as a [*occupation*].

(b) Mrs [*name*] was born on [*date*] and is employed as a [*occupation*].

(c) They married on [*date*]. Mr/Mrs [*name*]'s petition was issued on [*date*] and decree nisi of divorce was pronounced on [*date*]. Decree absolute of divorce has not yet been pronounced.

Available Pension Information

(a) Mr [*name*]'s pension
[*List and attach all of the information which you have available in respect of the husband's pension. It would be sensible to attach the relevant pages from Form E, any pension information which was exhibited to Form E or which has otherwise been provided and any completed Form P information*]

(b) Mrs [*name*]'s pension

[*Attach same relevant information*]

Requests for Further Information

We assume that it may be necessary for you to seek further information from both Mr and Mrs [*name*] in respect of their pensions and we would ask that you let us have your requests for information as soon as possible.

Civil Procedure Rules 1998

The court rules provide that your report must contain the following:

(a) The report must be addressed to the [*name*] County Court and not to [*name of solicitors*] or [*name of other solicitors*].

(b) The report must contain details of your qualifications and also details of any literature or any other material which you have relied upon in making your report.

(c) The report must contain a statement that you understand your duty to the court and that you have complied with that duty.

(d) The report must also contain a statement setting out the substance of all material instructions which you will be given and must also set out the facts and the instructions given to you which are material to the opinions expressed in your report.

(e) The report must be verified by a statement of truth as follows:

'I confirm that insofar as the facts I have stated in my report are within my own knowledge, I have made clear which they are and I believe them to be true and that the opinions I have expressed represent my true and complete professional opinion.'

Costs

Prior to the preparation of your report or carrying out any preliminary work, we should be grateful if you would provide us with an estimate of your costs. Once they are agreed, we would ask that you prepare your report.

Upon completion of your report, would you please invoice both [*name of solicitors*] and [*name of other solicitors*] for one half of your costs respectively.

Yours faithfully,   Yours faithfully,

[*Name of Solicitors*]   [*Name of solicitors*]
Solicitors for Mr [*name*]   Solicitors for Mrs [*name*]

Letter instructing a surveyor

[*Address*]   **Our Ref:**

Your Ref:

Date:

Family Direct Fax

Dear Sirs,

Re: [*Name of husband*] and [*Name of wife*]
      [*name*] **County Court – Case No.** [*number*]

You are instructed to prepare a report as a single joint expert for divorce proceedings ongoing in [*name*] County Court.

[*firm*] solicitors act for [*name*] and our details are as follows:
[*name and address of firm*]

[*firm*] solicitors act for [*name*] and their details are as follows:
[*name and address of firm*]

Nature of your Instructions

[You are being instructed pursuant to an order of District Judge [*name*] sitting at [*name*] County Court on [*date*]. The order provides as follows:
[*insert wording of order of the court*]

or

Although there are ongoing divorce proceedings, neither Mr and Mrs [*name*] have issued ancillary relief proceedings. Accordingly, you are being instructed to prepare your report to assist the parties in negotiating a settlement.

You are asked to prepare a report providing your opinion on the open market value of the property at [*date*], assuming the property is marketed over a reasonable period of time and a sale takes place between a willing vendor and a willing purchaser.]

[In addition to providing your opinion as to the open market value of the property, you are also asked to comment upon the following:

(i)   Whether you believe there is any work which could be carried out to enhance the value of the property such as remedial, decorative or more substantive work. If so, you are asked to provide your opinion as to the open market value of the property once such work has been completed. Please also provide your estimate of the cost of carrying out such work.

(ii)   Whether planning permission could be obtained to enhance the value of the property in any way. By way of example, planning permission to extend the property or to build another property in the grounds of the house. If you think that planning permission may be available, we should be grateful if you would provide your advice as to the most appropriate planning permission which should be sought and the impact that such planning permission would have upon the value of the property.]

Arrangements for Viewing the Property

The property is presently occupied by [*name*]. Would you please contact [him/her] direct on [*contact number*] to arrange an appointment to view the property.

[[*name*] would also wish to be in attendance when the inspection is carried out. Would you please also telephone [*name*] on [*contact number*] to arrange an appropriate time to view the property.]

Civil Procedure Rules 1998

The court rules provide that your report must contain the following:

(a) The report must be addressed to the [*name*] County Court and not to [*name of solicitors*] or [*name of other solicitors*].
(b) The report must contain details of your qualifications and also details of any literature or any other material which you have relied upon in making your report.
(c) The report must contain a statement that you understand your duty to the court and that you have complied with that duty.
(d) The report must also contain a statement setting out the substance of all material instructions which you will be given and must also set out the facts and the instructions given to you which are material to the opinions expressed in your report.
(e) The report must be verified by a statement of truth as follows:

> 'I confirm that insofar as the facts I have stated in my report are within my own knowledge, I have made clear which they are and I believe them to be true and that the opinions I have expressed represent my true and complete professional opinion.'

Costs

Prior to the preparation of your report or carrying out any preliminary work, we should be grateful if you would provide us with an estimate of your costs. Once they are agreed, we would ask that you prepare your report.

Upon completion of your report, would you please invoice both [*name of solicitors*] and [*name of other solicitors*] for one half of your costs respectively.

Yours faithfully,   Yours faithfully,

[*Name of Solicitors*]   [*Name of Solicitors*]
Solicitors for Mr [*name*]   Solicitors for Mrs [*name*]

APPENDIX 12

First Appointment order

Case No.

IN THE [*name*] COUNTY COURT

BETWEEN:

[*name*]

Applicant

and

[*name*]

Respondent

ORDER FOR FIRST APPOINTMENT

BEFORE District Judge [*name*] sitting in Chambers on [*date*]

UPON HEARING the solicitor for the Applicant and solicitor for the Respondent:

BY CONSENT IT IS ORDERED that:

1. The Respondent do respond to the Applicant's questionnaire dated [*date*], as amended by the District Judge, by 4:00pm on [*date*].
2. The Applicant do respond to the Respondent's questionnaire dated [*date*], as amended by the District Judge, by 4:00pm on [*date*].
3. [*surveyor's name*] shall be instructed to prepare a valuation of the former matrimonial home at [*address*] on the following basis:

    (a) The letter of instruction shall be agreed between the parties' solicitors and delivered to [*provide details*] by 4:00pm on [*date*].
    (b) [*surveyor's name*] shall file and serve their report by 4:00pm on [*date*].
    (c) The parties may raise questions with [*surveyor's name*] in respect of their report. Such questions must be served upon [*surveyor's name*] by 4:00pm on [*date*].
    (d) [*surveyor's name*] shall file and serve their replies to the parties' questions by 4:00pm on [*date*].

[Similar provisions can be included in respect of a jointly instructed accountant or actuary]

[The following provision can be used where either party is instructing their own expert, for example, in respect of a business valuation]

[4. The parties shall have leave to adduce expert evidence in respect of [*company*] Limited as follows:

    (a) The Applicant shall have leave to instruct [*accountants*]. Their report is to be filed and served by 4:00pm on [*date*].

    (b) The Respondent shall have leave to instruct [*accountants*]. Their report is to be filed and served by 4:00pm on [*date*].

    (c) The experts shall meet by 4:00pm on [*date*] with a view to drawing up a schedule of matters agreed and matters which are not agreed.

    (d) Such schedule shall be filed and served by 4:00pm on [*date*].]

5.   By 4:00pm on [*date*] the Applicant and Respondent shall file and serve narrative sworn statements limited to the following issues:

    (a) Conduct.

    (b) Contributions.

    (c) The relevant factors as contained in the checklist in s.25 Matrimonial Causes Act 1973 [*or as appropriate*]

6.   The matter to be listed for a Financial Dispute Resolution hearing with a time estimate of [*number*] hours [reserved to District Judge [*name*] if available] [at [*time*] o'clock on [*date*]] [on the first available date after [*date*], to be listed subject to counsels' availability. Counsels' clerks to file counsels' availability with the court no later than 4:00pm on [*date*]]. The parties are to attend at court no later than one hour before the time listed for the FDR hearing for the purpose of negotiation and discussion.

7.   Not less than seven days before the Financial Dispute Resolution hearing, the Applicant's solicitors shall file with the court a bundle, to be agreed if possible, in compliance with the President's Direction dated 27 July 2006 [*or as appropriate in accordance with local practice*].

8.   Costs in the case.

Notice of application for further directions

No. of matter: [*number*]

IN THE [*name*] COUNTY COURT

BETWEEN

[*name*]

Petitioner/Applicant

and

[*name*]

Respondent

NOTICE OF APPLICATION

TAKE NOTICE that the Applicant intends to apply to the District Judge sitting in Chambers on the [*day*] day of [*month*] 20[*year*], at [*time*] o'clock for an order in the following terms:

[The following are examples of applications which are relatively commonly made. The exact directions to be requested in any given case will depend upon the appropriate circumstances. The most common time to seek additional directions may be following on from the First Appointment once replies to questionnaire and expert evidence have been provided, or where it is decided that expert evidence is required if such issues were not apparent at the First Appointment]

[[1.]	The Respondent do file with the court and serve upon the Applicant's solicitors replies to the Applicant's supplemental questionnaire dated [*date*] (a copy of which is attached hereto) within 28 days of the date of this Order.]

[[2.]	The Applicant be granted leave to adduce the report of [*accountant*] in respect of [*company*] Limited dated [*date*].]

[[3.]	The parties be granted leave to instruct an accountant as a single joint expert to prepare and file a report in respect of [*company*] Limited on the following basis:

(a)	The terms of the instruction are to be given in accordance with the attached draft letter of instruction.

(b)	[*Name of proposed expert*] is to be instructed as a single joint expert. A copy of their CV and costs estimate is attached.

(c)	Such report is to be filed with the court and served upon the parties within 56 days of the date of the Order.]

[[4.]	The Respondent do serve upon [*name of expert*] and the Applicant's solicitors, the additional information requested by [*name of expert*] and set out in the attached schedule dated [*date*], such information to be served within 28 days of the date of this Order.]

[[5.]	The Respondent shall prepare a Scott Schedule setting out the items which he would wish to retain from the former matrimonial home at [*address*] and shall serve the Scott Schedule upon the Applicant's solicitors within 28 days of the date of this Order. The Applicant shall provide her comments upon the Scott Schedule, setting out the items that she would wish to retain from the matrimonial home, such revised schedule shall be served upon the Respondent's solicitors 28 days thereafter.]

[[6.] *[Such further directions as may be appropriate*]]

[[7.] The Respondent do pay the Applicant's costs of this application, to be summarily assessed.] *[An application for costs may not be appropriate – it will depend upon the specific applications being sought*]

The estimated length of the hearing of this application is *[number]* minutes.

Counsel will/will not be appearing on behalf of the Applicant.

Dated this *[day]* day of *[month]* 20*[year]*

....
[Solicitors for the Applicant]

To the District Judge
to the above named Respondent and his/her solicitors

Address all communications for the Court to: *[name and/or address]* (or to the Divorce Registry, First Avenue House, 42–49 High Holborn, London WC1V 6NP) quoting the number in the top right hand corner of this form. The Court Office is open from 10:00 am till 4:00 pm (4:30 pm at the Divorce Registry) on Mondays to Fridays only.

Notice of application for maintenance pending suit/interim periodical payments

No. of matter: [*number*]

IN THE [*name*] COUNTY COURT

BETWEEN

[*name*]

Petitioner/Applicant

and

[*name*]

Respondent

NOTICE OF APPLICATION

TAKE NOTICE that the Applicant intends to apply to the District Judge sitting in Chambers on the [*day*] day of [*month*] 20[*year*], at [*time*] o'clock for an order in the following terms:

1. The Respondent do pay maintenance pending suit and thereafter interim periodical payments to the Applicant, such payments to be made calendar monthly in advance by standing order.
2. The Respondent do pay to the Applicant arrears of maintenance pending suit backdated to [*date*], such arrears to be paid by the Respondent to the Applicant within 14 days of the date of the order.
3. The Respondent do pay the Applicant's costs of this application, to be summarily assessed.

The estimated length of the hearing of this application is [*number*] minutes.

Counsel will/will not be appearing on behalf of the Applicant.

Dated this [*day*] day of [*month*] 20[*year*]

....

[Solicitors for the Applicant]

To the District Judge
to the above named Respondent and his/her solicitors

Address all communications for the Court to: [*name and/or address*] (or to the Divorce Registry, First Avenue House, 42–49 High Holborn, London WC1V 6NP) quoting the number in the top right hand corner of this form. The Court Office is open from 10:00 am till 4:00 pm (4:30 pm at the Divorce Registry) on Mondays to Fridays only.

Notice of application for penal notice

No. of matter: [*number*]

IN THE [*name*] COUNTY COURT

BETWEEN

[*name*]

Petitioner/Applicant

and

[*name*]

Respondent

NOTICE OF APPLICATION

TAKE NOTICE that the Applicant intends to apply to the District Judge sitting in Chambers on the [*day*] day of [*month*] 20[*year*], at [*time*] o'clock for an order in the following terms:

1. The Respondent do file with the court and serve upon the Applicant's solicitors his [*Form E/Replies to Questionnaire/or as appropriate*] within seven days of personal service of this Order upon him.
2. A Penal Notice be attached to paragraph 1 of the Order.
3. The Respondent do pay the Applicant's costs of this application, to be summarily assessed.

The estimated length of the hearing of this application is [*number*] minutes.

Counsel will/will not be appearing on behalf of the Applicant.

Dated this [*day*] day of [*month*] 20[*year*]

....
[Solicitors for the Applicant]

To the District Judge
to the above named Respondent and his/her solicitors

Address all communications for the Court to: [*name and/or address*] (or to the Divorce Registry, First Avenue House, 42-49 High Holborn, London WC1V 6NP) quoting the number in the top right hand corner of this form. The Court Office is open from 10:00 am till 4:00 pm (4:30 pm at the Divorce Registry) on Mondays to Fridays only.

Notice of application for an adjournment

No. of matter: [*number*]

IN THE [*name*] COUNTY COURT

BETWEEN

[*name*]

Petitioner/Applicant

and

[*name*]

Respondent

NOTICE OF APPLICATION

TAKE NOTICE that the Applicant/Petitioner and the Respondent intend to apply BY CONSENT to the District Judge sitting in Chambers for an order in the following terms:

1. The FDR hearing listed at [*time*] o'clock on [*date*] be adjourned and re-listed on the first available date after [*date*], such hearing to be re-listed subject to counsels' availability, the parties to lodge with the court details of counsels' availability within seven days of the date of this Order.
2. The costs of this application to be in the case.

Dated this [*day*] day of [*month*] 20[*year*]

....
[Solicitors for the Applicant]

....
[Solicitors for the Respondent]

To the District Judge

Address all communications for the Court to: [*name and/or address*] (or to the Divorce Registry, First Avenue House, 42–49 High Holborn, London WC1V 6NP) quoting the number in the top right hand corner of this form. The Court Office is open from 10:00 am till 4:00 pm (4:30 pm at the Divorce Registry) on Mondays to Fridays only.

183

Offer letter

[*Address*]

Our Ref:

Your Ref:

Date:

Family Direct Fax

WITHOUT PREJUDICE

Dear Sirs,

Re: Mr and Mrs [*name*]

Mr [*name*] wishes to put forward proposals for settlement with a view to avoiding potentially significant future costs. He is hopeful that an agreement can be reached prior to the forthcoming FDR and therefore the costs of that hearing could be avoided.

Now that you have Mr [*name*]'s replies to questionnaire and expert evidence has been provided, you have sufficient information to advise Mrs [*name*] upon proposals for settlement. Mr [*name*] also wishes to put forward proposals which are realistic taking into account all of the circumstances of the case. Before setting out those proposals, he wishes to explain the basis for this offer as that should assist you in advising Mrs [*name*].

[*The reasoning in any offer will depend upon the circumstances of that given case. The following is an adaptable example*]

(a)   The matrimonial home is a large five-bedroom property which exceeds the reasonable housing needs of Mrs [*name*] and the children. It is the largest asset of the marriage and Mr [*name*] feels that it is appropriate for there to be a fair division of the equity. He is living in rented accommodation and wishes to be able to purchase a property for himself as soon as possible. In particular, it is important for him to have an established base for when the children stay with him overnight.

(b)   Looking at suitable alternative accommodation in the local area, Mr [*name*] estimates that Mrs [*name*] and the children could be adequately re-housed for approximately £[*amount*]. Taking into account stamp duty and the costs of purchase, that would mean that Mrs [*name*] would require a total sum of £[*amount*] to re-house her and the children.

(c)   As far as pension provision is concerned, as Mrs [*name*] is aware, a significant element of Mr [*name*]'s pension built up prior to the relationship. Mr [*name*] would, however, propose that there be an equal share of the pension provision built up during the course of the relationship.

(d)   As far as child support is concerned, Mr [*name*] is committed to meet his ongoing obligations towards the children. He would therefore propose to pay child support in accordance with the Child Support Agency formula.

(e)   Mr [*name*] acknowledges that he has an obligation to provide additional support to Mrs [*name*] at least until [*name of youngest child*] starts secondary education. Although Mrs [*name*] earns a modest income at the moment, Mr [*name*] feels that

Mrs [*name*] has a reasonable earning capacity and could significantly increase her income should he choose to do so. Likewise, as well as receiving child benefit, she is also eligible to receive child tax credits and working tax credits.

Taking into account the above factors, Mr [*name*] therefore proposes as follows:

1. The former matrimonial home be sold as soon as possible on the following basis:

   (a) Mr and Mrs [*name*] will have joint conduct of the sale of the property. In this regard, we would ask that Mrs [*name*] puts forward names of the estate agents whom she would prefer to market the property for sale so that they can be considered by Mr [*name*].

   (b) The property is to be marketed for sale at a price agreed by Mr and Mrs [*name*] after having received appropriate advice from estate agents.

   (c) Upon sale, the net proceeds are to be divided as follows:

   - In discharge of the costs of sale, to include estate agents' fees and expenses and legal fees.
   - In discharge of the mortgage secured upon the property in favour of [*bank/building society*].
   - In payment of the balance as to [*number*]% to Mr [*name*] and [*number*]% to Mrs [*name*].

2. There be a pension sharing order in respect of Mr [*name*]'s pension with [*pension provider*] so that Mrs [*name*] receives [*number*]% of the cash equivalent transfer value. The costs of sharing the pension are to be borne equally by Mr and Mrs [*name*].

3. Mrs [*name*] shall retain the investments and accounts in her name and Mr [*name*] will retain the investments and accounts in his name. The joint account with [*bank*] bank will be transferred into the sole name of Mr [*name*] and he shall retain the credit balance.

4. The contents of the former matrimonial home are to be retained by Mrs [*name*], although there are certain items which Mr [*name*] would wish to retain for himself. A schedule of those assets is enclosed with this letter. Mr [*name*] would propose that he removes his share of the contents upon sale of the property.

5. Mr [*name*] will pay child support to Mrs [*name*] for the benefit of each of the children of the family at the rate of £[*amount*] per month per child payable monthly in advance until the children respectively attain the age of 18 or cease full-time secondary education, whichever is the later.

6. Mr [*name*] will pay spousal maintenance to Mrs [*name*] at the rate of £[*amount*] per month payable monthly in advance until Mrs [*name*]'s remarriage, further order of the court or [*a specific date, for example, the youngest's child's 11ᵗʰ birthday*] whereupon Mrs [*name*]'s claims shall be dismissed and there is to be a direction that she shall not be able to apply for an extension of that term by virtue of s.28(1A) Matrimonial Causes Act 1973.

7. There is to be a dismissal of all of Mr [*name*]'s claims, including his claims under the Inheritance Act. There is to be a dismissal of all of Mrs [*name*]'s claims as to capital and pension provision. Her claims for maintenance and claims under the Inheritance Act are to be dismissed in accordance with paragraph 6 above.

8. Mr and Mrs [*name*] are each to pay their own costs.

We should be grateful if you would take Mrs [*name*]'s instructions as soon as possible in the hope that matters can be agreed forthwith. If it would assist, we would suggest that you telephone us to discuss this offer.

Yours faithfully,

APPENDIX 18

FDR bundle index

Case No. [*number*]

IN THE [*name*] COUNTY COURT

BETWEEN:

[*name*]

Applicant

and

[*name*]

Respondent

INDEX FOR BUNDLE FOR FDR HEARING
ON [*date*]

PRELIMINARY DOCUMENTS   **PAGE NO.**

1. Summary of the background to the hearing
2. Statement of the issues to be determined at the FDR hearing
3. Position statement of the Applicant Wife
4. Position statement of the Respondent Husband
5. Chronology
6. Skeleton argument prepared on behalf of Applicant wife
7. Skeleton argument prepared on behalf of Respondent Husband
8. List of essential reading

APPLICATIONS AND ORDERS

9. Applicant Wife's Form A dated [*date*]
10. First Appointment Order dated [*date*]
11. Applicant Wife's application for maintenance pending suit dated [*date*]
12. Maintenance pending suit order dated [*date*]

STATEMENTS AND AFFIDAVITS

13. Applicant Wife's Form E (without exhibits) sworn on [*date*]
14. Respondent Husband's Form E (without exhibits) sworn on [*date*]
15. Applicant Wife's sworn statement dated [*date*]
16. Respondent Husband's sworn statement dated [*date*]

FURTHER DISCLOSURE

17. Applicant Wife's replies to questionnaire (without exhibits) dated [*date*]
18. Respondent Husband's replies to questionnaire (without exhibits) dated [*date*]

EXPERTS' EVIDENCE

19. Valuation of [*company*] Limited prepared by [*accountant*] and dated [*date*]
20. Valuation of matrimonial home at [*address*] prepared by [*surveyor*] and dated [*date*]
21. Pension report prepared by [*pensions expert*] and dated [*date*]

PROPOSALS FOR SETTLEMENT

22. Applicant Wife's proposals as follows:-

    (a) Without prejudice offer dated [*date*]
    (b) Without prejudice offer dated [*date*]

23. Respondent Husband's proposals as follows:-

    (a) Without prejudice offer dated [*date*]
    (b) Without prejudice offer dated [*date*]

APPENDIX 19

Ancillary relief – pre-application protocol (25 May 2000)

1.   Introduction

1.1

1.1.1   Lord Woolf in his final Access to Justice Report of July 1996 recommended the development of pre-action protocols:

> to build on and increase the benefits of early but well informed settlement which genuinely satisfy both parties to dispute

1.1.2   Subsequently, in April 2000, the Lord Chancellor's Ancillary Relief Advisory Group agreed this Pre-Application Protocol.

1.2   The aim of the pre-action protocol is to ensure that:

(a)   Pre-application disclosure and negotiation takes place in appropriate cases.
(b)   Where there is pre-application disclosure and negotiation, it is dealt with

    i.   Cost effectively;
    ii.   In line with the overriding objective of the Family Proceedings (Amendments) Rules 1999;

(c)   The parties are in a position to settle the case fairly and early without litigation.

1.3   The court will be able to treat the standard set in the pre-application protocol as the normal reasonable approach to pre-application conduct. If proceedings are subsequently issued, the court will be entitled to decide whether there has been non-compliance with the protocol and, if so, whether non-compliance merits consequences.

2.   Notes of Guidance Scope of the Protocol

2.1   This protocol is intended to apply to all claims for ancillary relief as defined by FPR r 1(2). It is designed to cover all classes of case, ranging from a simple application for periodical payments to an application for a substantial lump sum and property adjustment order. The protocol is designed to facilitate the operation of what was called the pilot scheme and is from 5 June 2000 the standard procedure for ancillary relief applications.

2.2   In considering the option of pre-application disclosure and negotiation, solicitors should bear in mind the advantage of having a court timetable and court managed process. There is sometimes an advantage in preparing disclosure before proceedings are commenced. However, solicitors should bear in mind the objective of controlling costs and in particular the costs of discovery and that the option of pre-application disclosure and negotiation has risks of excessive and uncontrolled expenditure and delay. This option should only be encouraged where both parties agree to follow this route and disclosure is not likely to be an issue or has been adequately dealt with in mediation or otherwise.

2.3   Solicitors should consider at an early stage and keep under review whether it would be appropriate to suggest mediation to the clients as an alternative to solicitor negotiation or court based litigation.

2.4   Making an application to the court should not be regarded as a hostile step or a last resort, rather as a way of starting the court timetable, controlling disclosure and endeavouring to avoid the costly final hearing and the preparation for it.

First Letter

2.5   The circumstances of parties to an application for ancillary relief are so various that it would be difficult to prepare a specimen letter of claim. The request for information will be different in every case. However, the tone of the initial letter is important and the guidelines in para 3.7 should be followed. It should be approved in advance by the client. Solicitors writing to an unrepresented party should always recommend that he seeks independent legal advice and enclose a second copy of the letter to be passed to any solicitor instructed. A reasonable time limit for a response may be 14 days.

Negotiation and settlement

2.6   In the event of pre-application disclosure and negotiation, as envisaged in paragraph 2.2 an application should not be issued when a settlement is a reasonable prospect.

Disclosure

2.7   The protocol underlines the obligation of parties to make full and frank disclosure of all material facts, documents and other information relevant to the issues. Solicitors owe their clients a duty to tell them in clear terms of this duty and of the possible consequences of breach of the duty. This duty of disclosure is an ongoing obligation and includes the duty to disclose any material changes after initial disclosure has been given. Solicitors are referred to the Good Practice Guide for Disclosure produced by the Solicitors Family Law Association (obtainable from the Administrative Director, 366A Crofton Road, Orpington, Kent BR2 8NN).

3. The Protocol

General Principles

3.1   All parties must always bear in mind the overriding objective set out at FPR Rule 2.51B and try to ensure that all claims should be resolved and a just resolution achieved as speedily as possible without costs being unreasonably incurred. The needs of any children should be addressed and safeguarded. The procedures which it is appropriate to follow should be conducted with minimum distress to the parties and in a manner designed to promote as good a continuing relationship between the parties and any children affected as is possible in the circumstances.

3.2   The principle of proportionality must be borne in mind at all times. It is unacceptable for the costs of any case to be disproportionate to the financial value of the subject matter of the dispute.

3.3　Parties should be informed that where a court exercises a discretion as to whether costs are payable by one party to another, this discretion extends to pre-application offers to settle and conduct of disclosure. (Rule 44.3 Paragraph 1 of the Civil Procedure Rules 1998.)

Identifying the Issues

3.4　Parties must seek to clarify their claims and identify the issues between them as soon as possible. So that this can be achieved they must provide full, frank and clear disclosure of facts, information and documents which are material and sufficiently accurate to enable proper negotiations to take place to settle their differences. Openness in all dealings is essential.

Disclosure

3.5　If parties carry out voluntary disclosure before the issue of proceedings the parties should exchange schedules of assets, income, liabilities and other material facts, using Form E as a guide to the format of the disclosure. Documents should only be disclosed to the extent that they are required by Form E. Excessive or disproportionate costs should not be incurred.

Correspondence

3.6　Any first letter and subsequent correspondence must focus on the clarification of claims and identification of issues and their resolution. Protracted and unnecessary correspondence and 'trial by correspondence' must be avoided.

3.7　The impact of any correspondence upon the reader and in particular the parties must always be considered. Any correspondence which raises irrelevant issues or which might cause the other party to adopt an entrenched, polarised or hostile position is to be discouraged.

Experts

3.8　Expert valuation evidence is only necessary where the parties cannot agree or do not know the value of some significant asset. The cost of a valuation should be proportionate to the sums in dispute. Wherever possible, valuations of properties, shares etc should be obtained from a single valuer instructed by both parties. To that end, a party wishing to instruct an expert (the first party) should first give the other party a list of the names of one or more experts in the relevant speciality whom he considers are suitable to instruct. Within 14 days the other party may indicate an objection to one or more of the named experts and, if so, should supply the names of one or more experts whom he considers suitable.

3.9　Where the identity of the expert is agreed, the parties should agree the terms of a joint letter of instructions.

3.10　Where no agreement is reached as to the identity of the expert, each party should think carefully before instructing his own expert because of the costs implications. Disagreements about disclosure such as the use and identity of an expert may be better managed by the court within the context of an application for ancillary relief.

3.11　Whether a joint report is commissioned or the parties have chosen to instruct separate experts, it is important that the expert is prepared to answer reasonable questions raised by either party.

3.12　When experts' reports are commissioned pre-application, it should be made clear to the expert that they may in due course be reporting to the court and that they should therefore consider themselves bound by the guidance as to expert witnesses in Part 39 of the Civil Procedure Rules 1998.

3.13 Where the parties propose to instruct a joint expert, there is a duty on both parties to disclose whether they have already consulted that expert about the assets in issue.

3.14 If the parties agree to instruct separate experts the parties should be encouraged to agree in advance that the reports will be disclosed.

Summary

3.15 The aim of all pre-application proceedings steps must be to assist the parties to resolve their differences speedily and fairly or at least narrow the issues and, should that not be possible, to assist the Court to do so.

President's Direction: Court bundles (26 July 2000)

Family proceedings: Court bundles (universal practice to be applied in all courts other than the Family Proceedings Court)

1   The President of the Family Division has issued this practice direction to achieve consistency across the country in all family courts (other than the Family Proceedings Court) in the preparation of court bundles and in respect of other related matters.

Application of the practice direction

2.1 Except as specified in paragraph 2.4, and subject to specific directions given in any particular case, the following practice applies to:

   (a) all hearings of whatever nature (including but not limited to hearings in family proceedings, CPR Part 7 and Part 8 claims and appeals) before a judge of the Family Division of the High Court wherever the court may be sitting;
   (b) all hearings in family proceedings in the Royal Courts of Justice ("RCJ");
   (c) all hearings in the Principal Registry of the Family Division ("PRFD") at First Avenue House; and
   (d) all hearings in family proceedings in all other courts except for Family Proceedings Courts.

2.2 'Hearings' includes all appearances before a judge or district judge, whether with or without notice to other parties and whether for directions or for substantive relief.

2.3 This practice direction applies whether a bundle is being lodged for the first time or is being re-lodged for a further hearing (see paragraph 9.2).

2.4 This practice direction does not apply to:

   (a) cases listed for one hour or less at a court referred to in paragraph 2.1(c) or 2.1(d); or
   (b) the hearing of any urgent application if and to the extent that it is impossible to comply with it.

2.5 The Designated Family Judge responsible for any court referred to in paragraph 2.1(c) or 2.1(d) may, after such consultation as is appropriate (but in the case of hearings in the PRFD at First Avenue House only with the agreement of the Senior District Judge), direct that in that court this practice direction shall apply to all family proceedings irrespective of the length of hearing.

Responsibility for the preparation of the bundle

3.1 A bundle for the use of the court at the hearing shall be provided by the party in the position of applicant at the hearing (or, if there are cross-applications, by the party whose application was first in time) or, if that person is a litigant in person, by the first listed respondent who is not a litigant in person.

3.2 The party preparing the bundle shall paginate it. If possible the contents of the bundle shall be agreed by all parties.

Contents of the bundle

4.1 The bundle shall contain copies of all documents relevant to the hearing, in chronological order from the front of the bundle, paginated and indexed, and divided into separate sections (each section being separately paginated) as follows:

(a) preliminary documents (see paragraph 4.2) and any other case management documents required by any other practice direction;

(b) applications and orders;

(c) statements and affidavits (which must be dated in the top right corner of the front page);

(d) care plans (where appropriate);

(e) experts' reports and other reports (including those of a guardian, children's guardian or litigation friend); and

(f) other documents, divided into further sections as may be appropriate.

Copies of notes of contact visits should normally not be included in the bundle unless directed by a judge.

4.2 At the commencement of the bundle there shall be inserted the following documents ("the preliminary documents"):

(i) an up to date summary of the background to the hearing confined to those matters which are relevant to the hearing and the management of the case and limited, if practicable, to one A4 page;

(ii) a statement of the issue or issues to be determined (1) at that hearing and (2) at the final hearing;

(iii) a position statement by each party including a summary of the order or directions sought by that party (1) at that hearing and (2) at the final hearing;

(iv) an up to date chronology, if it is a final hearing or if the summary under (i) is insufficient;

(v) skeleton arguments, if appropriate, with copies of all authorities relied on; and

(vi) a list of essential reading for that hearing.

4.3 Each of the preliminary documents shall state on the front page immediately below the heading the date when it was prepared and the date of the hearing for which it was prepared.

4.4 The summary of the background, statement of issues, chronology, position statement and any skeleton arguments shall be cross-referenced to the relevant pages of the bundle.

4.5 The summary of the background, statement of issues, chronology and reading list shall in the case of a final hearing, and shall so far as practicable in the case of any other hearing, each consist of a single document in a form agreed by all parties. Where the parties disagree as to the content the fact of their disagreement and their differing contentions shall be set out at the appropriate places in the document.

4.6 Where the nature of the hearing is such that a complete bundle of all documents is unnecessary, the bundle (which need not be repaginated) may comprise only those documents necessary for the hearing, but

(i) the summary (paragraph 4.2(i)) must commence with a statement that the bundle is limited or incomplete; and

(ii) the bundle shall if reasonably practicable be in a form agreed by all parties.

4.7 Where the bundle is re-lodged in accordance with paragraph 9.2, before it is re-lodged:

    (a) the bundle shall be updated as appropriate; and
    (b) all superseded documents (and in particular all outdated summaries, statements of issues, chronologies, skeleton arguments and similar documents) shall be removed from the bundle.

Format of the bundle

5.1 The bundle shall be contained in one or more A4 size ring binders or lever arch files (each lever arch file being limited to 350 pages).

5.2 All ring binders and lever arch files shall have clearly marked on the front and the spine:

    (a) the title and number of the case;
    (b) the court where the case has been listed;
    (c) the hearing date and time;
    (d) if known, the name of the judge hearing the case; and
    (e) where there is more than one ring binder or lever arch file, a distinguishing letter (A, B, C etc).

Timetable for preparing and lodging the bundle

6.1 The party preparing the bundle shall, whether or not the bundle has been agreed, provide a paginated index to all other parties not less than 4 working days before the hearing (in relation to a case management conference to which the provisions of the Public Law Protocol [2003] 2 FLR 719 apply, not less than 5 working days before the case management conference).

6.2 Where counsel is to be instructed at any hearing, a paginated bundle shall (if not already in counsel's possession) be delivered to counsel by the person instructing that counsel not less than 3 working days before the hearing.

6.3 The bundle (with the exception of the preliminary documents if and insofar as they are not then available) shall be lodged with the court not less than 2 working days before the hearing, or at such other time as may be specified by the judge.

6.4 The preliminary documents shall be lodged with the court no later than 11 am on the day before the hearing and, where the hearing is before a judge of the High Court and the name of the judge is known, shall at the same time be sent by e-mail to the judge's clerk.

Lodging the bundle

7.1 The bundle shall be lodged at the appropriate office. If the bundle is lodged in the wrong place the judge may:

    (a) treat the bundle as having not been lodged; and
    (b) take the steps referred to in paragraph 12.

7.2 Unless the judge has given some other direction as to where the bundle in any particular case is to be lodged (for example a direction that the bundle is to be lodged with the judge's clerk) the bundle shall be lodged:

    (a) for hearings in the RCJ, in the office of the Clerk of the Rules, Room TM 9.09, Royal Courts of Justice, Strand, London WC2A 2LL (DX 44450 Strand);

(b) for hearings in the PRFD at First Avenue House, at the List Office counter, 3rd floor, First Avenue House, 42/49 High Holborn, London, WC1V 6NP (DX 396 Chancery Lane); and

(c) for hearings at any other court, at such place as may be designated by the Designated Family Judge or other judge at that court and in default of any such designation at the court office of the court where the hearing is to take place.

7.3 Any bundle sent to the court by post, DX or courier shall be clearly addressed to the appropriate office and shall show the date and place of the hearing on the outside of any packaging as well as on the bundle itself.

Lodging the bundle – additional requirements for cases being heard at First Avenue House or at the RCJ

8.1 In the case of hearings at the RCJ or First Avenue House, parties shall:

(a) if the bundle or preliminary documents are delivered personally, ensure that they obtain a receipt from the clerk accepting it or them; and

(b) if the bundle or preliminary documents are sent by post or DX, ensure that they obtain proof of posting or despatch.

The receipt (or proof of posting or despatch, as the case may be) shall be brought to court on the day of the hearing and must be produced to the court if requested. If the receipt (or proof of posting or despatch) cannot be produced to the court the judge may (i) treat the bundle as having not been lodged and (ii) take the steps referred to in paragraph 12.

8.2 For hearings at the RCJ:

(a) bundles or preliminary documents delivered after 11 am on the day before the hearing will not be accepted by the Clerk of the Rules and shall be delivered:

   (i) in a case where the hearing is before a judge of the High Court, directly to the clerk of the judge hearing the case;

   (ii) in a case where the hearing is before a Circuit Judge, Deputy High Court Judge or Recorder, directly to the messenger at the Judge's entrance to the Queen's Building (with telephone notification to the personal assistant to the Designated Family Judge, 020 7947 7155, that this has been done).

(b) upon learning before which judge a hearing is to take place, the clerk to counsel, or other advocate, representing the party in the position of applicant shall no later than 3pm the day before the hearing:

   (i) in a case where the hearing is before a judge of the High Court, telephone the clerk of the judge hearing the case;

   (ii) in a case where the hearing is before a Circuit Judge, Deputy High Court Judge or Recorder, telephone the personal assistant to the Designated Family Judge;

to ascertain whether the judge has received the bundle (including the preliminary documents) and, if not, shall organise prompt delivery by the applicant's solicitor.

Removing and re-lodging the bundle

9.1 Following completion of the hearing the party responsible for the bundle shall retrieve it from the court immediately or, if that is not practicable, shall collect it from the court within five working days. Bundles which are not collected in due time may be destroyed.

9.2 The bundle shall be re-lodged for the next and any further hearings in accordance with the provisions of this practice direction and in a form which complies with paragraph 4.7.

Time estimates

10.1 In every case a time estimate (which shall be inserted at the front of the bundle) shall be prepared which shall so far as practicable be agreed by all parties and shall:

    (a) specify separately (i) the time estimated to be required for judicial pre-reading and (ii) the time required for hearing all evidence and submissions and (iii) the time estimated to be required for preparing and delivering judgment; and

    (b) be prepared on the basis that before they give evidence all witnesses will have read all relevant filed statements and reports.

10.2 Once a case has been listed, any change in time estimates shall be notified immediately by telephone (and then immediately confirmed in writing):

    (a) in the case of hearings in the RCJ, to the Clerk of the Rules;

    (b) in the case of hearings in the PRFD at First Avenue House, to the List Officer at First Avenue House; and

    (c) in the case of hearings elsewhere, to the relevant listing officer.

Taking cases out of the list

11 As soon as it becomes known that a hearing will no longer be effective, whether as a result of the parties reaching agreement or for any other reason, the parties and their representatives shall immediately notify the court by telephone and by letter. The letter, which shall wherever possible be a joint letter sent on behalf of all parties with their signatures applied or appended, shall include:

    (a) a short background summary of the case ;

    (b) the written consent of each party who consents and, where a party does not consent, details of the steps which have been taken to obtain that party's consent and, where known, an explanation of why that consent has not been given;

    (c) a draft of the order being sought; and

    (d) enough information to enable the court to decide (i) whether to take the case out of the list and (ii) whether to make the proposed order.

Penalties for failure to comply with the practice direction

12 Failure to comply with any part of this practice direction may result in the judge removing the case from the list or putting the case further back in the list and may also result in a 'wasted costs' order in accordance with CPR Part 48.7 or some other adverse costs order.

Commencement of the practice direction and application of other practice directions

13 This practice direction replaces President's Direction (Family Proceedings: Court Bundles) [2000] 1 FLR 536 and shall have effect from 2 October 2006.

14 Any reference in any other practice direction to President's Direction (Family Proceedings: Court Bundles) [2000] 1 FLR 536 shall be read as if substituted by a reference to this practice direction.

15 This practice direction should where appropriate be read in conjunction with President's Direction (Human Rights Act 1998) [2000] 2 FLR 429 and with Practice Direction (Care Cases: Judicial Continuity and Judicial Case Management) appended to the Public Law Protocol [2003] 2 FLR 719. In particular, nothing in this practice direction is to be read as removing or altering any obligation to comply with the requirements of the Public Law Protocol.

This Practice Direction is issued:

(i) in relation to family proceedings, by the President of the Family Division, as the nominee of the Lord Chief Justice, with the agreement of the Lord Chancellor; and

(ii) to the extent that it applies to proceedings to which section 5 of the Civil Procedure Act 1997 applies, by the Master of the Rolls as the nominee of the Lord Chief Justice, with the agreement of the Lord Chancellor.

The Right Honourable
Sir Mark Potter
President of the Family Division & Head of Family Justice

The Right Honourable
Sir Anthony Clarke
Master of the Rolls & Head of Civil Justice

Best Practice Guide for Instructing a Single Joint Expert

Foreword by the President of the Family Division Her Honour Dame Elizabeth Butler-Sloss DBE

This is an excellent Practice Guide. It has my full support. I hope practitioners will take it to heart and observe the recommended procedures.

Foreword by Senior District Judge Gerald Angel

Following the introduction, on the 5th June 2000, of the revised ancillary relief procedure incorporating the Civil Procedure Rules about expert evidence, Lord Justice Thorpe, Chairman of the President's Ancillary Relief Advisory Group, constituted a working party to examine the topic of single joint experts in ancillary relief cases.

The working party, under the chairmanship of the Senior District Judge, comprised a High Court Family Division Judge, Mr Justice Bodey, District Judge Bird representing the Association of District Judges, Richard Freeman, representing the Academy of Experts, Nicholas Mostyn QC, representing the Family Law Bar Association and Richard Sax, representing the Solicitors Family Law Association, with Clive Buckley from the Principal Registry of the Family Division as its secretary. The working party met four times between October 2000 and October 2001. It set itself the task of examining whether it would be appropriate for there to be a protocol about Single Joint Experts in ancillary relief proceedings and if so, to settle its terms. In addition to examining a quantity of written material, the working party were provided with very valuable advice and assistance by Michael Cohen, Chairman Emeritus of the Academy of Experts and Geoffrey Bevans of the Royal Institution of Chartered Surveyors both of whom generously attended one of the meetings.

The working party concluded that it would recommend to the Advisory Group that there should be published Guidance about Single Joint Experts in ancillary relief proceedings. The final draft of the Guidance, to which each of the members of the working party contributed, was submitted to the President's Ancillary Relief Advisory Group at its meeting on the 24thApril 2002. The Advisory Group accepted the working party's proposal that the Guidance be published.

Best Practice Guide for instructing a single joint expert

1. The President's Practice Direction of the 25th May 2000 ([2000] 1 FLR 997), encouraged the appointment of a Single Joint Expert ('SJE') as follows:

    The introduction of expert evidence in proceedings is likely to increase costs substantially and consequently the court will use its powers to restrict the unnecessary use of experts. Accordingly, where expert evidence is sought to be relied upon, parties should if possible agree upon a single joint expert whom they can jointly instruct. Where parties are unable to agree upon the expert to be instructed the court will consider using its powers under Part 35 of the Civil Procedure Rules 1998 to direct that evidence be given by one expert only. In such cases, parties must be in a position at the first appointment or when the matter comes to be considered by the court to provide the court with a list of suitable experts or make submissions as to the method by which the expert is to be selected.

2. This Best Practice Guide is intended to promote efficiency, effectiveness and economy in the management of ancillary relief cases and to assist practitioners and experts as to the procedure to be adopted when instructions are given jointly to experts in applications for ancillary relief. It is equally applicable prior to the issue of proceedings. Throughout, the principle of proportionality must be a primary consideration.

3. An expert instructed by one party separately will not usually be appointable later as an SJE. Parties should therefore consider the costs implications before appointing an expert for their own side, rather than suggesting the appointment of an SJE to the other party.

4. If parties agree to appoint an SJE, then before instructions are given, they should:

    (1) obtain confirmation from the proposed expert:

        (a) that there is no conflict of interest;
        (b) that the matter is within the range of expertise of the expert;
        (c) that the expert is available to provide the report within a specified timescale;
        (d) of the expert's availability for attendance at any dates that are known to be relevant;
        (e) of any periods when the expert will not be available;
        (f) as to the expert's fee rate, basis of charging, other terms of business and best estimate of likely fee;
        (g) if applicable, that the expert will accept instructions on a publicly funded basis, and

    (2) (a) have agreed in what proportion the SJE's fee is to be shared between them (at least in the first instance) and when it is to be paid;
        (b) if applicable, have obtained agreement for public funding.

5. Where parties have not agreed on the appointment of an SJE before the relevant directions appointment, they should obtain the confirmations set out in 4(1) above, in respect of all experts they intend to put to the court for the purpose of CPR 35.7(3)(a).

6. Where the court directs a report by an SJE, the order should:

    (a) if the SJE has already been instructed, adopt the instructions already given or make such amendments to the instruction as the court thinks fit;
    (b) identify the SJE;
    (c) specify the task that the SJE is to perform;
    (d) provide that the instructions are to be contained in a jointly agreed letter;
    (e) specify the time within which the letter of instruction is to be sent;
    (f) specify the date by which the report must be produced;
    (g) provide for the date by which written questions may be put to the SJE and the date by which they must be answered;
    (h) make any such provision as to the SJE's fees which the court thinks appropriate.

7. The joint instructions to the SJE should reflect the proportionality principle and include:

    (a) basic relevant information;
    (b) any assumptions to be made;
    (c) the principal known issues;
    (d) the specific questions to be answered;
    (e) arrangements for attendance at a property, business or accountant's office or other place;
    (f) a copy of paragraphs 1.1 to 1.6 of the Practice Direction to CPR Part 35 (form and contents of expert's reports) and a copy of this Guide;
    (g) a copy of the relevant parts of the court order;
    (h) documents necessary for the expert's consideration of the case, sufficient for the purpose, clearly legible, properly sorted, paginated and indexed.

8. Upon receiving the joint letter of instruction, or subsequently should it become necessary to do so, the SJE should raise with the solicitors any issues or questions which may arise, including proportionality, lack of clarity or completeness in the instructions and the possible effect on fees of complying with the instructions.

9. Should a party wish to give supplementary instructions to the SJE, full consideration must be given to proportionality and to the possible effect on the timetable. Supplementary instructions should not be given to the SJE unless the other party has agreed or the court has sanctioned them.

9. All communications by the SJE should be addressed to both parties and the SJE should keep the parties informed of all material steps taken by, for example, copying all correspondence to each party.

10. Any meeting or conference attended by the SJE should be proportionate to the case and should normally be with both parties and/or their advisers. Unless both parties have agreed otherwise in writing, the SJE should not attend any meeting or conference that is not a joint one.

11. The report of the SJE should be served simultaneously on both parties.

12. Where the SJE considers that the proportionality principle cannot be complied with in preparing the report within the terms of reference, the SJE should give notice to the parties, identifying what is perceived to be the difficulty.

13. Where the difficulty cannot be resolved by the parties and the SJE, the SJE should file a written request to the court for directions pursuant to CPR 35.14.

14. As a last resort, the SJE may resign the joint appointment. In this event, the SJE should serve a concise statement of the reasons on both parties. Where the court has ordered his joint appointment the SJE should also serve the court with the statement.

APPENDIX 22

Civil Procedure Rules, Part 35, Experts and assessors

35.1 Duty to restrict expert evidence

Expert evidence shall be restricted to that which is reasonably required to resolve the proceedings.

35.2 Interpretation

A reference to an 'expert' in this Part is a reference to an expert who has been instructed to give or prepare evidence for the purpose of court proceedings.

35.3 Experts – overriding duty to the court

(1) It is the duty of an expert to help the court on the matters within his expertise.
(2) This duty overrides any obligation to the person from whom he has received instructions or by whom he is paid.

35.4 Court's power to restrict expert evidence

(1) No party may call an expert or put in evidence an expert's report without the court's permission.
(2) When a party applies for permission under this rule he must identify –

    (a) the field in which he wishes to rely on expert evidence; and
    (b) where practicable the expert in that field on whose evidence he wishes to rely.

(3) If permission is granted under this rule it shall be in relation only to the expert named or the field identified under paragraph (2).
(4) The court may limit the amount of the expert's fees and expenses that the party who wishes to rely on the expert may recover from any other party.

35.5 General requirement for expert evidence to be given in a written report

(1) Expert evidence is to be given in a written report unless the court directs otherwise.
(2) If a claim is on the fast track, the court will not direct an expert to attend a hearing unless it is necessary to do so in the interests of justice.

35.6 Written questions to experts

(1) A party may put to –

    (a) an expert instructed by another party; or
    (b) a single joint expert appointed under rule 35.7,

    written questions about his report.

(2) Written questions under paragraph (1) –

    (a) may be put once only;
    (b) must be put within 28 days of service of the expert's report; and
    (c) must be for the purpose only of clarification of the report,

unless in any case –

       (i) the court gives permission; or
      (ii) the other party agrees.

(3) An expert's answers to questions put in accordance with paragraph (1) shall be treated as part of the expert's report.

(4) Where –

    (a) a party has put a written question to an expert instructed by another party in accordance with this rule; and
    (b) the expert does not answer that question,

the court may make one or both of the following orders in relation to the party who instructed the expert –

       (i) that the party may not rely on the evidence of that expert; or
      (ii) that the party may not recover the fees and expenses of that expert from any other party.

35.7 Court's power to direct that evidence is to be given by a single joint expert

(1) Where two or more parties wish to submit expert evidence on a particular issue, the court may direct that the evidence on that issue is to given by one expert only.

(2) The parties wishing to submit the expert evidence are called 'the instructing parties'.

(3) Where the instructing parties cannot agree who should be the expert, the court may –

    (a) select the expert from a list prepared or identified by the instructing parties; or
    (b) direct that the expert be selected in such other manner as the court may direct.

35.8 Instructions to a single joint expert

(1) Where the court gives a direction under rule 35.7 for a single joint expert to be used, each instructing party may give instructions to the expert.

(2) When an instructing party gives instructions to the expert he must, at the same time, send a copy of the instructions to the other instructing parties.

(3) The court may give directions about –

    (a) the payment of the expert's fees and expenses; and
    (b) any inspection, examination or experiments which the expert wishes to carry out.

(4) The court may, before an expert is instructed –

    (a) limit the amount that can be paid by way of fees and expenses to the expert; and
    (b) direct that the instructing parties pay that amount into court.

(5) Unless the court otherwise directs, the instructing parties are jointly and severally liable (GL) for the payment of the expert's fees and expenses.

35.9 Power of court to direct a party to provide information

Where a party has access to information which is not reasonably available to the other party, the court may direct the party who has access to the information to –

(a)   prepare and file a document recording the information; and
(b)   serve a copy of that document on the other party.

35.10 Contents of report

(1)   An expert's report must comply with the requirements set out in the relevant practice direction.
(2)   At the end of an expert's report there must be a statement that –

    (a)   the expert understands his duty to the court; and
    (b)   he has complied with that duty.

(3)   The expert's report must state the substance of all material instructions, whether written or oral, on the basis of which the report was written.
(4)   The instructions referred to in paragraph (3) shall not be privileged (GL) against disclosure but the court will not, in relation to those instructions –

    (a)   order disclosure of any specific document; or
    (b)   permit any questioning in court, other than by the party who instructed the expert,

unless it is satisfied that there are reasonable grounds to consider the statement of instructions given under paragraph (3) to be inaccurate or incomplete.

35.11 Use by one party of expert's report disclosed by another

Where a party has disclosed an expert's report, any party may use that expert's report as evidence at the trial.

35.12 Discussions between experts

(1)   The court may, at any stage, direct a discussion between experts for the purpose of requiring the experts to –

    (a)   identify and discuss the expert issues in the proceedings; and
    (b)   where possible, reach an agreed opinion on those issues.

(2)   The court may specify the issues which the experts must discuss.
(3)   The court may direct that following a discussion between the experts they must prepare a statement for the court showing –

    (a)   those issues on which they agree; and
    (b)   those issues on which they disagree and a summary of their reasons for disagreeing.

(4)   The content of the discussion between the experts shall not be referred to at the trial unless the parties agree.
(5)   Where experts reach agreement on an issue during their discussions, the agreement shall not bind the parties unless the parties expressly agree to be bound by the agreement.

35.13 Consequence of failure to disclose expert's report

A party who fails to disclose an expert's report may not use the report at the trial or call the expert to give evidence orally unless the court gives permission.

35.14 Expert's right to ask court for directions

(1) An expert may file a written request for directions to assist him in carrying out his function as an expert.

(2) An expert must, unless the court orders otherwise, provide a copy of any proposed request for directions under paragraph (1)–

    (a) to the party instructing him, at least 7 days before he files the request; and

    (b) to all other parties, at least 4 days before he files it.

(3) The court, when it gives directions, may also direct that a party be served with a copy of the directions.

35.15 Assessors

(1) This rule applies where the court appoints one or more persons (an 'assessor') under section 70 of the Supreme Court Act 1981 or section 63 of the County Courts Act 1984.

(2) The assessor shall assist the court in dealing with a matter in which the assessor has skill and experience.

(3) An assessor shall take such part in the proceedings as the court may direct and in particular the court may –

    (a) direct the assessor to prepare a report for the court on any matter at issue in the proceedings; and

    (b) direct the assessor to attend the whole or any part of the trial to advise the court on any such matter.

(4) If the assessor prepares a report for the court before the trial has begun –

    (a) the court will send a copy to each of the parties; and

    (b) the parties may use it at trial.

(5) The remuneration to be paid to the assessor for his services shall be determined by the court and shall form part of the costs of the proceedings.

(6) The court may order any party to deposit in the court office a specified sum in respect of the assessor's fees and, where it does so, the assessor will not be asked to act until the sum has been deposited.

(7) Paragraphs (5) and (6) do not apply where the remuneration of the assessor is to be paid out of money provided by Parliament.

Extracts of the Matrimonial Causes Act 1973 (as amended at 1 October 2009)

Part II: Financial Relief for Parties to Marriage and Children of Family

Financial provision and property adjustment orders

21 Financial provision and property adjustment orders

(1) The financial provision orders for the purposes of this Act are the orders for periodical or lump sum provision available (subject to the provisions of this Act) under section 23 below for the purpose of adjusting the financial position of the parties to a marriage and any children of the family in connection with proceedings for divorce, nullity of marriage or judicial separation and under section 27(6) below on proof of neglect by one party to a marriage to provide, or to make a proper contribution towards, reasonable maintenance for the other or a child of the family, that is to say–

(a) any order for periodical payments in favour of a party to a marriage under section 23(1)(a) or 27(6)(a) or in favour of a child of the family under section 23(1)(d), (2) or (4) or 27(6)(d);

(b) any order for secured periodical payments in favour of a party to a marriage under section 23(1)(b) or 27(6)(b) or in favour of a child of the family under section 23(1)(e), (2) or (4) or 27(6)(e); and

(c) any order for lump sum provision in favour of a party to a marriage under section 23(1)(c) or 27(6)(c) or in favour of a child of the family under section 23(1)(f), (2) or (4) or 27(6)(f);

and references in this Act (except in paragraphs 17(1) and 23 of Schedule 1 below) to periodical payments orders, secured periodical payments orders, and orders for the payment of a lump sum are references to all or some of the financial provision orders requiring the sort of financial provision in question according as the context of each reference may require.

(2) The property adjustment orders for the purposes of this Act are the orders dealing with property rights available (subject to the provisions of this Act) under section 24 below for the purpose of adjusting the financial position of the parties to a marriage and any children of the family on or after the grant of a decree of divorce, nullity of marriage or judicial separation, that is to say–

(a) any order under subsection (1)(a) of that section for a transfer of property;

(b) any order under subsection (1)(b) of that section for a settlement of property; and

(c) any order under subsection (1)(c) or (d) of that section for a variation of settlement.

21A Pension sharing orders

(1) For the purposes of this Act, a pension sharing order is an order which–

    (a) provides that one party's–

        (i) shareable rights under a specified pension arrangement, or
        (ii) shareable state scheme rights,

    be subject to pension sharing for the benefit of the other party, and
    (b) specifies the percentage value to be transferred.

(2) In subsection (1) above–

    (a) the reference to shareable rights under a pension arrangement is to rights in relation to which pension sharing is available under Chapter I of Part IV of the Welfare Reform and Pensions Act 1999, or under corresponding Northern Ireland legislation,
    (b) the reference to shareable state scheme rights is to rights in relation to which pension sharing is available under Chapter II of Part IV of the Welfare Reform and Pensions Act 1999, or under corresponding Northern Ireland legislation, and
    (c) 'party' means a party to a marriage.

Ancillary relief in connection with divorce proceedings, etc

22 Maintenance pending suit

On a petition for divorce, nullity of marriage or judicial separation, the court may make an order for maintenance pending suit, that is to say, an order requiring either party to the marriage to make to the other such periodical payments for his or her maintenance and for such term, being a term beginning not earlier than the date of the presentation of the petition and ending with the date of the determination of the suit, as the court thinks reasonable.

23 Financial provision orders in connection with divorce proceedings, etc

(1) On granting a decree of divorce, a decree of nullity of marriage or a decree of judicial separation or at any time thereafter (whether, in the case of a decree of divorce or of nullity of marriage, before or after the decree is made absolute), the court may make any one or more of the following orders, that is to say–

    (a) an order that either party to the marriage shall make to the other such periodical payments, for such term, as may be specified in the order;
    (b) an order that either party to the marriage shall secure to the other to the satisfaction of the court such periodical payments, for such term, as may be so specified;
    (c) an order that either party to the marriage shall pay to the other such lump sum or sums as may be so specified;
    (d) an order that a party to the marriage shall make to such person as may be specified in the order for the benefit of a child of the family, or to such a child, such periodical payments, for such term, as may be so specified;

(e) an order that a party to the marriage shall secure to such person as may be so specified for the benefit of such a child, or to such a child, to the satisfaction of the court, such periodical payments, for such term, as may be so specified;

(f) an order that a party to the marriage shall pay to such person as may be so specified for the benefit of such a child, or to such a child, such lump sum as may be so specified;

subject, however, in the case of an order under paragraph (d), (e) or (f) above, to the restrictions imposed by section 29(1) and (3) below on the making of financial provision orders in favour of children who have attained the age of eighteen.

(2) The court may also, subject to those restrictions, make any one or more of the orders mentioned in subsection (1)(d), (e) and (f) above–

(a) in any proceedings for divorce, nullity of marriage or judicial separation, before granting a decree; and

(b) where any such proceedings are dismissed after the beginning of the trial, either forthwith or within a reasonable period after the dismissal.

(3) Without prejudice to the generality of subsection (1)(c) or (f) above–

(a) an order under this section that a party to a marriage shall pay a lump sum to the other party may be made for the purpose of enabling that other party to meet any liabilities or expenses reasonably incurred by him or her in maintaining himself or herself or any child of the family before making an application for an order under this section in his or her favour;

(b) an order under this section for the payment of a lump sum to or for the benefit of a child of the family may be made for the purpose of enabling any liabilities or expenses reasonably incurred by or for the benefit of that child before the making of an application for an order under this section in his favour to be met; and

(c) an order under this section for the payment of a lump sum may provide for the payment of that sum by instalments of such amount as may be specified in the order and may require the payment of the instalments to be secured to the satisfaction of the court.

(4) The power of the court under subsection (1) or (2)(a) above to make an order in favour of a child of the family shall be exercisable from time to time; and where the court makes an order in favour of a child under subsection (2)(b) above, it may from time to time, subject to the restrictions mentioned in subsection (1) above, make a further order in his favour of any of the kinds mentioned in sub-section (1)(d), (e) or (f) above.

(5) Without prejudice to the power to give a direction under section 30 below for the settlement of an instrument by conveyancing counsel, where an order is made under subsection (1)(a), (b) or (c) above on or after granting a decree of divorce or nullity of marriage, neither the order nor any settlement made in pursuance of the order shall take effect unless the decree has been made absolute.

(6) Where the court–

(a) makes an order under this section for the payment of a lump of sum; and

(b) directs–

(i) that payment of that sum or any part of it shall be deferred; or

(ii) that that sum or any part of it shall be paid by instalments,

the court may order that the amount deferred or the instalments shall carry interest at such rate as may be specified by the order from such date, not earlier than the date of the order, as may be so specified, until the date when payment of it is due.

24 Property adjustment orders in connection with divorce proceedings, etc

(1) On granting a decree of divorce, a decree of nullity of marriage or a decree of judicial separation or at any time thereafter (whether, in the case of a decree of divorce or of nullity of marriage, before or after the decree is made absolute), the court may make any one or more of the following orders, that is to say–

    (a) an order that a party to the marriage shall transfer to the other party, to any child of the family or to such person as may be specified in the order for the benefit of such a child such property as may be so specified, being property to which the first-mentioned party is entitled, either in possession or reversion;

    (b) an order that a settlement of such property as may be so specified, being property to which a party to the marriage is so entitled, be made to the satisfaction of the court for the benefit of the other party to the marriage and of the children of the family or either or any of them;

    (c) an order varying for the benefit of the parties to the marriage and of the children of the family or either or any of them any ante-nuptial or post-nuptial settlement (including such a settlement made by will or codicil) made on the parties to the marriage, other than one in the form of a pension arrangement (within the meaning of section 25D below);

    (d) an order extinguishing or reducing the interest of either of the parties to the marriage under any such settlement, other than one in the form of a pension arrangement (within the meaning of section 25D below);

subject, however, in the case of an order under paragraph (a) above, to the restrictions imposed by section 29(1) and (3) below on the making of orders for a transfer of property in favour of children who have attained the age of eighteen.

(2) The court may make an order under subsection (1)(c) above notwithstanding that there are no children of the family.

(3) Without prejudice to the power to give a direction under section 30 below for the settlement of an instrument by conveyancing counsel, where an order is made under this section on or after granting a decree of divorce or nullity of marriage, neither the order nor any settlement made in pursuance of the order shall take effect unless the decree has been made absolute.

24A Orders for sale of property

(1) Where the court makes under section 23 or 24 of this Act a secured periodical payments order, an order for the payment of a lump sum or a property adjustment order, then, on making that order or at any time thereafter, the court may make a further order for the sale of such property as may be specified in the order, being property in which or in the proceeds of sale of which either or both of the parties to the marriage has or have a beneficial interest, either in possession or reversion.

(2) Any order made under subsection (1) above may contain such consequential or supplementary provisions as the court thinks fit and, without prejudice to the generality of the foregoing provision, may include–

    (a) provision requiring the making of a payment out of the proceeds of sale of the property to which the order relates, and

(b) provision requiring any such property to be offered for sale to a person, or class of persons, specified in the order.

(3) Where an order is made under subsection (1) above on or after the grant of a decree of divorce or nullity of marriage, the order shall not take effect unless the decree has been made absolute.

(4) Where an order is made under subsection (1) above, the court may direct that the order, or such provision thereof as the court may specify, shall not take effect until the occurrence of an event specified by the court or the expiration of a period so specified.

(5) Where an order under subsection (1) above contains a provision requiring the proceeds of sale of the property to which the order relates to be used to secure periodical payments to a party to the marriage, the order shall cease to have effect on the death or re-marriage of, or formation of a civil partnership by, that person.

(6) Where a party to a marriage has a beneficial interest in any property, or in the proceeds of sale thereof, and some other person who is not a party to the marriage also has a beneficial interest in that property or in the proceeds of sale thereof, then, before deciding whether to make an order under this section in relation to that property, it shall be the duty of the court to give that other person an opportunity to make representations with respect to the order; and any representations made by that other person shall be included among the circumstances to which the court is required to have regard under section 25(1) below.

24B Pension sharing orders in connection with divorce proceedings etc

(1) On granting a decree of divorce or a decree of nullity of marriage or at any time thereafter (whether before or after the decree is made absolute), the court may, on an application made under this section, make one or more pension sharing orders in relation to the marriage.

(2) A pension sharing order under this section is not to take effect unless the decree on or after which it is made has been made absolute.

(3) A pension sharing order under this section may not be made in relation to a pension arrangement which–

(a) is the subject of a pension sharing order in relation to the marriage, or
(b) has been the subject of pension sharing between the parties to the marriage.

(4) A pension sharing order under this section may not be made in relation to shareable state scheme rights if–

(a) such rights are the subject of a pension sharing order in relation to the marriage, or
(b) such rights have been the subject of pension sharing between the parties to the marriage.

(5) A pension sharing order under this section may not be made in relation to the rights of a person under a pension arrangement if there is in force a requirement imposed by virtue of section 25B or 25C below which relates to benefits or future benefits to which he is entitled under the pension arrangement.

24C Pension sharing orders: duty to stay

(1) No pension sharing order may be made so as to take effect before the end of such period after the making of the order as may be prescribed by regulations made by the Lord Chancellor.

(2) The power to make regulations under this section shall be exercisable by statutory instrument which shall be subject to annulment in pursuance of a resolution of either House of Parliament.

24D Pension sharing orders: apportionment of charges

If a pension sharing order relates to rights under a pension arrangement, the court may include in the order provision about the apportionment between the parties of any charge under section 41 of the Welfare Reform and Pensions Act 1999 (charges in respect of pension sharing costs), or under corresponding Northern Ireland legislation.

25 Matters to which court is to have regard in deciding how to exercise its powers under ss.23, 24 and 24A

(1) It shall be the duty of the court in deciding whether to exercise its powers under section 23, 24, 24A or 24B above and, if so, in what manner, to have regard to all the circumstances of the case, first consideration being given to the welfare while a minor of any child of the family who has not attained the age of eighteen.

(2) As regards the exercise of the powers of the court under section 23(1)(a), (b) or (c), 24, 24A or 24B above in relation to a party to the marriage, the court shall in particular have regard to the following matters–

  (a) the income, earning capacity, property and other financial resources which each of the parties to the marriage has or is likely to have in the foreseeable future, including in the case of earning capacity any increase in that capacity which it would in the opinion of the court be reasonable to expect a party to the marriage to take steps to acquire;

  (b) the financial needs, obligations and responsibilities which each of the parties to the marriage has or is likely to have in the foreseeable future;

  (c) the standard of living enjoyed by the family before the breakdown of the marriage;

  (d) the age of each party to the marriage and the duration of the marriage;

  (e) any physical or mental disability of either of the parties to the marriage;

  (f) the contributions which each of the parties has made or is likely in the fore-seeable future to make to the welfare of the family, including any contribution by looking after the home or caring for the family;

  (g) the conduct of each of the parties, if that conduct is such that it would in the opinion of the court be inequitable to disregard it;

  (h) in the case of proceedings for divorce or nullity of marriage, the value to each of the parties to the marriage of any benefit which, by reason of the dissolution or annulment of the marriage, that party will lose the chance of acquiring.

(3) As regards the exercise of the powers of the court under section 23(1)(d), (e) or (f), (2) or (4), 24 or 24A above in relation to a child of the family, the court shall in particular have regard to the following matters–

  (a) the financial needs of the child;

  (b) the income, earning capacity (if any), property and other financial resources of the child;

  (c) any physical or mental disability of the child;

  (d) the manner in which he was being and in which the parties to the marriage expected him to be educated or trained;

  (e) the considerations mentioned in relation to the parties to the marriage in paragraphs (a), (b), (c) and (e) of subsection (2) above.

(4) As regards the exercise of the powers of the court under section 23(1)(d), (e) or (f), (2) or (4), 24 or 24A above against a party to a marriage in favour of a child of the family who is not the child of that party, the court shall also have regard–

   (a) to whether that party assumed any responsibility for the child's maintenance, and, if so, to the extent to which, and the basis upon which, that party assumed such responsibility and to the length of time for which that party discharged such responsibility;
   (b) to whether in assuming and discharging such responsibility that party did so knowing that the child was not his or her own;
   (c) to the liability of any other person to maintain the child.

25A Exercise of court's powers in favour of party to marriage on decree of divorce or nullity of marriage

(1) Where on or after the grant of a decree of divorce or nullity of marriage the court decides to exercise its powers under section 23(1)(a), (b) or (c), 24, 24A or 24B above in favour of a party to the marriage, it shall be the duty of the court to consider whether it would be appropriate so to exercise those powers that the financial obligations of each party towards the other will be terminated as soon after the grant of the decree as the court considers just and reasonable.

(2) Where the court decides in such a case to make a periodical payments or secured periodical payments order in favour of a party to the marriage, the court shall in particular consider whether it would be appropriate to require those payments to be made or secured only for such term as would in the opinion of the court be sufficient to enable the party in whose favour the order is made to adjust without undue hardship to the termination of his or her financial dependence on the other party.

(3) Where on or after the grant of a decree of divorce or nullity of marriage an application is made by a party to the marriage for a periodical payments or secured periodical payments order in his or her favour, then, if the court considers that no continuing obligation should be imposed on either party to make or secure periodical payments in favour of the other, the court may dismiss the application with a direction that the applicant shall not be entitled to make any future application in relation to that marriage for an order under section 23(1)(a) or (b) above.

25B Pensions

(1) The matters to which the court is to have regard under section 25(2) above include–

   (a) in the case of paragraph (a), any benefits under a pension arrangement which a party to the marriage has or is likely to have, and
   (b) in the case of paragraph (h), any benefits under a pension arrangement which, by reason of the dissolution or annulment of the marriage, a party to the marriage will lose the chance of acquiring,

   and, accordingly, in relation to benefits under a pension arrangement, section 25(2)(a) above shall have effect as if 'in the foreseeable future' were omitted.

(2) . . .

(3) The following provisions apply where, having regard to any benefits under a pension arrangement, the court determines to make an order under section 23 above.

(4) To the extent to which the order is made having regard to any benefits under a pension arrangement, the order may require the person responsible for the

pension arrangement in question, if at any time any payment in respect of any benefits under the arrangement becomes due to the party with pension rights, to make a payment for the benefit of the other party.

(5) The order must express the amount of any payment required to be made by virtue of subsection (4) above as a percentage of the payment which becomes due to the party with pension rights.

(6) Any such payment by the person responsible for the arrangement–

(a) shall discharge so much of his liability to the party with pension rights as corresponds to the amount of the payment, and

(b) shall be treated for all purposes as a payment made by the party with pension rights in or towards the discharge of his liability under the order.

(7) Where the party with pension rights has a right of commutation under the arrangement, the order may require him to exercise it to any extent; and this section applies to any payment due in consequence of commutation in pursuance of the order as it applies to other payments in respect of benefits under the arrangement.

(7A) The power conferred by subsection (7) above may not be exercised for the purpose of commuting a benefit payable to the party with pension rights to a benefit payable to the other party.

(7B) The power conferred by subsection (4) or (7) above may not be exercised in relation to a pension arrangement which–

(a) is the subject of a pension sharing order in relation to the marriage, or

(b) has been the subject of pension sharing between the parties to the marriage.

(7C) In subsection (1) above, references to benefits under a pension arrangement include any benefits by way of pension, whether under a pension arrangement or not.

25C Pensions: lump sums

(1) The power of the court under section 23 above to order a party to a marriage to pay a lump sum to the other party includes, where the benefits which the party with pension rights has or is likely to have under a pension arrangement include any lump sum payable in respect of his death, power to make any of the following provision by the order.

(2) The court may–

(a) if the person responsible for the pension arrangement in question has power to determine the person to whom the sum, or any part of it, is to be paid, require him to pay the whole or part of that sum, when it becomes due, to the other party,

(b) if the party with pension rights has power to nominate the person to whom the sum, or any part of it, is to be paid, require the party with pension rights to nominate the other party in respect of the whole or part of that sum,

(c) in any other case, require the person responsible for the pension arrangement in question to pay the whole or part of that sum, when it becomes due, for the benefit of the other party instead of to the person to whom, apart from the order, it would be paid.

(3) Any payment by the person responsible for the arrangement under an order made under section 23 above by virtue of this section shall discharge so much of his liability in respect of the party with pension rights as corresponds to the amount of the payment.

(4) The powers conferred by this section may not be exercised in relation to a pension arrangement which–

(a) is the subject of a pension sharing order in relation to the marriage, or
(b) has been the subject of pension sharing between the parties to the marriage.

25D Pensions: supplementary

(1) Where–

(a) an order made under section 23 above by virtue of section 25B or 25C above imposes any requirement on the person responsible for a pension arrangement ('the first arrangement') and the party with pension rights acquires rights under another pension arrangement ('the new arrangement') which are derived (directly or indirectly) from the whole of his rights under the first arrangement, and
(b) the person responsible for the new arrangement has been given notice in accordance with regulations made by the Lord Chancellor,

the order shall have effect as if it had been made instead in respect of the person responsible for the new arrangement.

(2) The Lord Chancellor may by regulations–

(a) in relation to any provision of sections 25B or 25C above which authorises the court making an order under section 23 above to require the person responsible for a pension arrangement to make a payment for the benefit of the other party, make provision as to the person to whom, and the terms on which, the payment is to be made,
(ab) make, in relation to payment under a mistaken belief as to the continuation in force of a provision included by virtue of section 25B or 25C above in an order under section 23 above, provision about the rights or liabilities of the payer, the payee or the person to whom the payment was due,
(b) require notices to be given in respect of changes of circumstances relevant to such orders which include provision made by virtue of sections 25B and 25C above,
(ba) make provision for the person responsible for a pension arrangement to be discharged in prescribed circumstances from a requirement imposed by virtue of section 25B or 25C above,
(c) . . .
(d) . . .
(e) make provision about calculation and verification in relation to the valuation of–

(i) benefits under a pension arrangement, or
(ii) shareable state scheme rights,

for the purposes of the court's functions in connection with the exercise of any of its powers under this Part of this Act,

. . . .

(2A) Regulations under subsection (2)(e) above may include–

(a) provision for calculation or verification in accordance with guidance from time to time prepared by a prescribed person, and
(b) provision by reference to regulations under section 30 or 49(4) of the Welfare Reform and Pensions Act 1999.

(2B) Regulations under subsection (2) above may make different provision for different cases.

(2C) Power to make regulations under this section shall be exercisable by statutory instrument which shall be subject to annulment in pursuance of a resolution of either House of Parliament.

(3) In this section and sections 25B and 25C above–

'occupational pension scheme' has the same meaning as in the Pension Schemes Act 1993;

'the party with pension rights' means the party to the marriage who has or is likely to have benefits under a pension arrangement and 'the other party' means the other party to the marriage;

'pension arrangement' means–

   (a) an occupational pension scheme,
   (b) a personal pension scheme,
   (c) a retirement annuity contract,
   (d) an annuity or insurance policy purchased, or transferred, for the purpose of giving effect to rights under an occupational pension scheme or a personal pension scheme, and
   (e) an annuity purchased, or entered into, for the purpose of discharging liability in respect of a pension credit under section 29(1)(b) of the Welfare Reform and Pensions Act 1999 or under corresponding Northern Ireland legislation;

'personal pension scheme' has the same meaning as in the Pension Schemes Act 1993;

'prescribed' means prescribed by regulations;

'retirement annuity contract' means a contract or scheme approved under Chapter III of Part XIV of the Income and Corporation Taxes Act 1988;

'shareable state scheme rights' has the same meaning as in section 21A(1) above; and

'trustees or managers', in relation to an occupational pension scheme or a personal pension scheme, means–

   (a) in the case of a scheme established under a trust, the trustees of the scheme, and
   (b) in any other case, the managers of the scheme.

(4) In this section and sections 25B and 25C above, references to the person responsible for a pension arrangement are–

   (a) in the case of an occupational pension scheme or a personal pension scheme, to the trustees or managers of the scheme,
   (b) in the case of a retirement annuity contract or an annuity falling within paragraph (d) or (e) of the definition of 'pension arrangement' above, the provider of the annuity, and
   (c) in the case of an insurance policy falling within paragraph (d) of the definition of that expression, the insurer.

25E The Pension Protection Fund

(1) The matters to which the court is to have regard under section 25(2) include–

   (a) in the case of paragraph (a), any PPF compensation to which a party to the marriage is or is likely to be entitled, and

(b) in the case of paragraph (h), any PPF compensation which, by reason of the dissolution or annulment of the marriage, a party to the marriage will lose the chance of acquiring entitlement to,

and, accordingly, in relation to PPF compensation, section 25(2)(a) shall have effect as if 'in the foreseeable future' were omitted.

(2) Subsection (3) applies in relation to an order under section 23 so far as it includes provision made by virtue of section 25B(4) which–

(a) imposed requirements on the trustees or managers of an occupational pension scheme for which the Board has assumed responsibility in accordance with Chapter 3 of Part 2 of the Pensions Act 2004 (pension protection) or any provision in force in Northern Ireland corresponding to that Chapter, and

(b) was made before the trustees or managers of the scheme received the transfer notice in relation to the scheme.

(3) The order is to have effect from the time when the trustees or managers of the scheme receive the transfer notice–

(a) as if, except in prescribed descriptions of case–

(i) references in the order to the trustees or managers of the scheme were references to the Board, and

(ii) references in the order to any pension or lump sum to which the party with pension rights is or may become entitled under the scheme were references to any PPF compensation to which that person is or may become entitled in respect of the pension or lump sum, and

(b) subject to such other modifications as may be prescribed.

(4) Subsection (5) applies to an order under section 23 if–

(a) it includes provision made by virtue of section 25B(7) which requires the party with pension rights to exercise his right of commutation under an occupational pension scheme to any extent, and

(b) before the requirement is complied with the Board has assumed responsibility for the scheme as mentioned in subsection (2)(a).

(5) From the time the trustees or managers of the scheme receive the transfer notice, the order is to have effect with such modifications as may be prescribed.

(6) Regulations may modify section 25C as it applies in relation to an occupational pension scheme at any time when there is an assessment period in relation to the scheme.

(7) Where the court makes a pension sharing order in respect of a person's shareable rights under an occupational pension scheme, or an order which includes provision made by virtue of section 25B(4) or (7) in relation to such a scheme, the Board subsequently assuming responsibility for the scheme as mentioned in subsection (2)(a) does not affect–

(a) the powers of the court under section 31 to vary or discharge the order or to suspend or revive any provision of it, or

(b) on an appeal, the powers of the appeal court to affirm, reinstate, set aside or vary the order.

(8) Regulations may make such consequential modifications of any provision of, or made by virtue of, this Part as appear to the Lord Chancellor necessary or expedient to give effect to the provisions of this section.

(9) In this section–

'assessment period' means an assessment period within the meaning of Part 2 of the Pensions Act 2004 (pension protection) (see sections 132 and 159 of that Act) or an equivalent period under any provision in force in Northern Ireland corresponding to that Part;

'the Board' means the Board of the Pension Protection Fund;

'occupational pension scheme' has the same meaning as in the Pension Schemes Act 1993;

'prescribed' means prescribed by regulations;

'PPF compensation' means compensation payable under Chapter 3 of Part 2 of the Pensions Act 2004 (pension protection) or any provision in force in Northern Ireland corresponding to that Chapter;

'regulations' means regulations made by the Lord Chancellor;

'shareable rights' are rights in relation to which pension sharing is available under Chapter 1 of Part 4 of the Welfare Reform and Pensions Act 1999 or any provision in force in Northern Ireland corresponding to that Chapter;

'transfer notice' has the same meaning as in section 160 of the Pensions Act 2004 or any corresponding provision in force in Northern Ireland.

(10) Any power to make regulations under this section is exercisable by statutory instrument, which shall be subject to annulment in pursuance of a resolution of either House of Parliament.

*Additional provisions with respect to financial provision and
property adjustment orders*

28 Duration of continuing financial provision orders in favour of party to marriage, and effect of remarriage or formation of civil partnership

(1) Subject in the case of an order made on or after the grant of a decree of a divorce or nullity of marriage to the provisions of sections 25A(2) above and 31(7) below, the term to be specified in a periodical payments or secured periodical payments order in favour of a party to a marriage shall be such term as the court thinks fit, except that the term shall not begin before or extend beyond the following limits, that is to say–

(a) in the case of a periodical payments order, the term shall begin not earlier than the date of the making of an application for the order, and shall be so defined as not to extend beyond the death of either of the parties to the marriage or, where the order is made on or after the grant of a decree of divorce or nullity of marriage, the remarriage of, or formation of a civil partnership by, the party in whose favour the order is made; and

(b) in the case of a secured periodical payments order, the term shall begin not earlier than the date of the making of an application for the order, and shall be so defined as not to extend beyond the death or, where the order is made on or after the grant of such a decree, the remarriage of, or formation of a civil partnership by, the party in whose favour the order is made.

(1A) Where a periodical payments or secured periodical payments order in favour of a party to a marriage is made on or after the grant of a decree of divorce or nullity of marriage, the court may direct that that party shall not be entitled to apply under section 31 below for the extension of the term specified in the order.

(1B) If the court–

    (a)   exercises, or has exercised, its power under section 22A at any time before making a divorce order, and

    (b)   gives a direction under subsection (1A) above in respect of a periodical payments order or a secured periodical payments order,

it shall provide for the direction not to take effect until a divorce order is made.

(2)   Where a periodical payments or secured periodical payments order in favour of a party to a marriage is made otherwise than on or after the grant of a decree of divorce or nullity of marriage, and the marriage in question is subsequently dissolved or annulled but the order continues in force, the order shall, notwithstanding anything in it, cease to have effect on the remarriage of, or formation of a civil partnership by, that party, except in relation to any arrears due under it on the date of the remarriage or formation of the civil partnership.

(3)   If after the grant of a decree dissolving or annulling a marriage either party to that marriage remarries whether at any time before or after the commencement of this Act or forms a civil partnership, that party shall not be entitled to apply, by reference to the grant of that decree, for a financial provision order in his or her favour, or for a property adjustment order, against the other party to that marriage.

29 Duration of continuing financial provision orders in favour of children, and age limit on making certain orders in their favour

(1)   Subject to subsection (3) below, no financial provision order and no order for a transfer of property under section 24(1)(a) above shall be made in favour of a child who has attained the age of eighteen.

(2)   The term to be specified in a periodical payments or secured periodical payments order in favour of a child may begin with the date of the making of an application for the order in question or any later date or a date ascertained in accordance with subsection (5) or (6) below but–

    (a)   shall not in the first instance extend beyond the date of the birthday of the child next following his attaining the upper limit of the compulsory school age (construed in accordance with section 8 of the Education Act 1996) unless the court considers that in the circumstances of the case the welfare of the child requires that it should extend to a later date; and

    (b)   shall not in any event, subject to subsection (3) below, extend beyond the date of the child's eighteenth birthday.

(3)   Subsection (1) above, and paragraph (b) of subsection (2), shall not apply in the case of a child, if it appears to the court that–

    (a)   the child is, or will be, or if an order were made without complying with either or both of those provisions would be, receiving instruction at an educational establishment or undergoing training for a trade, profession or vocation, whether or not he is also, or will also be, in gainful employment; or

    (b)   there are special circumstances which justify the making of an order without complying with either or both of those provisions.

(4)   Any periodical payments order in favour of a child shall, notwithstanding anything in the order, cease to have effect on the death of the person liable to make payments under the order, except in relation to any arrears due under the order on the date of the death.

(5) Where–

    (a) a maintenance *assessment* [calculation] ('the current *assessment* [calculation]') is in force with respect to a child; and

    (b) an application is made under Part II of this Act for a periodical payments or secured periodical payments order in favour of that child–

        (i) in accordance with section 8 of the Child Support Act 1991, and

        (ii) before the end of the period of 6 months beginning with the making of the current *assessment* [calculation]

the term to be specified in any such order made on that application may be expressed to begin on, or at any time after, the earliest permitted date.

(6) For the purposes of subsection (5) above, 'the earliest permitted date' is whichever is the later of–

    (a) the date 6 months before the application is made; or

    (b) the date on which the current *assessment* [calculation] took effect or, where successive maintenance *assessments* [calculations] have been continuously in force with respect to a child, on which the first of those *assessments* [calculations] took effect.

(7) Where–

    (a) a maintenance *assessment* [calculation] ceases to have effect or is cancelled by or under any provision of the Child Support Act 1991; and

    (b) an application is made, before the end of the period of 6 months beginning with the relevant date, for a periodical payments or secured periodical payments order in favour of a child with respect to whom that maintenance *assessment* [calculation] was in force immediately before it ceased to have effect or was cancelled,

the term to be specified in any such order made on that application may begin with the date on which that maintenance *assessment* [calculation] ceased to have effect or, as the case may be, the date with effect from which it was cancelled, or any later date.

(8) In subsection (7)(b) above–

    (a) where the maintenance *assessment* [calculation] ceased to have effect, the relevant date is the date on which it so ceased; and

    (b) where the maintenance assessment was cancelled, the relevant date is the later of–

        (i) the date on which the person who cancelled it did so, and

        (ii) the date from which the cancellation first had effect.

NB Words in italics are repealed and substituted by those in square brackets (Child Support, Pensions and Social Security Act 2000). In force (in certain cases): 3 March 2003 (SI 2003/192, arts.3, 8, Schedule). In force (remaining purposes): yet to be appointed (Child Support, Pensions and Social Security Act 2000, s.86(2)).

Variation, discharge and enforcement of certain orders, etc.

31 Variation, discharge, etc, of certain orders for financial relief

(1) Where the court has made an order to which this section applies, then, subject to the provisions of this section and of section 28(1A) above, the court shall have power to vary or discharge the order or to suspend any provision thereof temporarily and to revive the operation of any provision so suspended.

(2) This section applies to the following orders, that is to say–

    (a) any order for maintenance pending suit and any interim order for maintenance;

    (b) any periodical payments order;

    (c) any secured periodical payments order;

    (d) any order made by virtue of section 23(3)(c) or 27(7)(b) above (provision for payment of a lump sum by instalments);

    (dd) any deferred order made by virtue of section 23(1)(c) (lump sums) which includes provision made by virtue of–

        (i) section 25B(4), or

        (ii) section 25C, or

    (provision in respect of pension rights);

    (e) any order for a settlement of property under section 24(1)(b) or for a variation of settlement under section 24(1)(c) or (d) above, being an order made on or after the grant of a decree of judicial separation;

    (f) any order made under section 24A(1) above for the sale of property;

    (g) a pension sharing order under section 24B above which is made at a time before the decree has been made absolute.

(2A) Where the court has made an order referred to in subsection (2)(a), (b) or (c) above, then, subject to the provisions of this section, the court shall have power to remit the payment of any arrears due under the order or of any part thereof.

(2B) Where the court has made an order referred to in subsection (2)(dd)(ii) above, this section shall cease to apply to the order on the death of either of the parties to the marriage.

(3) The powers exercisable by the court under this section in relation to an order shall be exercisable also in relation to any instrument executed in pursuance of the order.

(4) The court shall not exercise the powers conferred by this section in relation to an order for a settlement under section 24(1)(b) or for a variation of settlement under section 24(1)(c) or (d) above except on an application made in proceedings–

    (a) for the rescission of the decree of judicial separation by reference to which the order was made, or

    (b) for the dissolution of the marriage in question.

(4A) In relation to an order which falls within paragraph (g) of subsection (2) above ('the subsection (2) order')–

    (a) the powers conferred by this section may be exercised–

        (i) only on an application made before the subsection (2) order has or, but for paragraph (b) below, would have taken effect; and

        (ii) only if, at the time when the application is made, the decree has not been made absolute; and

(b) an application made in accordance with paragraph (a) above prevents the sub-section (2) order from taking effect before the application has been dealt with.

(4B) No variation of a pension sharing order shall be made so as to take effect before the decree is made absolute.

(4C) The variation of a pension sharing order prevents the order taking effect before the end of such period after the making of the variation as may be prescribed by regulations made by the Lord Chancellor.

(5) Subject to subsections (7A) to (7G) below and without prejudice to any power exercisable by virtue of subsection (2)(d), (dd), (e) or (g) above or otherwise than by virtue of this section, no property adjustment order or pension sharing order shall be made on an application for the variation of a periodical payments or secured periodical payments order made (whether in favour of a party to a marriage or in favour of a child of the family) under section 23 above, and no order for the payment of a lump sum shall be made on an application for the variation of a periodical payments or secured periodical payments order in favour of a party to a marriage (whether made under section 23 or under section 27 above).

(6) Where the person liable to make payments under a secured periodical payments order has died, an application under this section relating to that order (and to any order made under section 24A(1) above which requires the proceeds of sale of property to be used for securing those payments) may be made by the person enti-tled to payments under the periodical payments order or by the personal represen-tatives of the deceased person, but no such application shall, except with the permission of the court, be made after the end of the period of six months from the date on which representation in regard to the estate of that person is first taken out.

(7) In exercising the powers conferred by this section the court shall have regard to all the circumstances of the case, first consideration being given to the welfare while a minor of any child of the family who has not attained the age of eighteen, and the circumstances of the case shall include any change in any of the matters to which the court was required to have regard when making the order to which the application relates, and–

(a) in the case of a periodical payments or secured periodical payments order made on or after the grant of a decree of divorce or nullity of marriage, the court shall consider whether in all the circumstances and after having regard to any such change it would be appropriate to vary the order so that payments under the order are required to be made or secured only for such further period as will in the opinion of the court be sufficient (in the light of any proposed exercise by the court, where the marriage has been dissolved, of its powers under subsection (7B) below) to enable the party in whose favour the order was made to adjust without undue hardship to the termination of those payments;

(b) in a case where the party against whom the order was made has died, the circumstances of the case shall also include the changed circumstances resulting from his or her death.

(7A) Subsection (7B) below applies where, after the dissolution of a marriage, the court–

(a) discharges a periodical payments order or secured periodical payments order made in favour of a party to the marriage; or

(b) varies such an order so that payments under the order are required to be made or secured only for such further period as is determined by the court.

(7B) The court has power, in addition to any power it has apart from this subsection, to make supplemental provision consisting of any of–

    (a)   an order for the payment of a lump sum in favour of a party to the marriage;

    (b)   one or more property adjustment orders in favour of a party to the marriage;

    (ba) one or more pension sharing orders;

    (c)   a direction that the party in whose favour the original order discharged or varied was made is not entitled to make any further application for–

        (i)   a periodical payments or secured periodical payments order, or

        (ii) an extension of the period to which the original order is limited by any variation made by the court.

(7C) An order for the payment of a lump sum made under subsection (7B) above may–

    (a) provide for the payment of that sum by instalments of such amount as may be specified in the order; and

    (b) require the payment of the instalments to be secured to the satisfaction of the court.

(7D) Section 23(6) above apply where the court makes an order for the payment of a lump sum under subsection (7B) above as they apply where it makes such an order under section 23 above.

(7E) If under subsection (7B) above the court makes more than one property adjustment order in favour of the same party to the marriage, each of those orders must fall within a different paragraph of section 21(2) above.

(7F) Sections 24A and 30 above apply where the court makes a property adjustment order under subsection (7B) above as they apply where it makes such an order under section 24 above.

(7G) Subsections (3) to (5) of section 24B above apply in relation to a pension sharing order under subsection (7B) above as they apply in relation to a pension sharing order under that section.

(8)   The personal representatives of a deceased person against whom a secured periodical payments order was made shall not be liable for having distributed any part of the estate of the deceased after the expiration of the period of six months referred to in subsection (6) above on the ground that they ought to have taken into account the possibility that the court might permit an application under this section to be made after that period by the person entitled to payments under the order; but this subsection shall not prejudice any power to recover any part of the estate so distributed arising by virtue of the making of an order in pursuance of this section.

(9)   In considering for the purposes of subsection (6) above the question when representation was first taken out, a grant limited to settled land or to trust property shall be left out of account and a grant limited to real estate or to personal estate shall be left out of account unless a grant limited to the remainder of the estate has previously been made or is made at the same time.

(10)   Where the court, in exercise of its powers under this section, decides to vary or discharge a periodical payments or secured periodical payments order, then, subject to section 28(1) and (2) above, the court shall have power to direct that the variation or discharge shall not take effect until the expiration of such period as may be specified in the order.

(11)   Where–

    (a) a periodical payments or secured periodical payments order in favour of more than one child ('the order') is in force;

    (b) the order requires payments specified in it to be made to or for the benefit of more than one child without apportioning those payments between them;

(c) a maintenance *assessment* [calculation] ('*the assessment* [the calculation]') is made with respect to one or more, but not all, of the children with respect to whom those payments are to be made; and

(d) an application is made, before the end of the period of 6 months beginning with the date on which *the assessment* [the calculation] was made, for the variation or discharge of the order,

the court may, in exercise of its powers under this section to vary or discharge the order, direct that the variation or discharge shall take effect from the date on which *the assessment* [the calculation] took effect or any later date.

(12) Where–

(a) an order ('the child order') of a kind prescribed for the purposes of section 10(1) of the Child Support Act 1991 is affected by a maintenance *assessment* [calculation];

(b) on the date on which the child order became so affected there was in force a periodical payments or secured periodical payments order ('the spousal order') in favour of a party to a marriage having the care of the child in whose favour the child order was made; and

(c) an application is made, before the end of the period of 6 months beginning with the date on which the maintenance *assessment* [calculation] was made, for the spousal order to be varied or discharged,

the court may, in exercise of its powers under this section to vary or discharge the spousal order, direct that the variation or discharge shall take effect from the date on which the child order became so affected or any later date.

(13) For the purposes of subsection (12) above, an order is affected if it ceases to have effect or is modified by or under section 10 of the Child Support Act 1991.

(14) Subsections (11) and (12) above are without prejudice to any other power of the court to direct that the variation of discharge of an order under this section shall take effect from a date earlier than that on which the order for variation or discharge was made.

(15) The power to make regulations under subsection (4C) above shall be exercisable by statutory instrument which shall be subject to annulment in pursuance of a resolution of either House of Parliament.

NB see note at section 28 for changes to sub-sections (11)–(12).

Extracts of the Family Proceedings Rules 1991 (as amended at 1 October 2009)

1.4 County court proceedings in principal registry

(1) Subject to the provisions of these rules–

   (a) matrimonial proceedings pending at any time in the principal registry which, if they had been begun in a divorce county court, would be pending at that time in such a court, shall be treated, for the purposes of these rules and of any provision of the County Court Rules 1981 and the County Courts Act 1984, as pending in a divorce county court and not in the High Court, and

   (b) civil partnership proceedings pending at any time in the principal registry which, if they had been begun in a civil partnership proceedings county court, would be pending at that time in such a court, shall be treated, for the purposes of these rules and of any provision of the County Court Rules 1981 and the County Courts Act 1984, as pending in a civil partnership proceedings county court and not in the High Court.

(2) Unless the context otherwise requires, any reference to a divorce county court or a civil partnership proceedings county court or a designated county court in any provision of these rules which relates to the commencement or prosecution of proceedings in . . ., or the transfer of proceedings to or from, such a court, includes a reference to the principal registry.

1.5 Computation of time

(1) Any period of time fixed by these rules, or by any rules applied by these rules, or by any decree, judgment, order or direction for doing any act shall be reckoned in accordance with the following provisions of this rule.

(2) Where the act is required to be done not less than a specified period before a specified date, the period starts immediately after the date on which the act is done and ends immediately before the specified date.

(3) Where the act is required to be done within a specified period after or from a specified date, the period starts immediately after that date.

(4) Where, apart from this paragraph, the period in question, being a period of seven days or less, would include a day which is not a business day, that day shall be excluded.

(5) Where the time so fixed for doing an act in the court office expires on a day on which the office is closed, and for that reason the act cannot be done on that day, the act shall be in time if done on the next day on which the office is open.

(6) In these rules 'business day' means any day other than–

   (a) a Saturday, Sunday, Christmas Day or Good Friday; or

   (b) a bank holiday under the Banking and Financial Dealings Act 1971, in England and Wales.

. . .

Ancillary relief

2.51B Application of ancillary relief rules

(1) The procedures set out in rules 2.51D to 2.71 ('the ancillary relief rules') apply to–

(a) any ancillary relief application,
(b) any application under section 10(2) of the Act of 1973, and
(c) any application under section 48(2) of the Act of 2004.

(2) In the ancillary relief rules, unless the context otherwise requires:

'applicant' means the party applying for ancillary relief;

'respondent' means the respondent to the application for ancillary relief;

'FDR appointment' means a Financial Dispute Resolution appointment in accordance with rule 2.61E.

2.51D The overriding objective

(1) The ancillary relief rules are a procedural code with the overriding objective of enabling the court to deal with cases justly.
(2) Dealing with a case justly includes, so far as is practicable–

(a) ensuring that the parties are on an equal footing;
(b) saving expense;
(c) dealing with the case in ways which are proportionate–

(i) to the amount of money involved;
(ii) to the importance of the case;
(iii) to the complexity of the issues; and
(iv) to the financial position of each party;

(d) ensuring that it is dealt with expeditiously and fairly; and
(e) allotting to it an appropriate share of the court's resources, while taking into account the need to allot resources to other cases.

(3) The court must seek to give effect to the overriding objective when it–

(a) exercises any power given to it by the ancillary relief rules; or
(b) interprets any rule.

(4) The parties are required to help the court to further the overriding objective.
(5) The court must further the overriding objective by actively managing cases.
(6) Active case management includes–

(a) encouraging the parties to co-operate with each other in the conduct of the proceedings;
(b) encouraging the parties to settle their disputes through mediation, where appropriate;
(c) identifying the issues at an early date;
(d) regulating the extent of disclosure of documents and expert evidence so that they are proportionate to the issues in question;
(e) helping the parties to settle the whole or part of the case;
(f) fixing timetables or otherwise controlling the progress of the case;
(g) making use of technology; and

(h) giving directions to ensure that the trial of a case proceeds quickly and efficiently.

2.52 Right to be heard on ancillary questions

A respondent may be heard on any question of ancillary relief without filing an answer and whether or not he has returned to the court office an acknowledgment of service stating his wish to be heard on that question.

2.53 Application by petitioner or respondent for ancillary relief

(1) Any application by a petitioner, or by a respondent who files an answer claiming relief, for–

    (a) an order for maintenance pending suit,
    (aa) an order for maintenance pending outcome of proceedings,
    (b) a financial provision order,
    (c) a property adjustment order,
    (d) a pension sharing order,

    shall be made in the petition or answer, as the case may be.

(2) Notwithstanding anything in paragraph (1), an application for ancillary relief which should have been made in the petition or answer may be made subsequently–

    (a) by leave of the court, either by notice in Form A or at the trial, or
    (b) where the parties are agreed upon the terms of the proposed order, without leave by notice in Form A.

(3) An application by a petitioner or respondent for ancillary relief, not being an application which is required to be made in the petition or answer, shall be made by notice in Form A.

2.54 Application by parent, guardian etc for ancillary relief in respect of children

(1) Any of the following persons, namely–

    (a) a parent or guardian of any child of the family,
    (b) any person in whose favour a residence order has been made with respect to a child of the family, and any applicant for such an order,
    (c) any other person who is entitled to apply for a residence order with respect to a child,
    (d) a local authority, where an order has been made under section 31(1)(a) of the Act of 1989 placing a child in its care,
    (e) the Official Solicitor, if appointed the guardian ad litem of a child of the family under rule 9.5, and
    (f) a child of the family who has been given leave to intervene in the cause for the purpose of applying for ancillary relief,

    may apply for an order for ancillary relief as respects that child by notice in Form A.

(2) In this rule 'residence' order has the meaning assigned to it by section 8(1) of the Act of 1989.

2.55 . . .

. . .

2.56 . . .

. . .

2.57 Children to be separately represented on certain applications

(1) Where an application is made to the High Court or a designated county court for an order for a variation of settlement, the court shall, unless it is satisfied that the proposed variation does not adversely affect the rights or interests of any children concerned, direct that the children be separately represented on the application, either by a solicitor or by a solicitor and counsel, and may appoint the Official Solicitor or other fit person to be guardian ad litem of the children for the purpose of the application.

(2) On any other application for ancillary relief the court may give such a direction or make such appointment as it is empowered to give or make by paragraph (1).

(3) Before a person other than the Official Solicitor is appointed guardian ad litem under this rule there shall be filed a certificate by the solicitor acting for the children that the person proposed as guardian has no interest in the matter adverse to that of the children and that he is a proper person to be such guardian.

2.58 . . .

. . .

2.59 Evidence on application for property adjustment or avoidance of disposition order

(1) . . .

(2) Where an application for a property adjustment order or an avoidance of disposition order relates to land, the notice in Form A shall identify the land and–

   (a) state whether the title to the land is registered or unregistered and, if registered, the Land Registry title number; and

   (b) give particulars, so far as known to the applicant, of any mortgage of the land or any interest therein.

(3) Copies of Form A and of Form E completed by the applicant, shall be served on the following persons as well as on the respondent to the application, that is to say–

   (a) in the case of an application for an order for a variation of settlement . . ., the trustees of the settlement and the settlor if living;

   (b) in the case of an application for an avoidance of disposition order, the person in whose favour the disposition is alleged to have been made;

   and such other persons, if any, as the district judge may direct.

(4) In the case of an application to which paragraph (2) refers, a copy of Form A shall be served on any mortgagee of whom particulars are given pursuant to that paragraph; any person so served may apply to the court in writing, within 14 days after service, for a copy of the applicant's Form E.

(5) Any person who–

   (a) is served with copies of Forms A and E pursuant to paragraph (3), or

   (b) receives a copy of Form E following an application made in accordance with paragraph (4), may, within 14 days after service or receipt, as the case may be, file a statement in answer.

(6) A statement filed under paragraph (5) shall be sworn to be true.

2.60 Service of statement in answer

(1) Where a form or other document filed with the court contains an allegation of adultery or of an improper association with a named person ('the named person'), the court may direct that the party who filed the relevant form or document serve a copy of all or part of that form or document on the named person, together with Form F.

(2) If the court makes a direction under paragraph (1), the named person may file a statement in answer to the allegations.

(3) A statement under paragraph (2) shall be sworn to be true.

(4) Rule 2.37(3) shall apply to a person served under paragraph (1) as it applies to a co-respondent.

2.61 Information on application for consent order for financial relief

(1) Subject to paragraphs (2) and (3), there shall be lodged with every application for a consent order under any of sections 23, 24 or 24A of the Act of 1973, or Parts 1, 2 and 3 of Schedule 5 to the Act of 2004, two copies of a draft of the order in the terms sought, one of which shall be indorsed with a statement signed by the respondent to the application signifying his agreement, and a statement of information (which may be made in more than one document) which shall include–

    (a) the duration of the marriage or civil partnership, as the case may be, the age of each party and of any minor or dependent child of the family;

    (b) an estimate in summary form of the approximate amount or value of the capital resources and net income of each party and of any minor child of the family;

    (c) what arrangements are intended for the accommodation of each of the parties and any minor child of the family;

    (d) whether either party has subsequently married or formed a civil partnership or has any present intention to do so or to cohabit with another person;

    (dd) where the order includes provision to be made under section . . . 25B or 25C of the Act of 1973 or under paragraphs . . . 25 or 26 of Schedule 5 to the Act of 2004, a statement confirming that the person responsible for the pension arrangement in question has been served with the documents required by rule 2.70(11) and that no objection to such an order has been made by that person within 21 days from such service;

    (e) where the terms of the order provide for a transfer of property, a statement confirming that any mortgagee of that property has been served with notice of the application and that no objection to such a transfer has been made by the mortgagee within 14 days from such service; and

    (f) any other especially significant matters.

(2) Where an application is made for a consent order varying an order for periodical payments paragraph (1) shall be sufficiently complied with if the statement of information required to be lodged with the application includes only the information in respect of net income mentioned in paragraph (1)(b) (and, where appropriate, a statement under paragraph (1)(dd)), and an application for a consent order for interim periodical payments pending the determination of an application for ancillary relief may be made in like manner.

(3) Where all or any of the parties attend the hearing of an application for financial relief the court may dispense with the lodging of a statement of information in accordance with paragraph (1) and give directions for the information which would otherwise be required to be given in such a statement to be given in such a manner as it sees fit.

2.61A Application for ancillary relief

(1) A notice of intention to proceed with an application for ancillary relief made in the petition or answer or an application for ancillary relief must be made by notice in Form A.
(2) The notice must be filed:

   (a) if the case is pending in a designated county court, in that court; or
   (b) if the case is pending in the High Court, in the registry in which it is proceeding.

(3) Where the applicant requests an order for ancillary relief that includes provision to be made by virtue of section 24B, 25B or 25C of the Act of 1973 or under paragraphs 15, 25 or 26 of Schedule 5 to the Act of 2004 the terms of the order requested must be specified in the notice in Form A.
(4) Upon the filing of Form A the court must:

   (a) fix a first appointment not less than 12 weeks and not more than 16 weeks after the date of the filing of the notice and give notice of that date;
   (b) serve a copy on the respondent within 4 days of the date of the filing of the notice.

(5) The date fixed under paragraph (4) for the first appointment, or for any subsequent appointment, must not be cancelled except with the court's permission and, if cancelled, the court must immediately fix a new date.

2.61B Procedure before the first appointment

(1) Both parties must, at the same time, exchange with each other, and each file with the court, a statement in Form E, which–

   (a) is signed by the party who made the statement;
   (b) is sworn to be true, and
   (c) contains the information and has attached to it the documents required by that Form.

(2) Form E must be exchanged and filed not less than 35 days before the date of the first appointment.
(3) Form E must have attached to it:

   (a) any documents required by Form E; . . .
   (b) any other documents necessary to explain or clarify any of the information contained in Form E; . . .
   (c) any documents furnished to the party producing the form by a person responsible for a pension arrangement, either following a request under rule 2.70(2) or as part of a 'relevant valuation' as defined in rule 2.70(4); and
   (d) any notification or other document referred to in paragraphs (2), (4) or (5) of rule 2.70A which has been received by the party producing the form.

(4) Form E must have no documents attached to it other than the documents referred to in paragraph (3).

(5) Where a party was unavoidably prevented from sending any document required by Form E, that party must at the earliest opportunity:

    (a) serve copies of that document on the other party; and

    (b) file a copy of that document with the court, together with a statement explaining the failure to send it with Form E.

(6) No disclosure or inspection of documents may be requested or given between the filing of the application for ancillary relief and the first appointment, except–

    (a) copies sent with Form E, or in accordance with paragraph (5); or

    (b) in accordance with paragraph (7).

(7) At least 14 days before the hearing of the first appointment, each party must file with the court and serve on the other party–

    (a) a concise statement of the issues between the parties;

    (b) a chronology;

    (c) a questionnaire setting out by reference to the concise statement of issues any further information and documents requested from the other party or a statement that no information and documents are required;

    (d) a notice in Form G stating whether that party will be in a position at the first appointment to proceed on that occasion to a FDR appointment.

(8) . . .

(9) At least 14 days before the hearing of the first appointment, the applicant must file with the court and serve on the respondent, confirmation of the names of all persons served in accordance with rule 2.59(3) and (4), and that there are no other persons who must be served in accordance with those paragraphs.

2.61C Expert evidence

CPR rules 35.1 to 35.14 relating to expert evidence (with appropriate modifications), except CPR rules 35.5(2) and 35.8(4)(b) apply to all ancillary relief proceedings.

2.61D The first appointment

(1) The first appointment must be conducted with the objective of defining the issues and saving costs.

(2) At the first appointment the district judge–

    (a) must determine–

        (i) the extent to which any questions seeking information under rule 2.61B must be answered; and

        (ii) what documents requested under rule 2.61B must be produced,

    and give directions for the production of such further documents as may be necessary;

    (b) must give directions about–

        (i) the valuation of assets (including, where appropriate, the joint instruction of joint experts);

        (ii) obtaining and exchanging expert evidence, if required; and

        (iii) evidence to be adduced by each party and, where appropriate, about further chronologies or schedules to be filed by each party;

    (c) must, unless he decides that a referral is not appropriate in the circumstances, direct that the case be referred to a FDR appointment;

    (d) must, where he decides that a referral to a FDR appointment is not appropriate, direct one or more of the following:

        (i)   that a further directions appointment be fixed;

        (ii)   that an appointment be fixed for the making of an interim order;

        (iii) that the case be fixed for final hearing and, where that direction is given, the district judge must determine the judicial level at which the case should be heard; . . .

        (iv) that the case be adjourned for out-of-court mediation or private negotiation or, in exceptional circumstances, generally;

    (e) in considering whether to make a costs order under rule 2.71(4), must have particular regard to the extent to which each party has complied with the requirement to send documents with Form E; and

    (f) may–

        (i)   make an interim order where an application for it has been made in accordance with rule 2.69F returnable at the first appointment;

        (ii)   having regard to the contents of Form G filed by the parties, treat the appointment (or part of it) as a FDR appointment to which rule 2.61E applies;

        (iii) in a matrimonial cause, in a case where an order for ancillary relief is requested that includes provision to be made under section 24B, 25B or 25C of the Act of 1973, direct any party with pension rights to file and serve a Pension Inquiry Form (Form P), completed in full or in part as the court may direct;

        (iv) in a civil partnership cause, in a case where an order for ancillary relief is requested that includes provision to be made under paragraphs 15, 25 or 26 of Schedule 5 to the Act of 2004, direct any civil partner with pension rights to file and serve a Pension Inquiry Form (Form P), completed in full or in part as the court may direct.

(3) After the first appointment, a party is not entitled to production of any further documents except in accordance with directions given under paragraph (2)(a) above or with the permission of the court.

(4) At any stage:

    (a) a party may apply for further directions or a FDR appointment;

    (b) the court may give further directions or direct that the parties attend a FDR appointment.

(5) Both parties must personally attend the first appointment unless the court orders otherwise.

2.61E The FDR appointment

(1) The FDR appointment must be treated as a meeting held for the purposes of discussion and negotiation and paragraphs (2) to (9) apply.

(2) The district judge or judge hearing the FDR appointment must have no further involvement with the application, other than to conduct any further FDR appointment or to make a consent order or a further directions order.

(3) Not later than 7 days before the FDR appointment, the applicant must file with the court details of all offers and proposals, and responses to them.

(4) Paragraph (3) includes any offers, proposals or responses made wholly or partly without prejudice, but paragraph (3) does not make any material admissible as evidence if, but for that paragraph, it would not be admissible.
(5) At the conclusion of the FDR appointment, any documents filed under paragraph (3), and any filed documents referring to them, must, at the request of the party who filed them, be returned to him and not retained on the court file.
(6) Parties attending the FDR appointment must use their best endeavours to reach agreement on the matters in issue between them.
(7) The FDR appointment may be adjourned from time to time.
(8) At the conclusion of the FDR appointment, the court may make an appropriate consent order, but otherwise must give directions for the future course of the proceedings, including, where appropriate, the filing of evidence and fixing a final hearing date.
(9) Both parties must personally attend the FDR appointment unless the court orders otherwise.

2.61F Costs

(1) Subject to paragraph (2), at every hearing or appointment each party must produce to the court an estimate in Form H of the costs incurred by him up to the date of that hearing or appointment.
(2) Not less than 14 days before the date fixed for the final hearing of an application for ancillary relief, each party must (unless the court directs otherwise) file with the court and serve on each other party a statement in Form H1 giving full particulars of all costs in respect of the proceedings which he has incurred or expects to incur, to enable the court to take account of the parties' liabilities for costs when deciding what order (if any) to make for ancillary relief.

2.62 Investigation by district judge of application for ancillary relief

(1) . . .
(2) An application for an avoidance of disposition order shall, if practicable, be heard at the same time as any related application for financial relief.
(3) . . .
(4) At the hearing of an application for ancillary relief the district judge shall, subject to rules 2.64, 2.65 and 10.10 investigate the allegations made in support of and in answer to the application, and may take evidence orally and may at any stage of the proceedings, whether before or during the hearing, order the attendance of any person for the purpose of being examined or cross-examined and order the disclosure and inspection of any document or require further statements.
(4A) A statement filed under paragraph (4) shall be sworn to be true.
(5) . . .
(6) . . .
(7) Any party may apply to the court for an order that any person do attend an appointment (an 'inspection appointment') before the court and produce any documents to be specified or described in the order, the inspection of which appears to the court to be necessary for disposing fairly of the application for ancillary relief or for saving costs.
(8) No person shall be compelled by an order under paragraph (7) to produce any document at an inspection appointment which he could not be compelled to produce at the hearing of the application for ancillary relief.

(9) The court shall permit any person attending an inspection appointment pursuant to an order under paragraph (7) above to be represented at the appointment.

2.63 ...

...

2.64 Order on application for ancillary relief

(1) Subject to rule 2.65 the district judge shall, after completing his investigation under rule 2.62, make such order as he thinks just.
(2) Pending the final determination of the application, and subject to rule 2.69F, the district judge may make an interim order upon such terms as he thinks just.
(3) RSC Order 31, rule 1 (power to order sale of land) shall apply to applications for ancillary relief as it applies to causes and matters in the Chancery Division.

2.65 Reference of application to judge

The district judge may at any time refer an application for ancillary relief, or any question arising thereon, to a judge for his decision.

2.66 Arrangements for hearing of application etc by judge

(1) Where an application for ancillary relief or any question arising thereon has been referred or adjourned to a judge, the proper officer shall fix a date, time and place for the hearing of the application or the consideration of the question and give notice thereof to all parties.
(2) The hearing or consideration shall, unless the court otherwise directs, take place in chambers.
(3) In a matrimonial cause, where the application is proceeding in a divorce county court which is not a court of trial or is pending in the High Court and proceeding in a district registry which is not in a divorce town, the hearing or consideration shall take place at such court of trial or divorce town as in the opinion of the district judge is the nearest or most convenient.
For the purposes of this paragraph the Royal Courts of Justice shall be treated as a divorce town.
(3A) In a civil partnership cause, where an application is proceeding in a civil partnership proceedings county court which is not a court of trial or pending in the High Court and proceeding in a district registry which is not in a dissolution town, the hearing or consideration shall take place at such court of trial or dissolution town as in the opinion of the district judge is the nearest or most convenient.

For the purposes of this paragraph the Royal Courts of Justice shall be treated as a dissolution town.

(4) In respect of any application referred to him under this rule, a judge shall have the same powers to make directions as a district judge has under these rules.

2.67 Request for periodical payments order at same rate as order for maintenance pending suit or outcome of proceedings

(1) Where at or after the date of a decree nisi of divorce or nullity of marriage or a conditional order of dissolution or nullity of civil partnership an order for maintenance pending suit or outcome of proceedings, as the case may be, is in

force, the party in whose favour the order was made may, if he has made an application for an order for periodical payments for himself in his petition or answer, as the case may be, request the district judge in writing to make such an order (in this rule referred to as a 'corresponding order') providing for payments at the same rate as those provided for by the order for maintenance pending suit or outcome of proceedings.

(2) Where such a request is made, the proper officer shall serve on the other spouse or civil partner, as the case may be, a notice in Form I requiring him, if he objects to the making of a corresponding order, to give notice to that effect to the court and to the applicant within 14 days after service of the notice on Form I.

(3) If the other spouse or civil partner does not give notice of objection within the time aforesaid, the district judge may make a corresponding order without further notice to that spouse or civil partner and without requiring the attendance of the applicant or his solicitor, and shall in that case serve a copy of the order on the applicant as well as on the other spouse or civil partner, as the case may be.

2.68 Application for order under section 37(2)(a) of Act of 1973 or paragraph 74(2) of Schedule 5 to the Act of 2004

(1) An application under section 37(2)(a) of the Act of 1973 or paragraph 74(2) of Schedule 5 to the Act of 2004 for an order restraining any person from attempting to defeat a claim for financial provision or otherwise for protecting the claim may be made to the district judge.

(2) Rules 2.65 and 2.66 shall apply, with the necessary modifications, to the application as if it were an application for ancillary relief.

2.69–2.69D . . .

. . .

2.69E Open proposals

(1) Not less than 14 days before the date fixed for the final hearing of an application for ancillary relief, the applicant must (unless the court directs otherwise) file with the court and serve on the respondent an open statement which sets out concise details, including the amounts involved, of the orders which he proposes to ask the court to make.

(2) Not more than 7 days after service of a statement under paragraph (1), the respondent must file with the court and serve on the applicant an open statement which sets out concise details, including the amounts involved, of the orders which he proposes to ask the court to make.

2.69F Application for interim orders

(1) A party may apply at any stage of the proceedings for an order for maintenance pending suit or outcome of proceedings, as the case may be, interim periodical payments or an interim variation order.

(2) An application for such an order must be made by notice of application and the date fixed for the hearing of the application must be not less than 14 days after the date the notice of application is issued.

(3) The applicant shall forthwith serve the respondent with a copy of the notice of application.

(4) Where an application is made before a party has filed Form E, that party must file with the application and serve on the other party, a draft of the order requested and a short sworn statement explaining why the order is necessary and giving the necessary information about his means.

(5) Not less than 7 days before the date fixed for the hearing, the respondent must file with the court and serve on the other party, a short sworn statement about his means, unless he has already filed Form E.

(6) A party may apply for any other form of interim order at any stage of the proceedings with or without notice.

(7) Where an application referred to in paragraph (6) is made with notice, the provisions of paragraphs (1) to (5) apply to it.

(8) Where an application referred to in paragraph (6) is made without notice, the provisions of paragraph (1) apply to it.

2.70 Pensions

(1) This rule applies where an application for ancillary relief has been made, or notice of intention to proceed with the application has been given, in Form A, or an application has been made in Form B, and the applicant or respondent has or is likely to have any benefits under a pension arrangement.

(2) When the court fixes a first appointment as required by rule 2.61A(4)(a),

    (a) in a matrimonial cause, the party with pension rights, and
    (b) in a civil partnership cause, the civil partner with pension rights,

shall within seven days after receiving notification of the date of that appointment, request the person responsible for each pension arrangement under which he has or is likely to have benefits to furnish the information referred to in regulation 2(2) of the Pensions on Divorce etc (Provision of Information) Regulations 2000.

(3) Within seven days of receiving information under paragraph (2) the party with pension rights or civil partner with pension rights, as the case may be, shall send a copy of it to the other party or civil partner, together with the name and address of the person responsible for each pension arrangement.

(4) A request under paragraph (2) above need not be made where the party with pension rights or the civil partner with pension rights is in possession of, or has requested, a relevant valuation of the pension rights or benefits accrued under the pension arrangement in question.

(5) In this rule, a relevant valuation means a valuation of pension rights or benefits as at a date not more than twelve months earlier than the date fixed for the first appointment which has been furnished or requested for the purposes of any of the following provisions:–

    (a) the Pensions on Divorce etc (Provision of Information) Regulations 2000;
    (b) regulation 5 of and Schedule 2 to the Occupational Pension Schemes (Disclosure of Information) Regulations 1996 and regulation 11 of and Schedule 1 to the Occupational Pension Schemes (Transfer Value) Regulations 1996;
    (c) section 93A or 94(1)(a) or (aa) of the Pension Schemes Act 1993;
    (d) section 94(1)(b) of the Pension Schemes Act 1993 or paragraph 2(a) (or, where applicable, 2(b)) of Schedule 2 to the Personal Pension Schemes (Disclosure of Information) Regulations 1987.

(6) Upon making or giving notice of intention to proceed with an application for ancillary relief which includes a request for a pension sharing order, or upon

adding a request for such an order to an existing application for ancillary relief, the applicant shall send to the person responsible for the pension arrangement concerned a copy of Form A.

(7) Upon making or giving notice of intention to proceed with an application for ancillary relief which includes an application for a pension attachment order, or upon adding a request for such an order to an existing application for ancillary relief, the applicant shall send to the person responsible for the pension arrangement concerned–

    (a) a copy of Form A;

    (b) an address to which any notice which the person responsible is required to serve on the applicant under the Divorce etc (Pensions) Regulations 2000 or the Dissolution etc (Pensions) Regulations 2005, as the case may be, is to be sent;

    (c) an address to which any payment which the person responsible is required to make to the applicant is to be sent; and

    (d) where the address in sub-paragraph (c) is that of a bank, a building society or the Department of National Savings, sufficient details to enable payment to be made into the account of the applicant.

(8) A person responsible for a pension arrangement on whom a copy of a notice under paragraph (7) is served may, within 21 days after service, require the party or civil partner with the pension rights, as the case may be, to provide him with a copy of section 2.13 of his Form E; and that party or civil partner must then provide that person with the copy of that section of the statement within the time limited for filing it by rule 2.61B(2), or 21 days after being required to do so, whichever is the later.

(9) A person responsible for a pension arrangement who receives a copy of section 2.13 of Form E as required pursuant to paragraph (8) may within 21 days after receipt send to the court, the applicant and the respondent a statement in answer.

(10) A person responsible for a pension arrangement who files a statement in answer pursuant to paragraph (9) shall be entitled to be represented at the first appointment, and the court must within 4 days of the date of filing of the statement in answer give the person notice of the date of the first appointment.

(11) Where the parties have agreed on the terms of an order and the agreement includes a pension attachment order, then unless service has already been effected under paragraph (7), they shall serve on the person responsible for the pension arrangement concerned–

    (a) the notice of application for a consent order under rule 2.61(1);

    (b) a draft of the proposed order under rule 2.61(1), complying with paragraph (13) below; and

    (c) the particulars set out in sub-paragraphs (b), (c) and (d) of paragraph (7) above.

(12) No consent order under paragraph (11) shall be made unless either–

    (a) the person responsible has not made any objection within 21 days after the service on him of such notice; or

    (b) the court has considered any such objection

and for the purpose of considering any objection the court may make such direction as it sees fit for the person responsible to attend before it or to furnish written details of his objection.

(13) An order for ancillary relief, whether by consent or not, which includes a pension sharing order or a pension attachment order, shall–

    (a) in the body of the order, state that there is to be provision by way of pension sharing or pension attachment in accordance with the annex or annexes to the order; and

    (b) be accompanied by an annex in Form P1 (Pension Sharing annex) or Form P2 (Pension Attachment annex) as the case may require; and if provision is made in relation to more than one pension arrangement there shall be one annex for each pension arrangement.

(14) . . .

(15) . . .

(16) A court which makes, varies or discharges a pension sharing order or a pension attachment order, shall send, or direct one of the parties to send, to the person responsible for the pension arrangement concerned–

    (a) a copy of–

        (i) in a matrimonial cause, the decree of divorce, nullity of marriage or judicial separation; or

        (ii) in a civil partnership cause, the conditional order of dissolution, nullity of civil partnership or the order of separation;

    (b) in the case of–

        (i) divorce or nullity of marriage, a copy of the certificate under rule 2.51 that the decree has been made absolute; or

        (ii) dissolution or nullity of civil partnership, a copy of the order making the conditional order final under rule 2.51A; and

    (c) a copy of that order, or as the case may be of the order varying or discharging that order, including any annex to that order relating to that pension arrangement but no other annex to that order.

(17) The documents referred to in paragraph (16) shall be sent–

    (a) in a matrimonial cause, within 7 days after–

        (i) the making of the relevant pension sharing or pension attachment order; or

        (ii) the decree absolute of divorce or nullity or decree of judicial separation,

    whichever is the later; and

    (b) in a civil partnership cause, within 7 days after–

        (i) the making of the relevant pension sharing or pension attachment order; or

        (ii) the final order of dissolution or nullity or order of separation,

    whichever is the later.

(18) In this rule–

    (a) in a matrimonial cause, all words and phrases defined in sections 25D(3) and (4) of the Act of 1973 have the meanings assigned by those subsections;

    (ab) in a civil partnership cause, all words and phrases defined in paragraphs 16(4) to (5) and 29 of Schedule 5 to the Act of 2004 have the meanings assigned by those paragraphs;

   (b) all words and phrases defined in section 46 of the Welfare Reform and Pensions Act 1999 have the meanings assigned by that section;

   (c) 'pension sharing order' means–

      (i) in a matrimonial cause, an order making provision under section 24B of the Act of 1973; and

      (ii) in a civil partnership cause, an order making provision under paragraph 15 of Schedule 5 to the Act of 2004; and

   (d) 'pension attachment order' means–

      (i) in a matrimonial cause, an order making provision under section 25B or 25C of the Act of 1973; and

      (ii) in a civil partnership cause, an order making provision under paragraph 25 and paragraph 26 of Schedule 5 to the Act of 2004.

2.70A Pension Protection Fund

(1) This rule applies where–

   (a) rule 2.70 applies; and

   (b) the party with pension rights or the civil partner with pension rights ('the member') receives or has received notification in compliance with the Pension Protection Fund (Provision of Information) Regulations 2005 ('the 2005 Regulations')–

      (i) from the person responsible for the pension arrangement, that there is an assessment period in relation to the pension arrangement; or

      (ii) from the Board that it has assumed responsibility for the pension arrangement or part of it.

(2) If the person responsible for the pension arrangement notifies or has notified the member that there is an assessment period in relation to the pension arrangement, the member must send to the other party or civil partner–

   (a) a copy of the notification; and

   (b) a copy of the valuation summary,

in accordance with paragraph (3).

(3) The member must send the documents referred to in paragraph (2)–

   (a) if available, when he sends the information received under rule 2.70(2); or

   (b) otherwise, within 7 days of receipt.

(4) If–

   (a) the pension arrangement is in an assessment period; and

   (b) the Board notifies the member that it has assumed responsibility for the pension arrangement, or part of it,
      the member must–

      (i) send a copy of the notification to the other party or civil partner within 7 days of receipt; and

      (ii) comply with paragraph (5).

(5) Where paragraph (4) applies, the member must–

  (a) within 7 days of receipt of the notification, request the Board in writing to provide a forecast of his compensation entitlement as described in the 2005 Regulations; and

  (b) send a copy of the forecast of his compensation entitlement to the other party or civil partner within 7 days of receipt.

(6) In this rule–

  (a) in a matrimonial cause, all words and phrases defined in section 25E(9) of the Act of 1973 have the meanings assigned by that subsection;

  (b) in a civil partnership cause, all words and phrases defined in paragraph 37 of Schedule 5 to the Act of 2004 have the meanings assigned by that paragraph; and

  (c) 'valuation summary' has the meaning assigned to it by the 2005 Regulations.

(7) Paragraph (18) of rule 2.70 shall apply to this rule as it applies to rule 2.70.

2.71 Costs orders

(1) CPR rule 44.3(1) to (5) shall not apply to ancillary relief proceedings.

(2) CPR rule 44.3(6) to (9) apply to an order made under this rule as they apply to an order made under CPR rule 44.3.

(3) In this rule 'costs' has the same meaning as in CPR rule 43.2(1)(a) and includes the costs payable by a client to his solicitor.

(4) (a) The general rule in ancillary relief proceedings is that the court will not make an order requiring one party to pay the costs of another party; but

  (b) the court may make such an order at any stage of the proceedings where it considers it appropriate to do so because of the conduct of a party in relation to the proceedings (whether before or during them).

(5) In deciding what order (if any) to make under paragraph (4)(b), the court must have regard to–

  (a) any failure by a party to comply with these Rules, any order of the court or any practice direction which the court considers relevant;

  (b) any open offer to settle made by a party;

  (c) whether it was reasonable for a party to raise, pursue or contest a particular allegation or issue;

  (d) the manner in which a party has pursued or responded to the application or a particular allegation or issue;

  (e) any other aspect of a party's conduct in relation to the proceedings which the court considers relevant; and

  (f) the financial effect on the parties of any costs order.

(6) No offer to settle which is not an open offer to settle shall be admissible at any stage of the proceedings, except as provided by rule 2.61E.

2.71 . . .

. . .

Barnsley	Northampton
Bath	Salford
Blackwood	Southampton
Bolton	Southport
Boston	Stafford
Bow	Staines
Bristol	Stoke-on-Trent
Bury	Taunton
Crewe	Teesside
Guildford	Trowbridge
Harrogate	Tunbridge Wells
Hertford	Willesden
Kingston	Wrexham
Maidstone	

Index

Accountants
  instruction 77–9, 169–71
Actuaries
  instruction 57–8, 81
Adjournments
  lump sum applications 52
  notice of application for 183
Age limits for child maintenance 63
Agreements between parties
  Xydhias agreements 91–2
  see also Post-nuptial agreements;
    Pre-nuptial agreements
Ancillary relief checklist 150–6
Antiques
  estimation of value 26
Appeals 137–8
  to county court 138
  to High Court 138–9
Application for ancillary relief *see*
  Procedure for ancillary relief

Bank accounts
  account numbers 30
  joint accounts 8, 30, 89–90
  separation agreement
    and 89–90
  statements 30
Barder events 141–2
Borrowing *see* Loans
Bundles
  final ancillary relief hearing 42
  financial dispute resolution (FDR)
    hearing 37, 186–7
  President's Direction 192–7
Businesses
  capital gains tax (CGT) on business
    assets 96
  commercial property 80
  estimation of value 27, 78–9, 169–71

  non-disclosure of sale of business
    interests 140
  separation agreement and 89

Capital claims 6
Capital gains tax (CGT)
  business assets 96
  current levels 95
  liabilities 26–7
  matrimonial home 95
  properties being sold 96
  tax year of separation 94–5
  transferring properties 96
Cars
  estimation of value 26
Child Support Agency (CSA) 26
Children
  child maintenance 7
  definition of 'child of the
    family' 63
  orders in favour of children 62–6
  school fees order 22
  separation agreement and 90
Chronology 31
Civil Procedure Rules (CPR) 20
  costs and funding of
    litigation 127–8
  expert evidence and 71–3, 201–4
Clean break orders 45, 67–8
Clients
  completion of Form E 25
  first meeting *see* First meeting
  goals 7
  health concerns 26
Cohabitation
  spousal maintenance and 48
Collaborative law 12, 103
Commercial property valuation 80
Company pension schemes 98

Conduct arguments 28, 46
  litigation conduct 125–6
Consent
  child maintenance orders 66
  consent orders 92–3, 106–8
Contributions 46
  estimation of value 28
Correspondence
  pre-action protocol 16
Costs and funding of litigation 11, 121–2
  Civil Procedure Rules (CPR) 127–8
  costs orders within family
    proceedings 125–7
  drafting statements of costs 128–30
  final ancillary relief hearing 43
  first appointment 35–6
  Form H 128
  information to be given to client
    119–21
  interim lump sum for costs 124–5
  legal aid 12
  litigation loans 122–3
  loans from friends or family 123
  maintenance pending suit orders and
    123–4
  negotiations and 100–1
  pre-action protocol 16
  proportionality of costs 110, 130–1
  provision for costs 111
  Sears Tooth agreement 122
Counsel
  instruction 42
Counselling 12
County court
  appeal to 138
  County Court Rules (CCR) 20
Courts
  approach to pre–nuptial agreements
    83–5
  county court 138
  failure to comply with court
    timetable 32–3
  family court 3–4
  general duty 44–6
  High Court 138–9
  inherent jurisdiction 118
  jurisdiction 3–4
  powers *see* Powers of the court
  undertakings to 92–3, 106
Credit cards
  separation agreement and 89–90
  statements 30–1
Cross-applications using Form A 24

Data collection 4
  pension information 4–5
  preservation, collation and copying of
    documents 5–6
  up-to-date information 5
Death
  variation of orders and 135–6
Delays
  failure to comply with court
    timetable 32–3
Disabled children
  maintenance orders 66
Disclosure 29
  basic principles 13–4
  further disclosure 17, 38–9
  non-disclosure 139–40
  pre-action protocol 14–7
  schedule 161–2
  settling cases without full disclosure
    17–8
  third party disclosure 39–41
Duress 18
Duxbury **funds** 52

Education
  child maintenance and 63
  school fees order 22, 65
Entrapment 31
Equality considerations 45, 46
Estimation of value *see* Valuation
Expenditure schedule 25, 27–8, 48, 165–6
Experts 34, 69
  accountants 77–9, 169–71
  Civil Procedure Rules and 71–3, 201–4
  final ancillary relief hearing 43
  identity 70
  instruction 16–7, 69–71, 76–7
  joint 70, 72, 74–6, 198–200
  pension experts 80–2, 172–4
  Practice Direction 35 73–4
  President's Best Practice Guide 74–6,
    198–200
  restriction of expert evidence 71
  surveyors 79–80, 175–6
  written questions to 72

**Failure to comply with court
  timetable** 32–3
Fairness 46
Family court jurisdiction 3–4
Family Law Protocol 131
Family proceedings
  costs orders within 125–7

Family Proceedings Rules 1991 20,
227–43
Final ancillary relief hearing 42–3
attendance of witnesses/experts 43
costs issues 43
preparation 41–2
Financial claims 6–7
voluntary disclosure 15–6
Financial disclosure *see* Disclosure
**Financial dispute resolution (FDR)
hearing** 14, 36
bundle 37, 186–7
conduct of hearing 38
first appointment as 32
steps to be taken in advance 36–7
First appointment 33
costs issues 35–6
order 177–8
practical steps for attending 35
practical steps for preparation
33–5
First appointment documents 29
chronology 31
Form G 32
questionnaire 29–31
statements of issues 31, 167–8
First meeting 1
basic information 2–3
checklist 143–9
concluding 11–2
data collection 4–6
financial claims 6–7
immediate action 7–8
interim financial provision 8–9
jurisdiction 3–4
letter to client following 157–9
letter to other spouse
following 160
occupation of the home 9–10
section 25 considerations 2–3
setting the scene 1–2
way forward 10–1
Foreign assets *see* Overseas assets
Form A 21
amending 22
cross–applications using Form A 24
drafting 21–2
example 163–4
filing 22–3
service 23–4
Form E 15–6, 113
additional disclosure and requests for
disclosure 29

basic principles 25
documents to be exhibited to 28–9
tips for completing 25–8
Form G 32
Form H 128
Form P 60
Freezing injunctions 117–8
Funding of litigation *see* Costs and
funding of litigation
Further directions
application for 179–80
Further disclosure 17, 38–9

General duty of the courts 44–6
Green Book 20

Health concerns 26
Hidden assets
tracing information 97–8
High Court
appeal to 138–9
Home
capital gains tax (CGT) and 95
estimation of value 26, 79–80
occupation of 9–10
sale of family home 54
separation agreement and 88–9
see also Property adjustment orders

Income
income claims 6–7
schedule of income needs 25, 27–8,
48, 165–6
Income support 9
Independent financial advisers
instruction 81–2
Inherent jurisdiction of court 118
Inherited assets 46
clean break orders and 67–8
estimation of value 28
Injunctions 10
freezing 117–8
to secure preservation of
assets 115–8
Inspection appointment
third party disclosure 39–40
Instalment payments 107
Instruction
accountants 77–9, 169–71
actuaries 57–8, 81
counsel 42
experts 16–7, 69–71, 76–7
independent financial advisers 81–2

pension experts 80–2, 172–4
surveyors 79–80, 175–6
Interest on lump sums 50, 107
Interim applications and orders 8–9, 109
  interim lump sums 50–1, 109, 124–5
  maintenance pending suit 21, 109–11,
  123–4, 133–5, 181
  notice of application for 181
  procedure for making application 112
  provision for legal fees 111

Joining of third parties 41
Joint accounts 8, 30, 89–90
Joint experts 70, 72, 74–6, 198–200
Joint tenancy
  severance 10
Jurisdiction 3–4
  child maintenance orders 62, 64–5
  inherent jurisdiction of court 118

Legal aid 12
Legal Services Commission 12
Limited resource cases
  lump sum orders 51
Loans 110
  from friends or family 123
  litigation loans 122–3
Lump sum orders 49–50, 106–7
  adjourning lump sum applications 52
  Duxbury funds 52
  factors to be taken into account 51
  instalment payments 107
  interest on lump sums 50, 107
  interim lump sums 50–1, 109, 124–5
  limited resource cases 51
  variation 53, 136–7

Maintenance
  agreement on 87
  children 62–6
  pending suit 21, 109–11, 123–4, 133–5,
  181
  spouse *see* Spousal maintenance
Mareva **(freezing) injunctions** 117–8
Matrimonial home *see* Home
Mediation 12, 102–3
Money laundering requirements 12
Mortgages 8
  service of Form A on mortgagees 23–4

Negotiations
  collaborative law 12, 103
  kitchen table agreements 102

making proposals 100
mediation 12, 102–3
open/without prejudice offers
  100–1, 126–7
roundtable meetings 103–4
tactics 104–5
telephone 101–2
when to start 99
who makes first offer 99–100
'No order' principle 125–6, 128
Non–disclosure 139–40

Occupation of the home 9–10
Occupational pensions 98
Online accounts 8
Open offers 42, 126–7
Overriding objective 20, 130–1
Overseas assets 96–7
  sale 97
  taxation 97
  valuation 97

Penal notice
  notice of application for 182
Pensions
  acting for the party with pension
  rights 59
  application to court 58–9
  attachment 60–1
  company schemes 98
  dividing the benefits 57
  drafting the order 61–2
  Form P 60
  implementation of pension
  order 62
  instructing an actuary 57–8, 81
  instruction of pension experts 80–2,
  172–4
  nature of available orders 55
  pension information 4–5, 21, 27
  service of Form A on pension
  providers 23–4
  sharing 24, 56
  valuation of pension rights 57
  variation of order 136
  what pension provider may
  do 59–60
Periodical payments order 46–7, 107–8
  Duxbury funds 52
  interim 181
  secured periodical payments 49
  separation agreement and 88
  variation 133–5

Personal items
  estimation of value 26
Post-nuptial agreements 87
  Edgar v *Edgar* case 87–8
  maintenance agreement 87
  separation agreement 87, 88–91
Powers of the court
  child maintenance orders 62–6
  clean break 67–8
  general duty of the courts 44–6
  lump sum orders 49–53
  orders available under MCA 1973 44
  pension orders 55–62
  property adjustment 53–5
  secured periodical payments 49
  spousal maintenance 46–8
Pre-action protocol 11, 19
  correspondence 16
  financial disclosure 14–7
  instruction of experts 16–7
  text 188–91
Pre-nuptial agreements 83
  advising and drafting 85–7
  court's approach 83–5
  reform proposals 85
Preservation of assets
  injunctions for 115–8
Procedure for ancillary relief
  applications for directions/further
    disclosure 38–9
  failure to comply with court
    timetable 32–3
  Family Proceedings Rules 1991 20
  final ancillary relief hearing 42–3
  financial dispute resolution hearing
    36–8
  first appointment 33–6
  first appointment documents 29–32
  Form A 21–4, 163–4
  Form E 15–6, 25–9
  interim applications and orders 112
  pre-action protocol *see* Pre-action
    protocol
  preparation for final ancillary relief
    hearing 41–2
  reasons for making application 19
  third party disclosure 39–41
Property adjustment orders 21
  sale of family home 54
  settlement of property 54–5
  transfers of property 53–4
  variation 55
Proportionality of costs 110, 130–1

Questionnaire
  first appointment document 29–31

Reasonable requirements 45
Reasons for making application 19
Rehearings *see* Setting aside final
  orders
Re–marriage 24, 48
Reopening litigation *see* Setting aside
  final orders
Resolution Code of Practice 11
Roundtable meetings 103–4
Rules of the Supreme Court (RSC) 20

Sale of family home 54
School fees order 22, 65
Sears Tooth **agreement** 122
Secured periodical payments 49
Segal orders 65
Separation
  agreement on 87, 88–91
  child maintenance orders and 66
Setting aside final orders 139
  intervening events 141–2
  non-disclosure 139–40
Settlement of cases
  negotiations *see* Negotiations
  offer letter 184–5
  open offers 42, 126–7
  parameters for settlement 37
  without full disclosure 17–8
Settlement of property 54–5
Severance of joint tenancy 10
Solicitors' Code of Conduct 119
Spousal maintenance
  cohabitation and 48
  income needs 48
  level of payments 47–8
  periodical payments order 46–7
  timing of application 47
Statements of issues 31, 167–8
Subpoenas 40–1
Summonses
  witnesses 40, 41
Surveyors
  instruction 79–80, 175–6
Sworn statements 113
  applicant's 113–4
  respondent's 114–5

Taxation
  capital gains *see* Capital gains tax
    (CGT)

interest on lump sums 107
overseas assets 97
Telephone negotiations 101–2
Termination of payment 136
Third party disclosure 39
application for subpoena/witness
summons 40–1
inspection appointment 39–40
joining of third parties 41
Timescale 11
Tracing information 97–8

Undertakings 92–3, 106

Valuation 69–70
businesses 27, 78–9, 169–71
commercial property 80
contributions 28
home 26, 79–80
inherited assets 28
overseas assets 97
pension rights 57
personal items 26
Variation 132–3
child maintenance orders 65
clean break orders and 68

consideration of circumstances 135
death and 135–6
lump sum orders 53, 136–7
maintenance pending suit 133–5
pension orders 136
periodical payments order 133–5
procedure 136
property adjustment orders 55
termination of payment 136
Voluntary disclosure 15–6

Welfare benefits 27
income support 9
Wills 10
Without prejudice offers
100–1, 126–7
Witnesses
final ancillary relief hearing 43
summonses 40, 41
see also Experts

Xydhias **agreements** 91–2